AF265156

Bird Watching Tips and Secrets

Keith A. Lee

ISBN: 978-0-578-68893-0

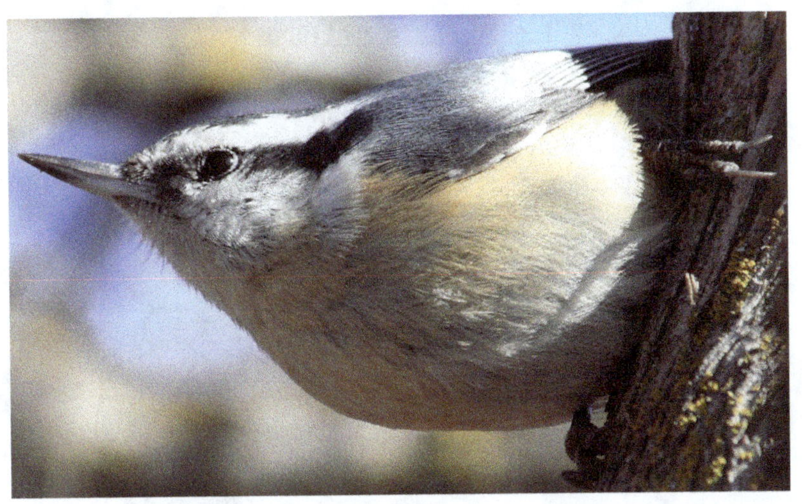

CONTENTS

<u>Favorite Birds</u>

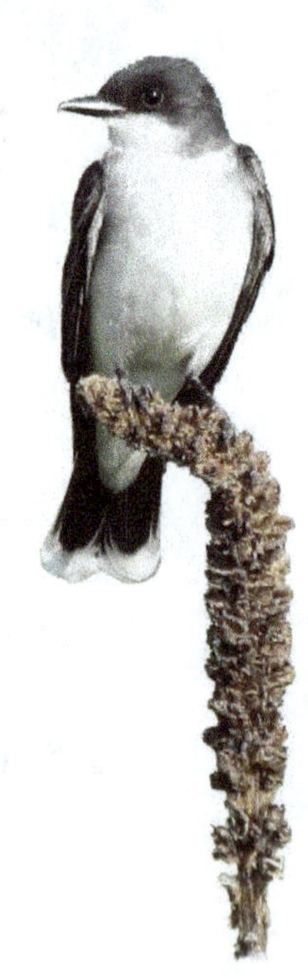

My Fascination with Birdwatching

As a boy growing up in Missoula, Montana, I was captivated by the ever-changing variety of colorful birds visiting our yard. I associated spring with robins hopping around our lawn searching for worms. I can remember the first time I saw a mud and weed nest with the characteristic light blue robin eggs in it. It was around this time that I first saw a hummingbird fly to its nest—a tiny lichen-covered nest with two small white eggs in it. I was fascinated, and although I did not know it, I had become a bird watcher.

Other visitors to the yard were waxwings, sparrows, House Finches, Downy Woodpeckers, starlings, and several kinds of hummingbirds. There were many more but these are the ones that stick in my mind.

I learned to recognize many by their musical songs and calls, and even by their shapes and silhouettes.

We would get huge flocks of Evening Grosbeaks and Cedar Waxwings that would feed on the berry trees in our yard. They seem to especially like the Mountain Ash berries.

In early evening we could watch swallows and bats zooming through the sky catching insects. We had many different trees in our yard, and there was always a chorus of sound and color from the many different birds. I also became interested in photography at an early age, and owned a studio for several years. Photographing birds for this book was a lot of fun. Quite a few years ago I started the web site All-birds. com, so it was a natural progression for me to write a book.

Introduction to Bird watching

The most important thing about bird watching is that you should enjoy yourself. Bird watching is one of the fastest growing hobbies in America and around the world. Around 60 million people feed birds in the US. A national survey of Fishing, Hunting, and Wildlife Associated Recreation found that nearly 48 million Americans are bird watchers. The only outdoor hobby that is more popular is gardening, and the two combine naturally. Birding is enjoyed by all ages. For our flying friends, the benefit is reliable food sources provided by feeders. This is a fascinating hobby whether you just want to observe birds in your yard or a local park, or get more serious, and take birding vacations to remote areas.

Birds are probably the most fun to watch of all animals. They have spectacular colors that are simply unmatched. The dazzling colors of hummingbirds, peacocks, or parrots are in a class of their own. Their streamlined anatomy gives them the ability to fly with grace, and ease. Their songs and calls are enchanting melodies that rival the music of any animal, brightening up even dreary days.

Even their eggs are varied and colorful.

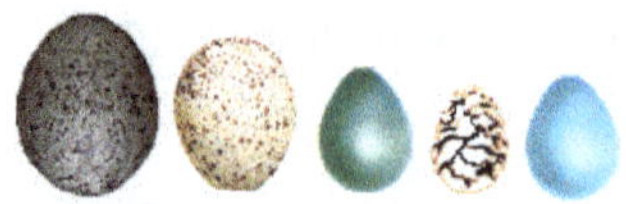

Behavior
Some birds have fascinating social behaviors such as courtship rituals,

which may include exotic dances, feeding courtships, or making elaborate nests, and bowers. In a Cedar Waxwing dance, the pair will hop from side to side while passing a berry back and forth. The male hornbill has strange behavior in which he locks his mate into a tree cavity for weeks at a time. Killdeers will pretend to have a broken wing to lure predators away from their nest. Nuthatches will spread their wings and point their bills at other another bird to challenge it. This is often seen at bird feeders.

With experience many birds can be identified by their behavior. Many birds fly, walk, or swim in identifiable ways that can be detected from far away. How does the bird forage? Nuthatches climb up and down tree trunks. Juncos and towhees like to forage on the ground. Flycatchers will sit on a high perch scanning for insects. Birds like House wrens will cock their tail over their back. Sandpipers constantly bob up and down. Woodpeckers fly in an undulating pattern where they rest, and sink between wing flaps. Tree swallows are very graceful flyers that may be seen skimming over the surface of water. Birds of prey like eagles and hawks may be seen soaring high in the air.

Preening
Birds need to keep their feathers clean and in good shape. Most people know that birds will splash around in water to clean their feathers. They also preen in order to smooth their feathers and remove dirt and parasites. During this process they spread oil from a gland at the base of their tail over their feathers. This helps protect the feathers and makes them somewhat waterproof. Many birds dust bathe, using fine dust to clean their feathers. Many birds can also be seen sunbathing, where they spread their wings and feathers and sprawl in the sun. All this makes them awesome entertainers. Who would not be awed by the sight and sound of migrating geese or the sight of huge flocks of blackbirds as they fly in waves across the sky? The size and shape of birds is virtually infinite, from hummingbirds, owls, woodpeckers, pelicans, eagles, and birds of prey, to the flightless ostrich. They are all fascinating.

Getting Started with Bird watching

For those new to the hobby, the best place to start may be your own backyard and neighborhood. Watch the behavior of local birds and learn to identify them. When you go into the wild you may notice many of the same birds you see in your backyard. If you are a beginner, it is helpful to start by going out with experienced birders to learn what to look for.

There are many bird groups you can join. The Audubon Society and American Birding Association are probably the best known. These groups offer birding information in the form of magazines, newsletters, and guided trips. You can find birding books and songs recorded on CDs in local bookstores or online. The clubs should also have lists of birds in your area, and can tell you hotspots you can visit.

Keeping a birding log can be fun. One benefit of keeping track of birds and the sounds they make is that in a short time you will be able to identify them by their shape or song. Many birdwatchers use software such as Aves Bird Watcher. You can create and maintain a list of bird species along with feeding habits, nesting, and courtship details.

Where and When to See Birds
Luckily for us, many popular songbirds visit backyard feeders and birdbaths. This makes a yard designed with birds in mind one of the best places to watch birds.   Watching the entertaining antics of birds feeding and bathing from your lawn chair or a window can be very enjoyable.

Habitats
While it is possible to watch birds any time and any place, it is helpful to know when, and where to look. Learning the preferred habitats of birds in your area will increase the number of birds you see and make your birding more enjoyable. If you know that meadowlarks are likely to be found in open grassy areas, and dippers forage along streambeds, you may look for them if you are in those types of habitats.

You are more likely to see specific birds at certain times of the day. For example, songbirds are easier to see two to three hours after dawn or just before sunset. This is when songbirds are most actively feeding. Many small birds will be silent or even hidden during the rest of the day. After sunup is the best time to see eagles and hawks. Visibility is best for hunting at this time, and they can soar on the thermal currents from the warmed air. Birds like owls are more likely to be seen in the evening. Many shorebirds and waders rest at high tide and feed when the water rises or falls.

All birds need food, water, and shelter, but needs or habits will vary with each species. Crossbills' natural food comes from conifer trees. Cranes need to be around water. Red-winged Blackbirds fasten their nests to reeds such as cattails. A meadowlark's nest is a grass dome built on the ground. Nuthatches, woodpeckers, and Brown Creepers are more likely to be seen on tree trunks. Dippers will be found in mountain streams hopping from rock to rock or diving for aquatic insects. Learning the needs of a specific bird will tell you what their natural habit is and where to look for it.

Seasons
There are advantages to each season. To see birds in full colorful breeding plumage, the best time to watch is in spring when they migrate to their nesting grounds. Most birds breed in the summer, so that is when you can watch them build their nests and raise their young. This is also when they will be the most visible. Later in the summer when they are molting they remain more concealed. Fall is the most difficult time to identify birds because of the change in plumage.

Birding Technique and Skills
It goes without saying that watching birds in the wild takes more patience than watching them in your backyard. If you are walking it the woods, try walking a little ways, then stopping for a few minutes to look around. Scan the forest from bottom to top. Some birds prefer to stay in the underbrush, some prefer the middle, and still others will remain in treetops. You might want to just sit for a while on a stump or log. Often birds that might be spooked as you walk through might reveal themselves if you are still for a while. Birds have a comfort zone that they will not let you enter. For each species this zone is different. The way to learn this zone is with practice and experience. Birds are likely to be alarmed by noise or sudden movement, so move slowly and quietly. Watch the vegetation for movement that may give away a bird's location. Birds have sharper senses than we do so they probably know you are there, but they have to see you as non-threatening. Watch for signs of alarm in birds, a freeze in posture, or half raised wings. These are signs to stop moving until the bird calms down or back away if necessary. If you are walking, and you see birds flee into bushes as you approach try staying still for a few minutes. When birds perceive that you are not a threat they may come out of hiding. Often their curiosity will bring them quite close to you and you can get great pictures.

Clothes
If you are walking though a wooded area, just wear clothes you would wear on any hike or field trip. It is a good idea to avoid fabrics that squeak, rustle, or snag easily. Many people like to wear a hat to keep the sun out of their eyes.

Choosing a Bird Field Guide

Use a good field guide to identify birds. Roger Tory Peterson has written several good ones. Look for clear color pictures that make it easy to recognize one bird from another. Next to each picture should be detailed descriptions of each bird's anatomy, habits, and what it eats. The guide should have information about what habitat each bird lives in.   Many guides have maps showing the range of different birds along with their migration patterns.

Bird watching Equipment

Some items that might make bird watching more enjoyable are binoculars, a camera, some kind of system for keeping notes, a good field guide, and maybe a backpack, which is handy for carrying water, snacks, insect repellent, or even camera gear.

Binoculars

A good magnification range for binoculars is 7x35 or 8×40. The first number is the amount of magnification. Objects will look 7 times closer with a 7x lens. The second part of the number is the diameter of the lens. A larger lens will allow more light to come in and the image will be clearer, making it easier to see small birds in shaded areas.

Bird watching binoculars may have either a porro prism or a roof prism. With the porro, the outer lens is offset from the eyepiece so the light follows a z-pattern. The roof prism type have the prism on top, making them more durable but also more expensive.

Try out a few to see which is best for you. Keep in mind that the larger the binoculars the more they will weigh, and carrying them can get tiresome. Try to get a wide comfortable neck strap. Look for binoculars that are easy to focus, with a central focusing ring so you can follow moving birds. Also make sure the binoculars can focus on close objects. Many birders who want more magnification are using spotting scopes instead of binoculars.

Using binoculars

It is best to search for birds using only your eyes first because you have a wider range of vision with your naked eye. Once you locate a bird you can use the binoculars to get a better view. Often when you raise your binoculars you will not be able to find the bird you were watching. Here is the trick I use. Try to find a landmark such as a tree limb close to where you see the bird. While keeping your eyes on the bird, raise your binoculars to your eyes. If you do not see the bird, remember where it was in relation to the landmark and look for it in that area.

Note taking
Birders often keep lists or journals of the birds they see. The most common list bird watchers keep is the life list. This can be simply a list of all the bird species you have seen along with the dates. You may want to create and maintain a list of bird species, habitats they are found in, taxonomy, feeding habits, nesting, courtship details, and much more.

Sound recording
Recording the songs of birds you encounter can be fun. Sound recording equipment can run from a few hundred dollars to several thousand. It is best to start out small, but many people get hooked on it, and before long they have a lot of money invested. Since the microphone is what captures the birds' sound, it is the first piece of equipment you need to consider. Many just use a hand held recorder but for more serious birders there are two types of systems. One is a handheld directional mike called a shotgun mike, so named because it looks like a long gun barrel. These are easy to pack on a trip, and using them is a simple as pointing them at the bird you are trying to record. The second is a mike in a parabolic reflector or dish. The dish can be anywhere from one to a few feet in diameter. When pointed at a bird all the sound waves that strike the dish are funneled to the center where the mike is. This type of system is a little more cumbersome, but the sound will be clearer, especially for soft sounds, or those in the distance. This is because the dish can collect hundreds of times more sound energy than the shotgun mike. Though this provides a stronger signal, the sound can also be a bit distorted with parabolic reflectors. The next two pieces of equipment needed are the recorder, and headphones. There are many options for sound equipment. A good place to start is searching for shotgun mikes for bird recording on Google. This will bring up links for reviews and prices for all the

different types of bird recording equipment.

Bird Identification Clues

For beginning bird watchers, using pictures and descriptions in a good field guide to identify birds is a good place to start. Many birds are hard to distinguish from each other, so study an unfamiliar bird thoroughly before consulting your field guide. Expert bird watchers learn to keep these pictures and descriptions, as well as other clues, in their head. There are some basic clues you can look and listen for, such as the bird's shape or silhouette, its plumage and coloration, its behavior, its song or calls, and the habitat it is found in. Look to see if there are identifiable field marks, such as wing bars, eye rings, or crowns. The shape of the beak is often a big clue. Also consider the time of the year; their plumage will change during different seasons.

Size

While not always the case, size can be a good indicator of the species of the bird you are watching or trying to identify. Learn the general size of common bird types to help you with identification. As an example, most songbirds such as robins, bluebirds, or cardinals fit into a certain size group. Raptors or birds of prey like eagles, hawks, and owls will usually be larger. Birds like ducks, herons, Canadian Geese or other waterfowl will fit another size. Although this is very general, it can help you pick out a single bird that is a different size than the others in a group or flock.

Silhouette - Shape and Size

Bird shape and posture are the most important characteristics used to identify birds. Most experts can identify a bird from its shape or silhouette because this does not change like their plumage does. Each bird family has a certain shape and size, and many birds are identifiable by outline alone.

By placing the bird you see into a particular family, you will narrow down the number of possible birds. Take a look at the silhouette section of this book. Things to look for are: Is the body shape compact, stocky, or thin? Is the beak conical like a cardinal or long and narrow like a humming bird? Are the wings thin and pointed like a swallow? Or broad and rounded like a hawk? The tail of a bird can have many variations. The tail can be notched like a swallow, long and pointed like a Mourning dove, or rounded like a Blue Jay. The legs can be long like a Blue heron or short like a duck. Birds of prey will have distinctive hooked beaks and claws or talons for tearing meat. Almost everyone can identify an owl, eagle, or duck just from the shape of their heads.

Color and Plumage

Most people get into bird watching to see the beautiful colors. The marks that distinguish one bird from another are called field marks. These include such things as breast spots, wing bars (thin lines

along the wings), eye rings, eyebrows (lines over the eyes), eye lines
(lines through the eyes), and many others. Birds like cardinals, Blue
Jays, parrots, and orioles can all be identified by color. Examples
of birds that can be identified at a distance by patterns are the Red
winged blackbird, with its distinctive red shoulder, the Red headed
woodpecker, or flying waterfowl.

Bird Beaks
Look at the shape of a bird's bill in low light. Cardinals, finches, and
sparrows have short conical bills.   Woodpeckers have rigid powerful
bills to chip away at wood. Hawks, eagles, and owls have sharp,
hooked bills for tearing meat. Shorebirds have slender bills for probing
into the sand. Birds such as ducks have flat bills useful for filtering.
Most people are familiar with the long thin beak of a hummingbird.
Take a look at the anatomy section to learn about the specialization of
beaks and feet.

Bird Shape Identification (Silhouettes)

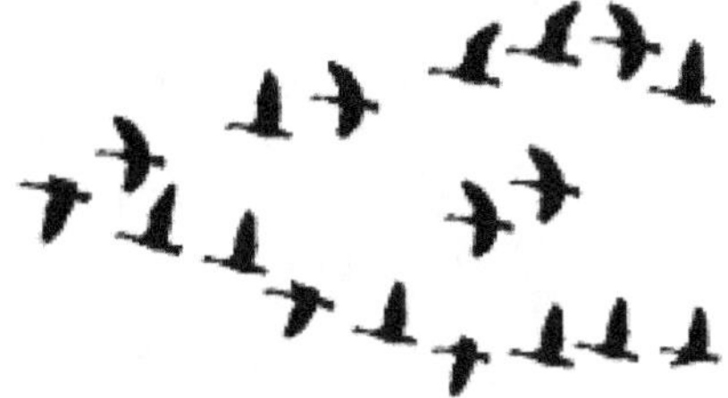

Identifying birds and bird families is often done from a distance by
observing the shape or silhouette. Visual categories can be helpful.
While you may not be able to identify a bird exactly by this method,
shapes may help you at least identify a bird's family.

To use the silhouettes find which of the five groups the bird you are
looking at fits into. Learning shapes can help you identify birds.

Five Bird Groups

Predatory Birds

Eagles, Hawks, Falcons, Owls and Vultures are in this group.

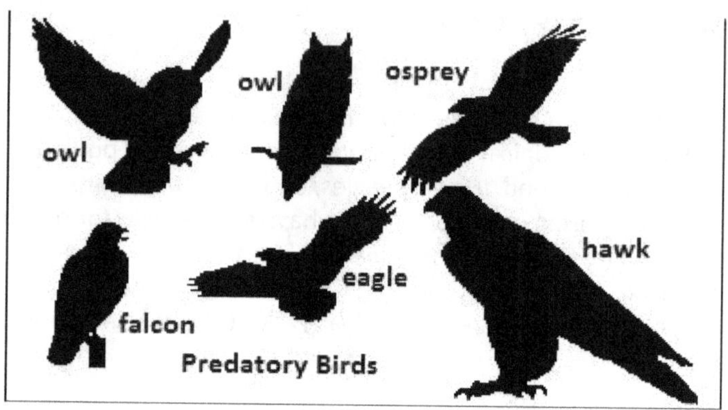

Song Birds - Perching land birds-Passerines

Perching land birds are the birds we know as songbirds, flying from one perch to another. This group has the largest number of birds, and many are hard to sort by shape.

Blackbirds, Bluebirds, Chickadees, Creepers, Corvids, Larks, Nuthatches, Cardinals, Finches, Gnatcatchers, Grosbeaks, Mockingbirds, Meadowlarks, Phoebes, Orioles, Pipits, Robins, Shrikes, Starlings, Vireos, Sparrows, Swallows, Tanagers, Thrushes, Thrashers, Tyrant, Flycatchers, Waxwings, Wagtails, Wrens.

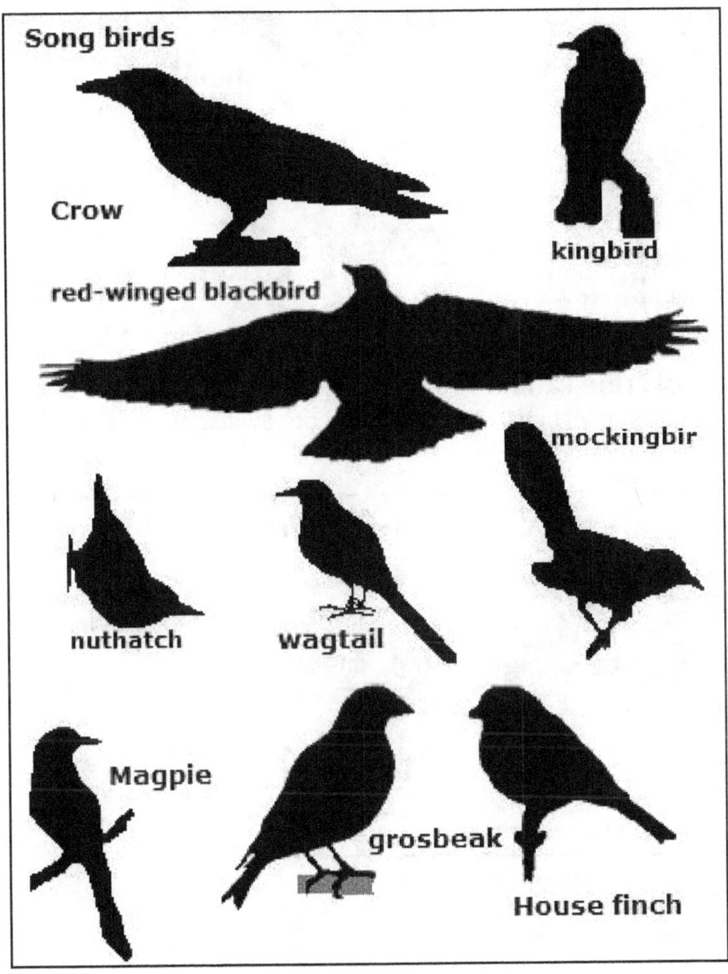

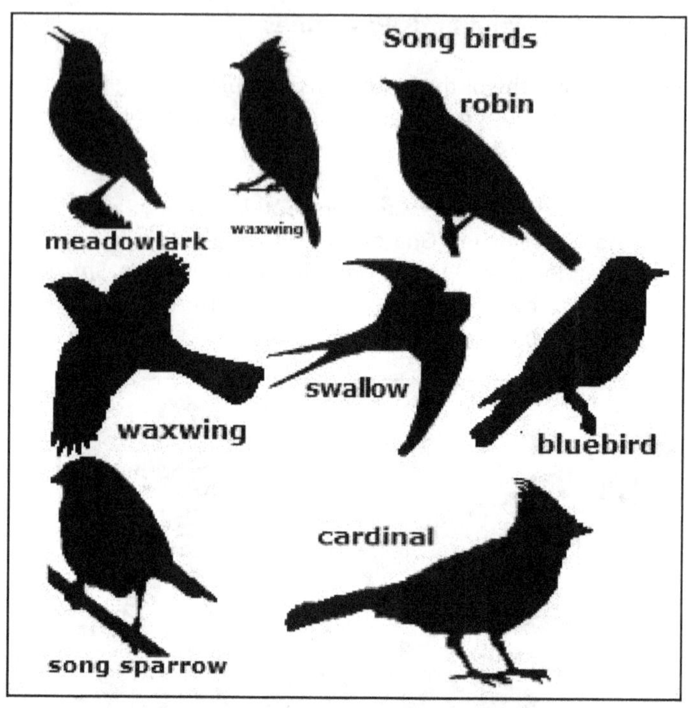

Non-passerine Land Birds
Cuckoos, Hummingbirds, Kingfishers, Parrots, Swifts, Woodpeckers.

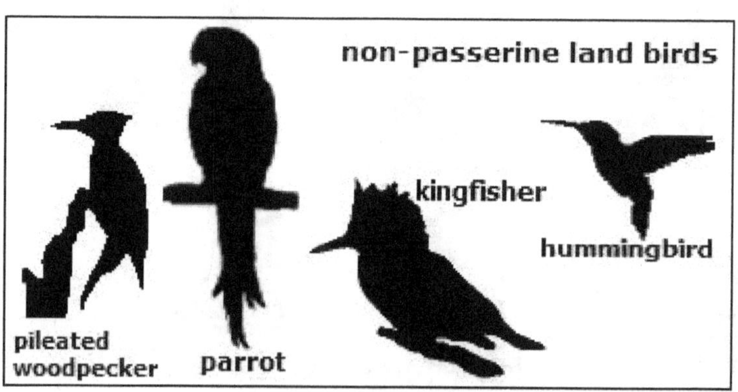

Waterfowl & Marshland Birds

Most water birds seldom go far from wetlands. Those that do, like Gulls, can be easily recognized by their shape.

Water Birds Include:

- **Aerialists** like gulls have long slender wings. They fly long distances and you can see them scanning the water or shore for food.

- **Swimmers** such as ducks have wide bodies and webbed feet. Their flight is swift and direct. On the water their profile is easily recognizable.

- **Shorebirds** such as sandpipers and plovers can be seen on beaches or shores probing for food. Many have long slender legs for wading and slender bills for probing.

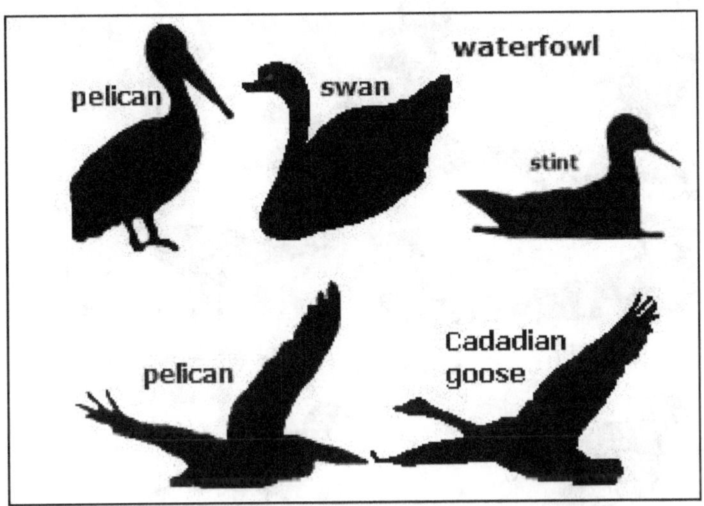

Waterfowl & Marshland Birds

-

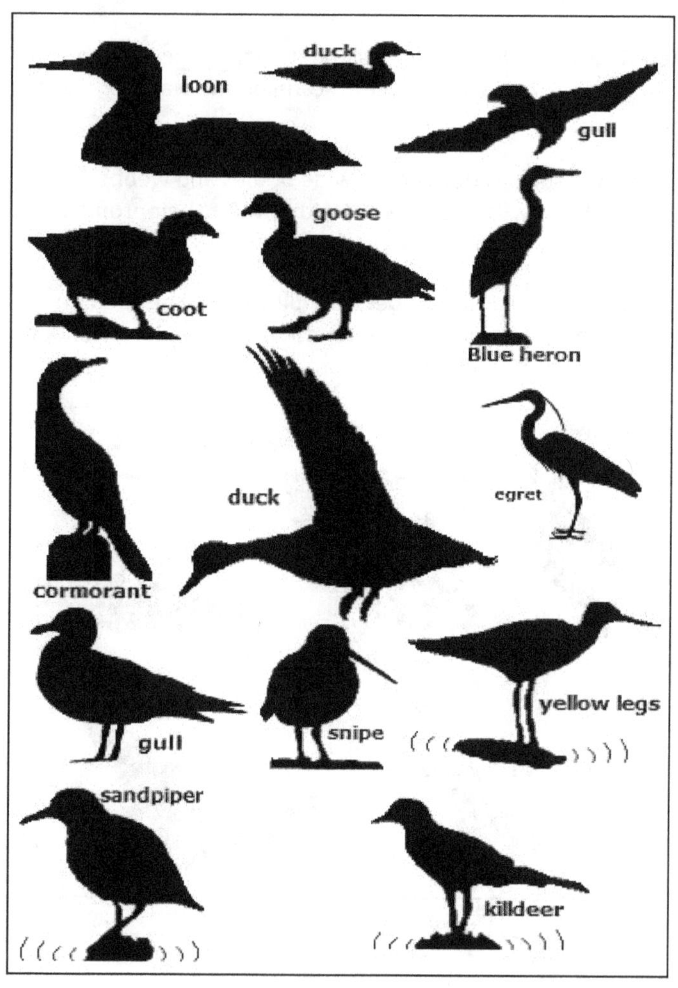

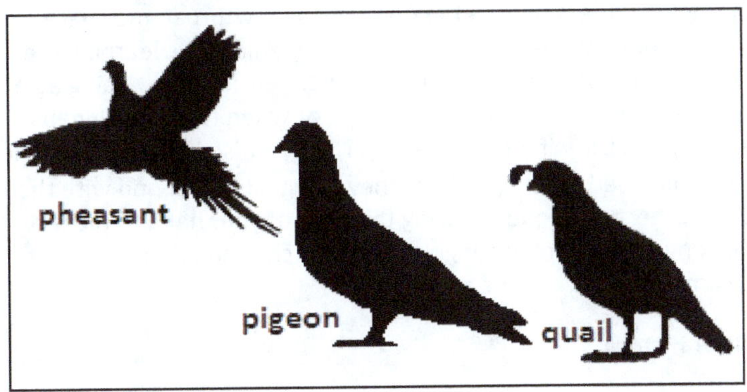

Birds Songs and Calls

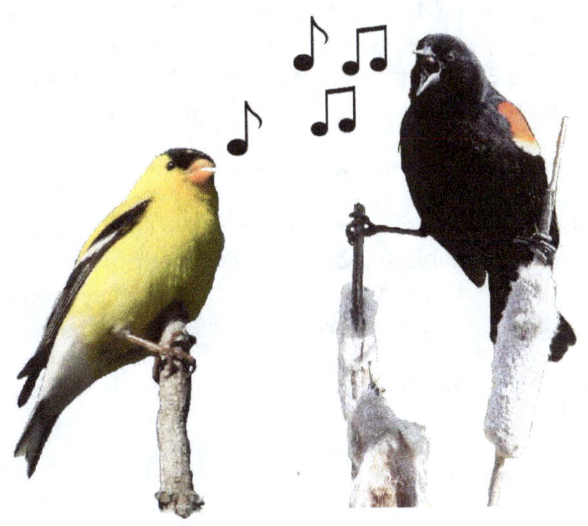

No matter where we live, the songs of birds brighten up our days. This is nature's orchestra at its best. The early morning chirps of a robin or chickadee delight us, and the sound of a honking flock of migrating geese inspire us. There is an incredible diversity. Some birds have their songs encoded at birth, while others learn their songs, either from their father or from birds around them. Some of those that learn their songs only learn when they are young, and others keep learning their entire life. Some species may sing the same song but have different dialects from one area to another. Some birds, such as the Brown thrasher, may have hundreds or thousands of different songs, while others such as the Common yellowthroat, may have as little as one. While bird watching is very enjoyable, learning the songs and calls of birds adds an exciting dimension to it. Being able to identify unseen birds from a distance or when they are hidden in the bush, and listening to their songs is very satisfying. Many people do what is called spishing, where they make a (spis) sound with their lips. Another technique is kissing the back of your hand to make a squeaking sound. Some songbirds such as chickadees and warblers will come to check out the sound.

A Bit of History

The first known recording of bird song was by Ludwig Koch in 1889. At the time Ludwig was eight years old. He recorded the Indian Shama, a member of the Thrush family. Many years later, after Dr. Koch moved to Britain from Germany, he worked with E.M Nicholson. E.M Nicholson became the director of the Nature Conservancy creating the book *Songs of Wild Birds*. Dr. Koch's sound recordings became the base for the BBC's natural history library. As you can imagine, the recording equipment at that time was very cumbersome.

Communication of Bird Songs and Calls

Songs and calls play a very important role in the lives of birds. Of all the ways birds communicate, sound is probably the most important. Because birds do not have a strong sense of smell, they rely on vision and sound. Sound is ideal for low light or over long distances.

Basic Difference between Songs and Calls

Songs 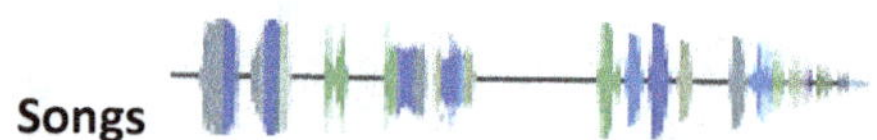

Songs are more musical and complex then calls. They are usually only produced by the male. Males often learn these songs from their fathers or by listening to nearby males. Because they learn these musical phrases, regional dialects are often developed. A male's song may get richer and more varied as he gains more experience with age. This gives him a bit of an edge over younger birds. When the female chooses a mate, she will evaluate his health and maturity by this song. With most birds the song can be associated with breeding. The male is singing to find or communicate with his mate and to claim and protect his territory by warning other males to stay away. Social bonding of pairs may also be aided with songs. The majority of the singing is in early morning. The birds will be quiet during the middle of the day, and start up again in late afternoon, although there are some species that will sing all day long. Songbirds such as warblers may have different songs for attracting mates than they do for protecting their territory. Some birds, such as meadowlarks, will sing a duet in which each partner contributes phrases to the song. A male Red-winged blackbird will sing while the female will chatter back at him. Male songbirds may do what is known as countersinging during territorial deputes. In this contest each bird will match the other bird's song types. One bird famous for this is the Marsh Wren.

Some songbirds are known for imitating the sounds of other birds and animals. Mockingbirds will even imitate machinery. European Starlings, catbirds, and thrashers are imitators. Blue Jays will imitate the call of a hawk. There are two types of songs. The loud primary song we usually hear is a male singing, and then there are soft songs that are called whisper songs.

Calls

Calls are usually not as musical as songs. They are usually only a few short notes and may be heard throughout the year. Birds use calls to communicate many things to each other and between members of a flock or family. Contact calls may be used to give others information such as a bird's location. There are calls for aggression, warning, identification, flocking, hunger, to announce a food source, and many others. Young birds give begging calls to get their parents to feed them. Many species will have calls that specify a certain type of predator in the area. Some calls are understood by more than one species. A fascinating study conducted recently by scientists at the universities of Washington and Montana found that nuthatches understand chickadee calls. When chickadees warn that predatory bird is near, the nuthatches will band together with them to surround the predator in an attempt to drive it away.

Although calls are used for communication, that communication is only about the present. Here is an example of what I mean. You may tell a friend you left your keys at his house yesterday. Birds have not developed the mental capacity for the past, and can only communicate something happening right now, such as a warning call.

Learning to Recognize Bird Sounds

Many people buy tapes or CDs of bird sounds, both for enjoyment, and to learn the different songs. Check bird shops and bookstores for these. You can find sounds for almost any bird by searching sounds from web sites such as FindSounds.com. Many of these can be downloaded for your own use. Some people like to record sounds themselves. Bird sound recording equipment can be found on the internet.

The more ways you have to identify a bird the more you will enjoy, and the more success you will have at bird watching.

Their colorful plumage makes most birds easy to identify if you can get a good look at them. If the birds are in the brush, a long distance away, or in poor light it is more difficult. Because of the effects of shadows, lighting, and changes in plumage visual identification is often not as reliable as identification from songs and calls.

The best place to start learning birdcalls is in your backyard. If you walk through a wooded area there may be such a stream of different calls it is hard to pick one out. By observing the birds in your backyard, and listening, you can learn to pick them out in a forest or wooded area. This, combined with the learning their shapes, can make your birding experience more fun and rewarding.

Sound Production

Birds have a sound-producing organ called the syrinx. The syrinx is near the bottom of their windpipe, where it divides into the main bronchial tubes that lead to the lungs. The membranes are like the skin of a drum and vibrate as air is pushed out through them. Pairs of muscles control the tension on the membranes to change the sound characteristics. The number and complexity of these muscles vary with different species, and in fact between male and female. The syrinx is divided into two compartments, one for each lung. These can be controlled separately, and sounds from each can be combined. This is why birds like starlings and mockingbirds can make such varied sounds, and are such good imitators.

Birds' Hearing is also Important
Birds' hearing is much the same as ours. One big advantage is that birds have developed a sense of time resolution, which is about 10 times better than ours. What does this mean? Several separate notes

in sequence may sound to us like one long note. Because of their time resolution ability, they hear the note separated into the smaller segments. This allows more information to be communicated. One way to visualize this is to compare it to a piece of movie film. When run through a projector we can't see the separation. Scientists today use sound spectrographs to study these.

Below is visual image of a simple robin chirp as it looks in a sound editor. It sounds to us like two notes. In the image you can see the separation that birds can hear.

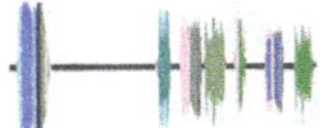

Other sounds

There of course sounds other than songs or calls. Here are a few:

Woodpeckers have specialized bills and neck muscles for hammering on tree trunks. In addition to drilling holes they use this to send sound signals. Woodpeckers and grouse both use drumming to claim a territory and attract a mate, just like songbirds use their song. Grouse beat their wings to make the sound. The Common snipe will climb high in sky then dive down at a slant with its tail feathers spread. The air rushing through will cause the outer feathers to vibrate creating a drumming sound. It has been described as a siren or bleating sound.

Owls and herons snap their bills to show aggression or if alarmed.

Bird Anatomy & Bird Parts

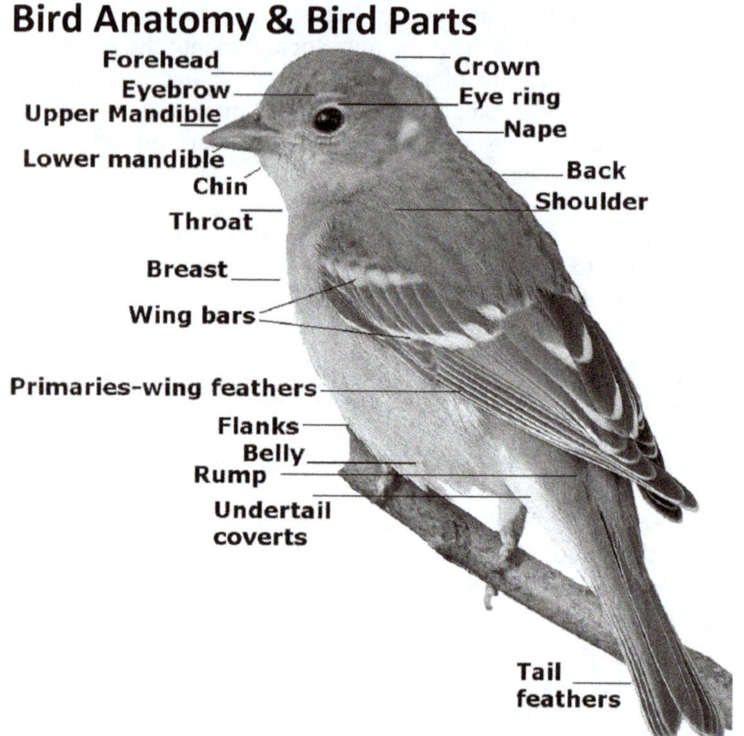

While learning the shapes and silhouettes of birds is helpful in identifying them at a distance, learning the anatomy of birds provides clues to where they live and what they eat. If you see a bird that has red bars, it is helpful if you know what part of the bird is red.

Designed for flight

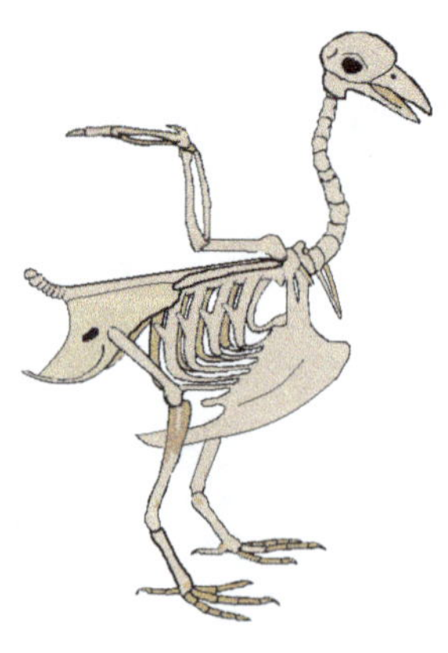

Birds are one of the few animals that have developed the ability to fly. Every part from the skeleton to the feathers has evolved to aid in flight. The skeleton, while using the same general design of other vertebrates has some distinct differences. The skull is very light in proportion to the rest of the body because there are no teeth for chewing, no heavy jaw, nor any jaw muscles. The gizzard performs the job of grinding up food. This means the skull is usually around 1 percent of the body weight.

25

The bones are hollow with strut-like structures inside. This makes them light while still making them strong enough for flight. The forelimbs have developed into wings.

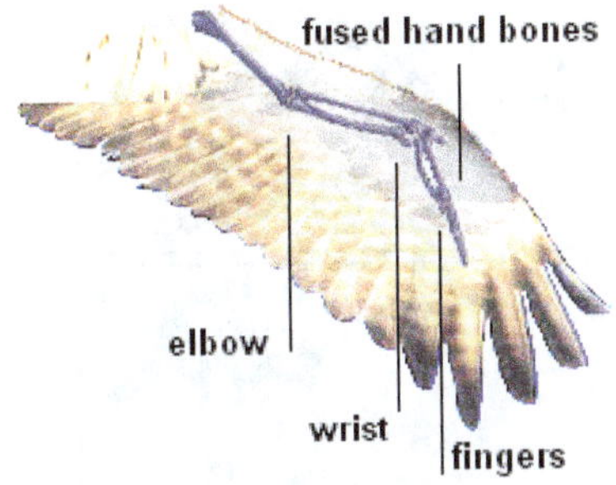

The wings are composed of the humerus, or upper arm, and the radius, or ulna, which makes up the forearm with wrist, and hand bones. The forearm supports the secondary feathers and the fused wrist, and hand bones support the primary feathers. The joints have added strength because they have limited movement.

The skeleton has many modifications to allow birds to walk on their hind legs. The muscles have also evolved for flight. The important muscles for flight run between the upper arm and the breast. There are two pairs of flight muscles. The larger pair called the pectoralis major contracts for the down stroke. The pectoralis minor handles the upstroke, which needs far less power.
The body is the third part of this design for flight. It is very streamlined to reduce friction. The smooth surface of the feathers reduces the friction even more.

The tail consisting entirely of feathers aids in maneuvering. The legs will usually be tucked under the body when flying so they don't affect the flight.

Beaks, Legs, and Feet

Beaks of birds are varied, depending on the species and are specialized for their particular diet. In most birds beaks are light to save weight for flight. Bird beaks are bony structures covered with keratin, much like our fingernails. Just like bird beaks, the feet and legs of birds are specialized, depending on each bird's habits, and lifestyle.

Here are examples of a few of the specialized beaks and feet.

The hard beak of a woodpecker is good for drilling holes.
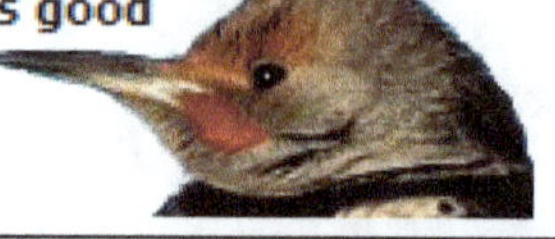

Birds with short, thin beaks such as swallows usually eat insects.
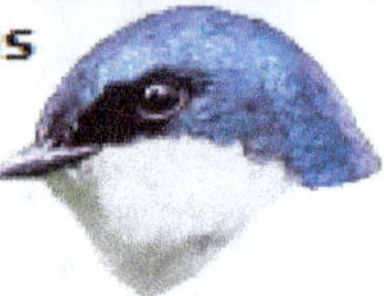

A thick, short, or conical beak is good for cracking seeds. Buntings, Cardinals, Grosbeaks, Towhees, Finches. …
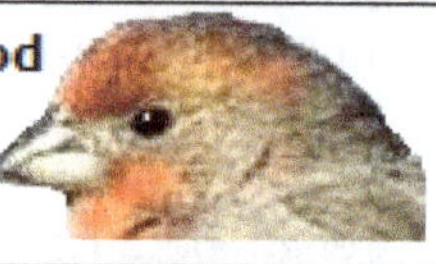

The bills of crossbills have lower and upper mandibles crossed, making it easier for them to eat pinecone seeds. They start at the bottom of a cone and spiral upward, opening each scale, and removing the seeds with their tongues.
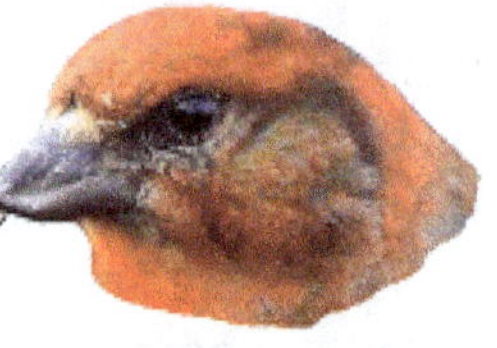

Parrots have a different kind of conical bill good for cracking seeds
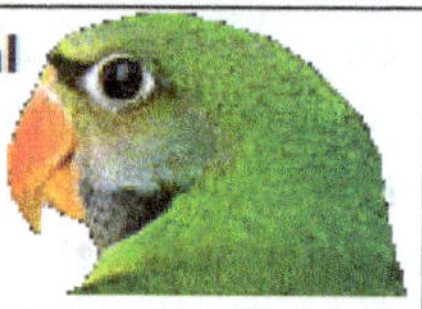

A pelican's pouch is used to scoop fish. When the fish is caught the pouch contracts to squeeze water.
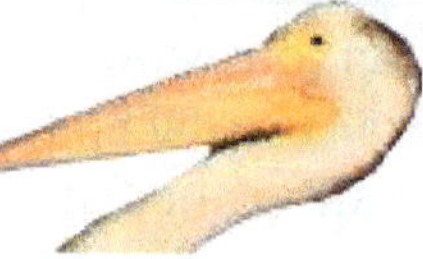

Birds such as thrashers and wrens, with slender, curved bills can probe for insects.
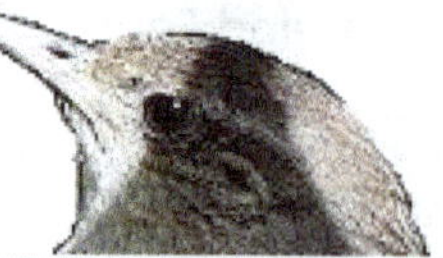

Straight, slender bills are very versatile. Large birds like crows are often omnivores. Small birds will feed largely on insects.
The list includes blackbirds, bluebirds, robins, chickadees, crows, grackles, jays, magpies, mockingbirds, meadowlarks, orioles and thrushes.

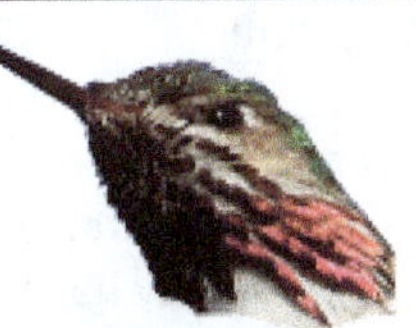

Humming birds have long, thin beaks for getting nectar from flowers.

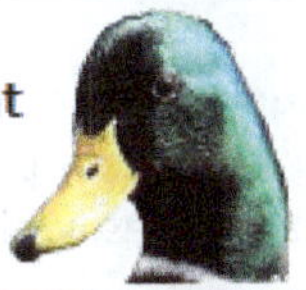

Birds such as ducks use their webbed feed to swim and their flat beak to filter food from water.

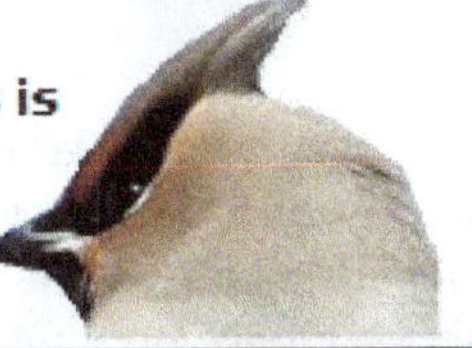

A broad, flat bill such as that of flycatchers, shrikes, or waxwings is good for catching flying insects.

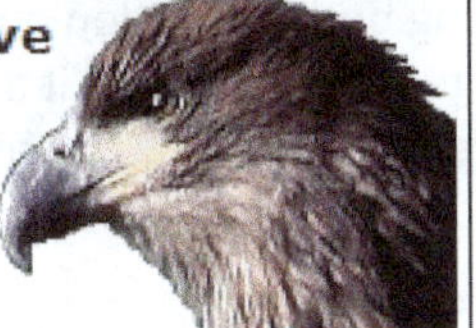

Birds like hawks, owls, or eagles have sharp hooked beaks, and powerful claws for tearing meat and eating other animals.

Bird Feet and Legs

Birds that have long legs, such as the heron, walk or wade more than they fly. Most birds have four toes, three that face forward, and one rearward. Birds that have two toes facing forward and two toes facing rearward usually hang onto the sides of trees. Birds that swim like ducks will have webbed feet. Predatory birds like eagles and hawks will have strong talons. They are usually not very good runners.

Here are a few of the many varied types of feet.

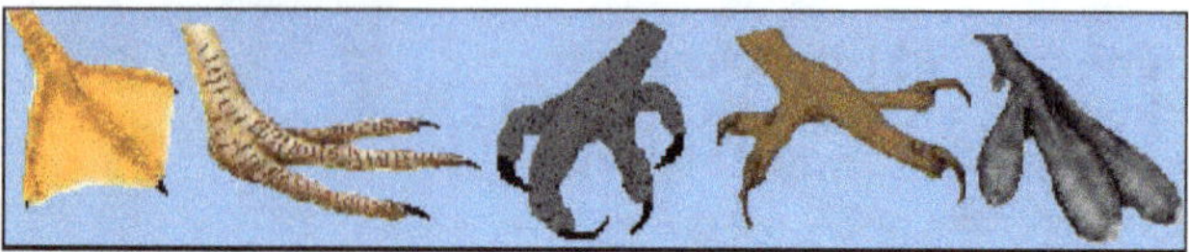

Digestive system

Birds are very active animals. They use a lot of energy and consume food at a very rapid rate. Small birds may eat a third of their body weight in a day. They have specially evolved digestive systems with organs like the gizzard not found in other animals.

Birds can be herbivores, carnivores, or omnivores. The herbivores feed on seeds, fruit, and other plants, and have a more complex digestive system then carnivores, which feed on meat.

Lungs

Another thing that is different in birds are the lungs. In other vertebrates, the lungs consist of sacs. Birds have extensions to the lungs called air sacs. Inhaled air passes through the air sacs, and back through the lungs. With this system, oxygen is transferred to the blood during both inhalation and exhalation. This gives birds better use of oxygen for flying, and it allows them to get by with smaller lungs than other vertebrates. This also aids birds that dive and need to hold their breath for long periods.

Sight

Birds' eyes are much larger in relation to their heads than ours, giving them the ability to see fine detail. They process what they see faster than we do, and they are better at detecting movement. Birds can't roll their eyes like humans so they must turn their heads. When a robin cocks its head to one side, it is looking in that direction. Having both monocular and binocular vision, birds' eyes work together to see straight ahead as well as working independently. This gives some birds an extremely wide field of vision, even allowing some birds to see both in front and in back of themselves. Birds such as waterfowl or pigeons have very little binocular vision but wide monocular vision. Some birds such as the kingfisher have droplets of color oil in the retinas that diminish the glare of water when they are fishing. Others such as raptors have eyes more towards the front of their heads giving them better binocular vision, letting them judge distance better.

Plumage and Colors

While their colors are a thing of beauty to us, these distinctive colors are a matter of survival to birds. Their colors help them attract mates and protect them from predators.

Females of most species choose their mates and are attracted to the male with the most colorful plumage. The color of the male will become muted when breeding season ends. The female will usually be duller than the male, and this helps protect her from predators while she is nesting. The markings of many birds give them camouflage, allowing them to blend in with their surroundings. A Ruffed Grouse matches his surroundings so well it becomes almost invisible. Many birds have counter shading to help protect them. The back, which is exposed to light, is darker than the breast, which is in shadow. The shade of sides will fade gradually from light below to dark above. Many birds have lighter under parts, and darker upper parts. This gradual change in color makes them less conspicuous.

All adult birds molt at least once a year. Molting is a process where old feathers are replaced by new feathers. As much as a third of the bird's body weight is replaced during molting so they need a lot of protein. Many songbirds molt near the end of the summer, and they can look a bit ragged at this time.

Bird Brain

The brains of birds have also developed for flight. The cerebellum is the part that is responsible for co-ordination of movement. Because birds make extremely fast moves at very high speeds, this part of the brain is large. The cerebral hemispheres, which let the bird perform complex behavior patterns, is also very large. Many birds are quite intelligent, even using tools, and having social communication.

Bird Intelligence

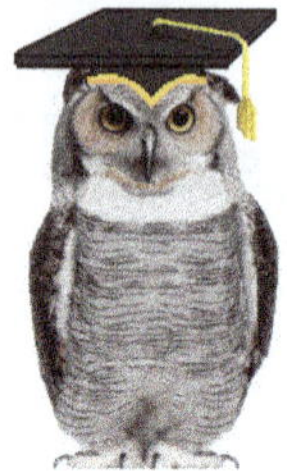

We have all heard someone called birdbrain or featherhead, indicating they were dim-witted or brainless.

As it turns out birds have gotten a bum rap. When compared to other animals some birds are actually pretty smart. A good example is the corvids or the crow family. In the *Audubon Society of Encyclopedia of North American Birds*, ornithologist John K. Terres says corvids have achieved the highest degree of intelligence of any birds. Irene Pepperber, known for her studies in animal recognition, has written that corvid's cognitive abilities are equal to those of many primates such as chimps and gorillas.

There is a little disagreement over just which one of this family is the smartest. Some say the American crow is at the top of the list, others say it is the raven, and still other say jays or jackdaws. Whoever is right, it is agreed that corvids are smart.

Some say mynas and parrots are just as intelligent, if even a little brighter. Everyone is familiar with the ability to mimic songs, calls and other sounds many birds have, but they can do more than that.

There is one study of a parrot that was able to identify more than 100 items by name. In addition the bird could also tell similarities and differences. If shown 3 triangles of different colors and asked what is the same or different, the bird would give the correct answer (shape or color) four out of 5 times. Birds such as nutcrackers will hide thousands of seeds, and the birds will remember where they stored them as much as 9 months later.

Learning Ability

Some say birds are nothing more than living robots, with everything they do programmed into their genes from birth. There is evidence, however, that suggests that while this is true, certain birds have advanced learning abilities. For instance, some birds, such as jackdaws, do not automatically recognize what animals are predators. They learn it from their parents. Many songbirds are able to learn and teach vocal communication, the skill that makes human language possible. When chickadees announce the presence of a predator, nuthatches will join with them to mob and chase the predator away. Research by psychologist Helmut Prior shows that magpies have self-recognition, a trait previously thought to only exist in higher orders of mammals. The researchers placed colored dots on the necks of magpies. When the birds saw the dots in a mirror they would try to remove them.

Bird Brains

The cerebral cortex is the main area of intelligence for most animals. Birds have a relatively small cortex. In the 1960s, neurologist Stanley Cobb discovered that birds use a part of the brain, which mammals do not have, as their main area of intelligence. This is the hyperstriatum and is at the front of a bird's brain. It was found that the larger this part of the brain was, the better birds did on tests to measure intelligence.

Not surprisingly, corvids are the group of birds where this is the largest. In fact their brain to body ratio equals that of dolphins and is almost the same as ours.

Social Behavior: A Sign of Intelligence

Scientists say the more social animals are, the smarter they tend to be. Aside from humans and other primates, dolphins and whales are at the top of this list. Parrots and corvids are also highly social.

John Marzluff and Russell Balda studied Pinyon jays and charted their genealogy. Pinyon jays live in troops, which consist of many clans. In the fall the troops will congregate into flocks of thousands of birds. Later they will again separate into the original clans.

Corvids, such as crows, ravens, and magpies may separate into a family group for things like nesting, and territory defense, and then congregate into huge flocks. These flocks, which may include a variety of birds such as crows, magpies, and jackdaws, can get very large. There are sites in central U.S. that get flocks that are estimated to have as many as 10 million crows.

Intelligence experts say this kind of social interaction requires superior intelligence. The reason is that for this to happen the birds must not only be able to recognize and remember companions but must also be able to notice, and interpret small changes in appearance and behavior.

Play and Games

Yes, birds are even known to play games and even intentionally tell lies. Examples of games played are drop and catch, where one bird will drop a stick another will catch it. If one bird hangs upside down and passes an object from its feet to its beak and back again, others are likely to do the same thing. This shows the ability to learn behaviors. One game played is where a bird will stand on a mound, and hold a stick while another tries to take it from him. An example of what would be considered a lie is some birds will use a call normally meant to signal that a predator is around to scare other birds away from a food source.

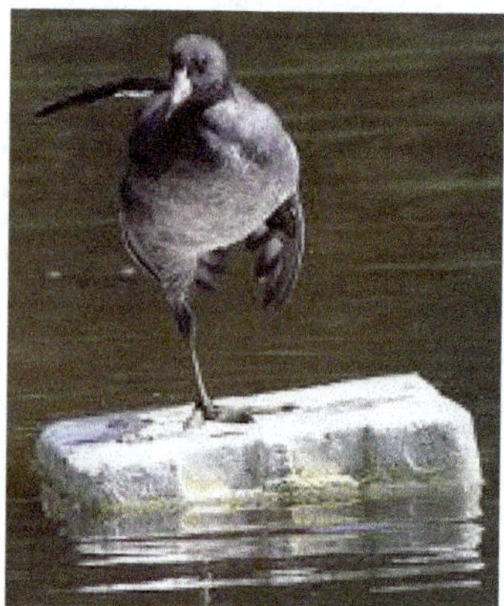

I once observed a coot playing on a foam box top. It started with two other coots pushing him around as he stood on the top. When the other birds tired of this, he continued without them. The coot would flap his wings until the box top was moving forward. He would then stand on one foot and ride the top until it stopped. When it stopped, he would start flapping again. He repeated this process many times.

Teamwork

Some birds will cooperate while hunting. An example is what could be called bait and switch.

Two or more birds discover another animal with something they would like to eat. One bird will land and distract the animal maybe by pecking at its tail. As soon as the animal turns, the other bird swoops in and takes the food. There is even teamwork between species. An example is when birds such as chickadees and nuthatches work together to drive away a predator.

Use of Tools

Obviously birds use material to build nests, but the use of tools goes beyond that.

Crows have been known to steal fish from ice fishermen by using their beaks and feet to pull up the lines when the men were not looking. Some birds have been observed using twigs to probe for grubs they could not reach. They may even use a bit of invention by bending or shaping the twig for this purpose.

Even more fascinating are some types of birds that seem to use bait for fishing. In this instance they will drop an insect in the water and wait for a fish to surface. Some birds such as jays will wedge a nut into forked branches to make it easier to crack. American crows have been observed dropping rocks or holding them in their beaks while they pound on nuts to open them.

Crows in Japan have an interesting way of cracking nuts. They will wait at a traffic light. When the traffic stops, they will run out and place a nut in front of a car tire. When the traffic stops again they will retrieve their cracked nut.

Honeyguide

African Honeyguides are small birds named for their habit of leading people to beehives. The birds will call and fly backwards to get the people to follow them. After the people open the hive and retrieve the honey, the birds feed on the leftover honey and larvae.

Please Pass the Ant

Birds often clean their feathers—this is one good use of a birdbath. This preening, as it is called, both cleans and repairs the feathers so

they are better for flying and insulation. It also helps fight parasites.
Most birds will spread oil form the preen gland during this process.
Some do what is called **anting**. This is where they pick up an ant and
rub it through their feathers or even sit in ants. It is thought that the
formic acid from ants works as a repellent for fleas and lice.

Where did I put that?

In experiments jays have been shown to remember exactly where
they hid acorns. In one study jays were able to find seeds almost a
year after they hid them. It is thought that they remember these by
forming and storing detailed image maps of the surrounding area.

Attracting Birds to Your Yard

Food water and shelter are the keys to enticing birds to your yard.
Aside from the obvious things like providing food and water, there
are many things you can do to attract birds. As the saying goes, if you
build it they will come. The right landscaping will attract a large variety
of birds.

Many birds are attracted to edge environments where trees and
shrubs surround an open area.   Choose trees with various sizes and
shapes. The idea here is to offer a sanctuary with food, water, and
shelter. A big reason birds are attracted to edge areas is that there
are more birds that nest on the ground and in shrubs than there are
that use cavities. The bushes and shrubs also provide shelter for them
to hide in as well as food such as insects or berries.   A yard that has
natural foods is better for birds and will attract more of them then if
your feeders are the only source.

You can easily create this kind of environment in your yard. Plant a
variety of trees and shrubs around the edges of your yard. If you plant
shrubs that produce berries, you give birds one more reason to come
to your yard. Birds prefer a yard that is not manicured, so holding
back on the trimming will increase the number of birds that visit your
yard. Even a partially decayed tree stump left on your property can
be inviting to cavity nesters. By boring a 1 1/8 inch hole in a sheltered
side of a stump you might tempt chickadees to finish the excavation
and build a nest there. If they do, they will probably be back next year.
Many people place a brush pile near their feeders to provide cover for
small birds. Brush piles will be used to hide from predators and for
protection from weather all year long.

Deciduous plants, whose leaves drop off in winter, offer areas for
nesting in spring, and summer as well as a variety of foods to help
them get through the winter.

A good place to put bird feeders is near your water.

Attracting Hummingbirds

Hummingbirds are attracted to bright colors, especially red and orange. If you have hummingbirds around, they will most likely come if you plant flowers. Put up a feeder where they can find it. Once they find a feeder, they will usually keep coming back.

Nesting Areas

Most people want to attract songbirds to their yards. One way to do this is to provide places for them to nest. By putting up birdhouse, you not only have the joy of watching the birds, you become part of the solution to a growing problem. Today as never before, natural habitats for bird nesting are being destroyed. More and more bird species are threatened by extinction everyday. In October of 2019 the Audubon Society estimated that two thirds of birds in North America are threatened by extinction. The large numbers of people becoming interested in bird watching are critical to the survival of some species.

The most common type of nesting that people provide is birdhouses. This is good for cavity nesters; however, many birds nest in shrubs or trees, and on or in the ground. Of these, ground nesting is the most common followed by shrubs, and trees. A grassy area of your yard that is left in a natural state may entice birds such as juncos to nest there. Since birds tend to return to an area they previously nested in, it may take a while before they start using a newly landscaped yard. Once they do nest there, they will probably keep coming back. Birds that use birdhouses are more likely to move into a new house right away, because it is often difficult to find a suitable cavity. In addition to landscaping, some people provide nesting materials. A suet holder can be stuffed with things like string, feathers, and small pieces of cloth. Place it somewhere the birds can see it such as on a pole and chances are you will see birds taking building material from it. In a dry season birds that use mud in their nests such as robins, phoebes, or swallows may use a pan of mud placed in a protected but accessible place. Providing areas for birds to nest on your property becomes more helpful to birds as time goes on. With increases in population in cities and the countryside, many valuable nesting sites are disappearing.

There is even an economic advantage for farmers when birds nest on their property. Birds are voracious eaters of insects. In areas where the loss of crops due to injurious insects has been great, there have been efforts to increase bird populations in farmlands and orchards. One pair of chickadees in an orchard will eat thousands of harmful insect eggs. Even birds that feed mainly on seeds usually feed their young insects. For the first days of their existence, they may eat more than their weight in food a day. Parents will start the feeding at sun up and not stop all day. Young birds will gain 20 to 50 percent of their weight during this period.

One shining example of how successful providing nesting sites can be is bluebirds. Bluebird populations across the U.S. were declining rapidly. Because of a nationwide effort to put up birdhouses, and start bluebird trails many areas that were losing these precious little birds are seeing a comeback.

Platform Nesting

Many birds such as robins, phoebes, or Barn swallow nest on platforms or shelves on buildings. A platform can easily be built, and attached to a building. It is best if it is under an eve or something to help protect it from the weather.

Birdhouses & Nest Boxes

Basic Birdhouse Plan

Each bird species has their own requirements for dimensions so whether you are buying or building a birdhouse, consider the needs of the bird the house is for.

Where to put a birdhouse, the types of birds it may attract, and other information is below the nest box plan. Design and construction of your birdhouse or nest box is important. Just as important is where you put the birdhouse.

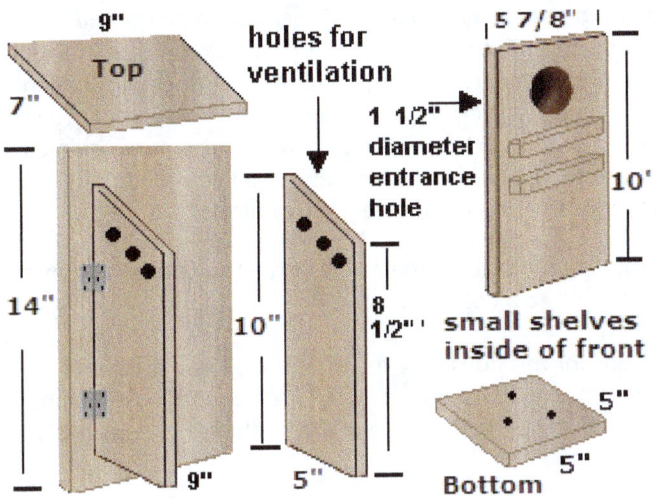

The tools needed for the above nest box are a handsaw or power saw, hammer, screwdriver, and electric drill with 1/4 inch bit, and wood boring bit for making the entrance hole.

Wood that is 5/8 to 3/4 inch thick will insulate the young birds and eggs from excessive heat and cold. Try to avoid pressure treated lumber since it can be harmful to birds. The roof of the birdhouse should slope so rain drains off. Let it over lap the sides and front by around 1½ inch. It helps to score a 1/8th inch groove in the underside of the roof about an inch from the front. This is a drip line. Attach two small shelves inside the front. This helps the young birds learning to fly. Drill several ¼ inch ventilation holes in the sides above the level of the opening. Hinge the top, or one side so you can open it for cleaning, inspection, and removal of old nests. The birdhouse should be cleaned at least once a year. You can use metal hinges for this or a piece of rubber or leather works for the top. If you use the side for this attach a latch to keep it closed.

Finally, drill some ¼ inch holes in the bottom for drainage. Do not add a perch as this can attract predators and the adult birds may leave. Galvanized nails or screws will last longer than ordinary nails. Gluing all the joints before you nail them will extend the life of your birdhouse. Seal the sides with sealant as you build to make the box both windproof and waterproof.

Painting the box is not necessary. Some colors may even discourage birds from nesting.

If you do paint the box keep in mind that lead-based paints and creosote can be harmful to birds. Dull, light colors reflect heat, and are less conspicuous to predators. You should seal the sides with sealant as you build, to make the box both windproof and waterproof. You can use a coat of linseed oil to keep the wood from drying out. Again be careful because some wood preservatives can be harmful to birds. If you do use a preservative, do not treat the inside.

Before assembling the pieces, drill a hole at the top of the back board so you can attach it to a pole or tree.

The dimensions for this house are for bluebirds. There are over two dozen birds in North America that will nest in birdhouses. The dimensions for other birdhouses are in the Birdhouse dimensions table.

While most birdhouses are made of wood, you can buy aluminum houses for martins. Many people make birdhouses out of gourds for wrens and martins.

Where to Put Your Birdhouse

Try to place the birdhouse where it is shaded from the hot sun. A little morning sun will not hurt. Most birds like a clear flight path into the nest box. To attract birds you might try placing a small amount of grass or a piece of dried moss inside. If possible have the hole facing away from the prevailing wind so rain does not blow in.

Different habitats attract different birds. Observe the bird you want to attract in its natural habitat and try to recreate it. There are many things you can do in your yard. One thing you can do is provide bird feeders and water. Do not put the food to close to the birdhouse or they may not use it for fear of predators. You may even want to plant trees or shrubs, birds can perch on to survey the feeder for predators from a safe distance.

If You Build It They Will Come

The light level changes caused by early late winter and early spring affect the hormones of birds, and they start their breeding behavior. The males will start singing and trying to attract mates. You may see them checking your birdhouse out. They will land and peer into the opening. Any other cavities such as a hole in a tree or opening in a clothesline post will also be investigated.

Once they decide on a house they will start to bring nesting material. Usually this means they will nest here but the birds could still choose a different location.

Predators and Unwanted Competitors

This is a good place to mention competitors that many people consider a nuisance. Starlings and sparrows were both imported to the U.S. They are both very aggressive cavity nesters and often take over houses that other birds might nest in. Neither bird is protected by law, unlike most other birds. Sometimes repeatedly removing their nesting material will persuade them to go elsewhere. Some people resort to buying traps to get rid of them.

Not all birds will use a birdhouse or nest box. Those that do will want protection from predators, and easy access to food and water. Birds have many predators.

Raccoons and snakes are very common predators that are a danger to the birds, their young, and eggs. Claw marks on your birdhouse or nesting material pulled from the entrance are signs that you may have a raccoon around.

Dogs may attack young birds during nesting season.

Cats are always a danger. If you have a cat, try using a bell collar. The period when young birds are learning to fly is one of the most dangerous for them, and they may be unable to escape the clutches of a cat. When the house is occupied a cat may reach in and attack young birds or even catch parents trying to protect their young. Some people have had success by wrapping a piece of tin around a tree or post creating a cat guard, so the cat can't climb up.

Squirrels can damage the birdhouse. If they get in, they can eat the eggs. A predator guard of sheet metal added to the entrance hole will usually take care of this.

Birdhouses mounted on metal poles are less vulnerable to predators than houses nailed to tree trunks or hung from tree limbs. Many people smear the poles with a petroleum jelly and hot pepper mixture. A 2-foot section of 4 inch PVC pipe around the pole will help with raccoons and squirrels. This will also help if you have a squirrel problem on a bird feeder. If you have snakes, in addition to the PVC pipe, spread a few shovels of sharp gravel around the base.

Another advantage to mounting your birdhouse on a steel pole is you can easily move anywhere you want.

Many **insects** lay their eggs and pupate in birdhouses. You should inspect your birdhouses for signs of gypsy moths, blowflies, ants, gnats, bees, and wasps.
Coating the inside of the roof with bar soap will help keep bees and wasps from attaching their nests. Birdhouses should be cleaned out each spring and after nesting prevent a buildup of parasites and mites. Plugging the holes in winter is also a good idea, as it will discourage mice or starlings from living in the house.

Number of Birdhouses

It's a good idea to have several houses because there is always a shortage of available cavities, and a number of birds will compete for the same house. Do not place the nest boxes too close together, as this creates unwanted competition. Too many in one location can also be a problem.

Birds That Will Not Use a Nest Box

Many birds such as cardinals or orioles will not use birdhouses. You can still attract them to bird feeders and water. If you do they may stay and nest in nearby trees. For types of food visit the Food - Feeding section.

Another good choice for a free birdhouse is natural gourds. Many people grow their own gourds, and they are very attractive nest boxes.

Birdhouse or Nest Box Dimensions

When deciding on the dimensions for your birdhouse, consider what that bird might use in its natural environment. Primary cavity nesters such as woodpeckers, chickadees, and nuthatches control the size of the hole by using their bills to chisel a hole in a tree. Other cavity nesting birds called secondary nesters use cavities that are either already there or were created by primary cavity nesters. Secondary nesters are birds such as bluebirds, swallows, and titmice. For many birds you want a hole large enough that they can easily come in and out, but small enough that it keeps out predators and birds like starlings, which are very aggressive and will monopolize your birdhouse. An opening 1 9/16 inches or smaller will usually keep starlings out.

The inside should accommodate the size of nest a particular species builds. There should be enough distance from the hole so predators cannot reach in and get the babies, yet not too much distance to prevent young birds from looking out and being fed by the parents.

Box Dimensions

Bird	Box floor inches	Box height inches	Entrance height inches	Entrance diameter inches	Placement height feet
Bluebird	5x5	8-12	6-10	1-1/2	4-6
Chickadees	4x4	8-10	6-8	1-1/8	6-15
Flycatcher	6x6	8-12	6-10	1-3/4	5-15
House wrens	4x4	6-8	4-6	1-1/4	6-10
Kestrel	9x9	14-16	10-12	3	15-30
Northern Flicker	7x7	16-18	14-16	2-1/2	6-20
Nuthatches	4x4	8-10	6-8	1-1/4	5-15
Purple Martin	6x6	6	1-2	2-1/4	6-20
Titmice	4x4	10-12	6-10	1-1/4	5-15
Tree and Violet-Green Swallows	5x5	6-8	4-6	1-1/2	5-15
Barn Owls	10x18	15-18	4	6	12-18
Screech Owls	8x8	12-15	9-12	3	10-30
Downy Woodpecker	4x4	8-10	6-8	1-1/4	6-20

Hairy
Woodpecker   6x6   12-15   9-12   1-1/2   8-20

Lewis's
Woodpecker   7x7   16-18   14-16   2-1/2   12-20

Pileated
Woodpecker   8x8   16-24   12-20   3x4   15-25

Red-Headed
Woodpecker   6x6   12-15   9-12   2   10-20

Warbler   5x5   6   4-5   1-1/8   4-8

Yellow- bellied
Sapsucker   5x5   12-15   9-12   1-1/2   10-20

Birds below use nesting shelves instead of nest box
Swallow - American Robin - Phoebes

Feeding Birds & Bird Foods

Feeding birds and watching them at feeders is enjoyable for people
of all ages. For birds the benefit is a reliable food source provided
by feeders. Many birds depend on feeders to get them through the
winter.

All birds need food, water, and shelter, but they all have different
nutritional needs. If you are looking for specific types of birds, you are
more likely to find them if you look in their normal habitat. You will
also have more success in your backyard or garden if you are feeding
the birds what they like.

Natural foods that birds eat include insects, worms, berries, fruit,
flower nectar, nuts, seeds, tree sap, buds of trees and shrubs, fish,
small animals, other birds, and eggs. They even scavenge dead
animals.

You can get a clue what a bird eats by the type of beak or bill the bird
has. A thick cone-shaped bill is good for cracking seeds. Examples of
these birds are cardinals, grosbeaks, finches, sparrows, and towhees.
These birds eat seeds all year long, eating insects when seeds are
scarce.

For a look at different types of bird beaks see the anatomy section.

Other factors that determine a bird's diet include flight habits, sight, and hearing. For example, birds such as the swallow that feeds while flying rely mostly on insects for food. The eyesight of eagles and hawks lets them see prey from great distances. The hearing of an owl helps it detect rodents in darkness. A heron not only has ability to see fish, but it is able to allow for refraction of the water. Robins can see and hear slight movements of earthworms.

Seasons

Since the availability of food plays a large role in determining what a bird eats, seasonal changes make a difference. When fruits are ripe, the birds feed on fruit. Insects are more plentiful at certain times of a year. Birds are great opportunists and will eat what is available. Most migrating birds will eat to help build fat for their migration. To entice birds to stay all year, you will need to provide food for them all year. During winter small birds eat all day long because they burn food up rapidly keeping warm, so they need a constant supply. It is more difficult for many birds to find food in the winter months. When there is heavy snow on the ground, the supply of food for seed-eating birds may be hard to find or get to. Ice and snow can make it difficult for birds that depend on getting insects and their eggs from beneath bark. This can be a great time to observe them since they may become tamer if they need to use feeders more.

Garden
The best way to develop a backyard that will attract birds is to observe the birds in the wild. Birds like natural habitats. A garden that looks like the bird's natural habit is more likely to be visited by birds then one with excessive pruning. The reason nest boxes are used by birds is they have the same function as tree cavities in the wild. By watching birds in their natural surroundings, you will get a good idea of where to put your nest box or feeder.

Feeding Hummingbirds

Their unique habits and beautiful jewel colors make hummingbirds one of the most popular birds to watch. The two main sources of food for hummingbirds are nectar and small insects. They will visit all flowers but are especially attracted to red, orange, and bright pink. To attract these little bird jewels, plant flowering annuals, perennials, and shrubs.

There are many different hummingbird feeders sold, or you can make your own. Hummingbirds love sugar water. Here is a simple formula: about 1 part white sugar to 4 parts water. Boil the water, add the sugar until it dissolves, and let it cool. Once you get hummingbirds coming to you feeders fill them daily. You should clean them every few days. Rinse them with hot water. A little vinegar added to the water will help fight mold.

Unfortunately, insects also like sugar water. For a hanging feeder, a little petroleum jelly on the wire will keep ants away. Flying insects are a little harder. Try a small amount of the jelly around feeder openings. You can also get bee guards—plastic grates that cover the openings. Other birds such as sparrows, woodpeckers, and chickadees will also visit the feeders, especially if there is a perch for them.

Hand Feeding

It comes as a surprise to many people that wild birds will eat out of your hand. Birds such as chickadees, nuthatches, Downy Woodpeckers, hummingbirds and others will eat out of your hand. The trick here is to get them used to you being around the feeder. They will soon start to feed even if you are there. Once they do this, stand still and hold out your hand with seeds in it, and hopefully they will start to land on your hand.

Providing Food for Birds

Many songbirds are attracted to seeds. There are many good feeders you can buy, or you can just design your own. The main food bird feeders provide are grains, seeds, nuts, and fats in the form of suet. It is best to provide a mix of sizes. Niger, billet, and sunflower seeds make a good mix. Certain birds like robins will be attracted to pieces of fruit. You could put the fruit on a stick. Many birds like bakery products.

In addition to bird feed, it is good to provide grit. Birds do not have teeth and depend on hard particles in their gizzards to grind up their food. You can get grit at bird feed stores and garden centers. Some forms of grit are ground oyster shells, sand with particles of quartz, and crushed eggshells. Grit will also give the birds calcium, which is essential to birds' diets, especially during nesting season when they need more calcium to produce strong eggs. Spread the grit on the ground, or put it in small containers away from the feeders to avoid bird droppings.

Seeds and Grains

Birdseed can be found in a variety of retail stores. Many experienced bird watchers will avoid much of commercial mixes because they have inexpensive seeds in them that the birds will not eat.

You can attract specific birds by offering only feed you know they will eat. One way to find out what the bird you want to attract eats is to put containers of different foods out, and watch which food they eat. Preferences do change though, so you may want to test at different times of the year. To get started go with the most popular feed.

Sunflower

Black oil sunflower was designed specifically to feed wild birds. It is all black with a thin papery shell. Most songbirds that eat sunflower prefer it. It is good for the birds because it is rich in oil and fat, which helps birds through cold winter nights. It is also a good buy because 70 percent of the seed is meat. It can be put in feeders or just thrown on the ground.

Sunflower hearts can be purchased unshelled to lessen the mess. They are more expensive than shelled seeds, but they last significantly longer. They do not last long if exposed to the weather so it is best to only use them in feeders.

Safflower

This seed will help you attract favorite birds and discourage unpopular birds. It has hard shells, and some birds like starlings have more trouble eating it. Other birds like cardinals, chickadees, and nuthatches love it. It is also good for birds because it is rich in oil. Like sunflower seeds, this can be offered either in feeders or spread on the ground.

Niger Seed

This small black seed is a favorite of certain birds like goldfinches, and Pine siskin. Many other birds will prefer other seeds. Again the best way to know is to test.

Millet

This is a small, round, shiny cream-colored seed, found often in mixed birdseed. Birds like sparrows, cardinals, and juncos will eat this.

Corn

There are a number of forms corn can be offered in. Northern cardinals, sparrows, blackbirds, and many others love cracked corn. Corn cobs, or corn meal mush are also popular. This makes a great winter food because the high carbohydrates are good for keeping birds warm.

Nutmeats

Nuts are a great winter food because they are high in calories, and fat. Some birds may have trouble with harder shelled nuts. Peanuts have a lighter shell than most.

Other Bird Foods

Suet

Next to black oil sunflower, suet is a favorite of people who feed birds. Woodpeckers, nuthatches, bluebirds, chickadees, and many other birds are attracted to suet. Beef suet is the best. You can get it from a butcher. If you are going to melt it, ask the butcher to grind it for you. Suet cakes can be made with all kinds of tasty treats in them. Heat the suet to melt it. Let it cool a little to thicken, and add your ingredients. You can add raisins, peanut butter, fruits, and cornmeal. Pour the mixture in to small containers and store in a freezer. If you don't like the work, you can buy commercial suet cakes. They have the advantage of not spoiling as fast, but many birds prefer the soft homemade cakes.

Baked Goods

Most birds love baked goods such as white bread crumbs, doughnuts, crackers, pancakes, and more.

Fruit and Jelly

A bowl with cut fruit and jelly will attract robins, mockingbirds, orioles, and many others. Try putting half an orange on a stick.

Mealworms

Orioles, warblers, Purple martins, and other birds will come for mealworms. Wild bird supplies, pet stores, and fish bait shops will have mealworms.

Sugar Water

As mentioned earlier, this is great for hummingbirds. Many other birds also like it. Grosbeaks, cardinals, finches, woodpeckers, and chickadees are just few of the birds that will come to sugar water feeders.

Water
One of the best ways to attract a variety of birds to your yard is to
have a clean source of water such as a shallow birdbath, or small pond
for them to drink and bathe in. Most birds cannot resist water and
will make frequent trips to a water source. Songbirds usually prefer
water close to a protective cover like shrubs or trees. They like the
water far enough from vegetation so that they can keep an eye on
what is around them, and close enough for them to dive for cover if
they detect predators. They will check out the water from a close by
tree, and then dive down for a drink or splash. Another consideration
in summer is having the water at least partially shaded so it does not
get to hot. The birds will splash in the water to clean their feathers.
During cleaning most birds rub oil from their preen gland on their
feathers. Some do what is called anting, where they rub an ant on
their feathers to help fight parasites. This is thought by some to fall
under the use of tools, and be a sign of intelligence.

To accommodate the bathing of different sizes of birds, make sure the
edges of the birdbath slope gradually upward towards the edge. If
your water source has varying levels of shallow and deep water, it will
be used by a wider variety of birds, as smaller birds will need shallower
water to bathe and splash in. Many birdbaths have smooth, slippery
edges. It is best to have roughened material so birds can have firm
footing.

The sound of running water is hard for birds to resist. You can use
a pump in your birdbath or pond to get water flowing. Observing
birds around water in the wild will aid you in creating a spot in your
backyard or garden that will attract them. You can buy a birdbath, or it
is easy to make a small pool. Use an old barrel, a plastic pool, or line a
hole in the ground with plastic sheeting. Try providing water in winter
too since many natural sources will be frozen.

Bird Feeders

The more feeders and nest boxes you have, the more birds you will
have in your yard. You can get numerous styles of both in a wide price
range.
The cheaper wood feeders held together with staples will fall apart.
Squirrels also tend to eat these. Good quality feeders are held
together with screws and are often made with kiln dried cedar or pine.
Feeders should be kept clean so it is a good idea to consider how easy
a feeder is to fill or clean.

Platform feeders

Birds like the openness of platform feeders but the food will get scattered easily so it doesn't last as long. They can also be messy. Just about any flat object such as piece of plywood can be used. You can easily add raised sides to it to make a tray. Make it into a fly through feeder by attaching a roof to it. Put the feeder on a pole or hang it in a tree.

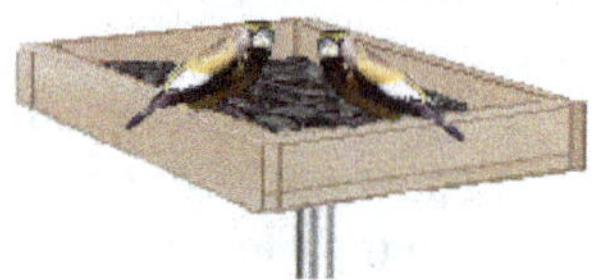

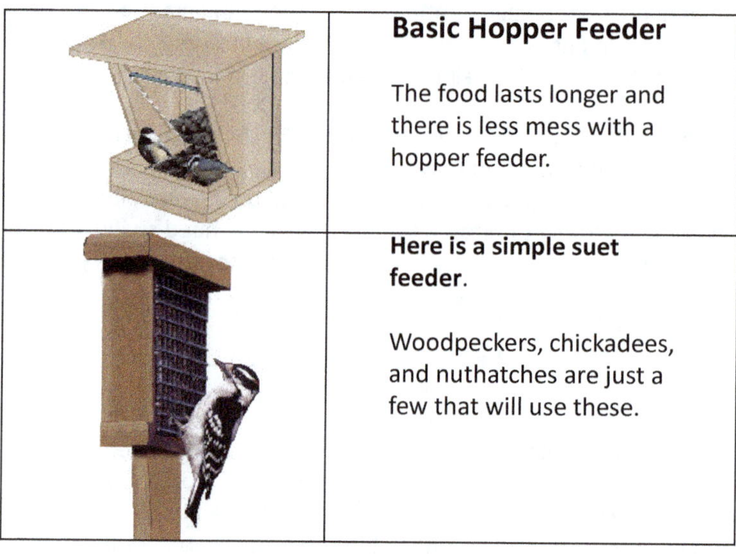

Basic Hopper Feeder

The food lasts longer and there is less mess with a hopper feeder.

Here is a simple suet feeder.

Woodpeckers, chickadees, and nuthatches are just a few that will use these.

Other types of popular feeders are wire mesh or tube feeders. Tube feeders are good for smaller birds like finches or sparrows. The wire mesh is good for peanuts and will attract birds like woodpeckers, Blue Jays and chickadees.

Keeping Feeders Clean

Birds do carry diseases and dirty feeders can transmit them to other birds. To clean the feeders, remove the old seed. A small brush may be helpful. Soak the feeder in water and a small amount of bleach. Shake feeders or use a stick to remove seed clogs before filling feeders. Rake up hulls and droppings under feeders regularly.

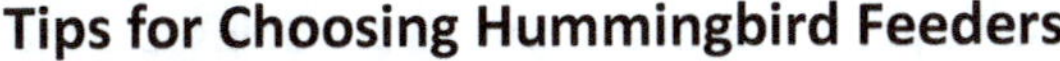

Tips for Choosing Hummingbird Feeders

There are many shapes and sizes to choose from. Designs such as pie or saucer shaped, tubes and many others. Some have perches for the little birds to land on. While most feeders will attract birds, there are some basic guidelines to follow that will make both you and the hummingbirds happy.

Here are some tips:

- Probably the most important design feature to look for is ease of disassembly and cleaning. The larger ones are easier to clean. A dishrag and a small bottlebrush such as an old toothbrush will work. Pipe cleaners are also good for cleaning. There are special brushes sold for cleaning hummingbird feeder ports.
  Wash your hummingbird feeders thoroughly with hot, soapy water, and rinse completely every time you refill them. Keep an eye out for molds.

- Perches are great. Hummingbirds use a tremendous amount of energy hovering and prefer to sit when they feed if they are able to do so.

- Red is the most attractive color to hummingbirds. You are better off not coloring the sugar water.

- Ants love sugar so look for built in ant moats. You can also get add-on ant moats.

- Bees and wasps are also pests that love nectar. Bee guards will help. The most attractive color to bees and wasps is yellow. Some shapes such as saucer feeders will discourage bees.
  Smear a bit of petroleum jelly around the feeder port to discourage both ants and bees.

- Rain guards help if you get a hummingbird feeder with feeding ports located on top of the solution reservoir. Rain will dilute and possibly contaminate the mixture. You can also get rain guards to hang on your feeder.

- Saucer feeders are better than bottle feeders in direct sunlight. Bottle feeders will leak as they warm up. The sun will cause the sugar solution to spoil rapidly.

Where to Put Hummingbird Feeders

Place your feeders where hummingbirds are most likely to see them, such as near flowers. Flowers offer the birds energy in exchange for pollination. Feeders make a good substitute. They also eat insects and spiders for protein.

After they get in the habit of visiting, you can move it closer to a window if you want. This not only lets you watch the birds but you can see when the sugar is low.

If you have a garden area with flowers hummingbirds like, that is a good place.

Once hummingbirds discover where a feeder is, the birds will keep coming back daily even bringing their young. They will return year after year to the same feeders. During migration the traffic can increase. Many people like to put the feeders by a window so they can watch. You can get window feeders that attach to the window.

If your feeder is within 15 feet of a window, move it so it is only a few inches away. Windows are dangerous because the birds will fly into them. They are less likely to if the feeder is either farther than 15 feet or just a few inches from the window.

Hummingbirds are more likely to visit your feeders if there is cover close by. They spend a great deal of time perched in trees or bushes where they are protected. They prefer to fly only a short distance food.

A shady spot keeps feeders cool and reduces spoilage. On the other hand the hummingbird's colors come out in sunlight. The answer is a compromise. Try to a place where the feeder is in shade for a good part of the day.

Sometimes a single hummingbird will dominate a feeder so spreading several around is a good idea.

Sugar solution

The standard recipe for sugar water is 1 part white sugar to 4 parts water. Bring water to a boil over low heat and stir in the sugar. Boiling kills mold spores, but do not over boil. Cool the mixture and fill the feeder. Store sugar water in the refrigerator.

Do not use honey because it spoils easily and has bacteria in it that can cause a fatal fungal tongue disease.

Photographing Birds

Learn how to photograph birds to make bird watching more fun. There is a rush of excitement when you capture the bird in a photo just the way you wanted. Even though there are countless photos of that bird, it is a great feeling when you took it yourself. Bird photography is easy to get hooked on.

Yes, there will be plenty of bad photos, but the good ones make it worth it. Here are a few photography tips.

Patience in Bird Photography

Photographing birds requires patience. Most birds are afraid of people, and all species have their own comfort zone. With a little time, you can learn the comfort zone of the birds you are photographing. If you get to close and scare them off, many birds will come back if you just sit still for a while.

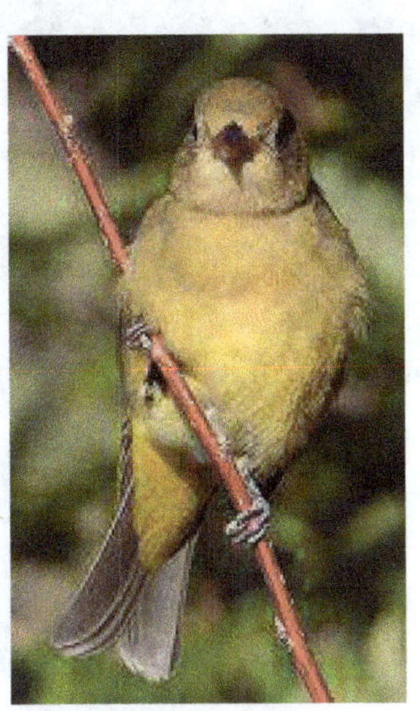

 Once they perceive that you are not a threat you may be able to get closer. Sometimes they will be curious and come close to study you, creating interesting opportunities, as when this tanager came in to look at me.

Type or Style

Your reason for photographing birds may determine your style, and the kind of equipment you use. If you are just recording the kinds of birds you see, you don't need to get as close, and you can use less expensive equipment then you need for high quality prints.

My approach to bird photography is usually to just walk through a wooded area and photograph the birds I see. I like taking handheld shots. I know that I could get better quality images if I used a tripod but the experience with a handheld camera is much more enjoyable. I am able to respond faster to a bird that perches next to me, and move with the bird when it moves.

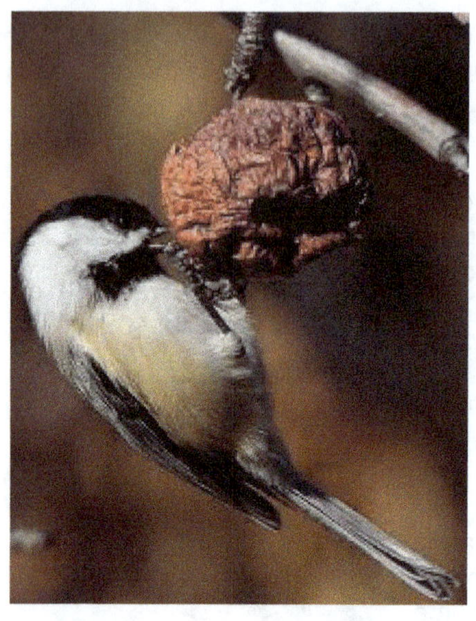

The chickadee in this photo landed on an apple above me and was only there for a few seconds. While I would have liked to have time to make adjustments, if my camera had been on a tripod I wouldn't have even gotten the shot. It's true you can get more crystal clear images with a tripod, but you lose some flexibility. Most birds are highly active and they are not going to pose for you. Birds like chickadees are usually fluttering all over the place.

Photographing Birds in Flight

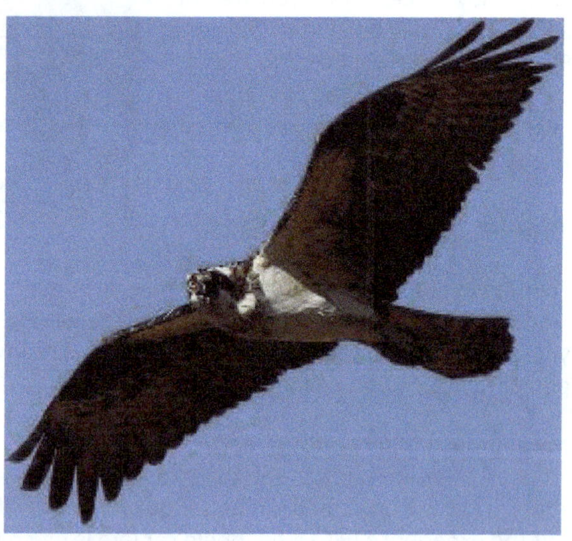

Photographing birds in flight can be fun. Many digital cameras have a tracking function. With these you focus on the bird, and then as you track it the lens will keep focus. There are basically two ways to photograph flying birds.

The first is to focus on a point in the bird's flight path and snap the shot as it goes by. The second is to track the bird with your camera. A fast shutter speed of at least 1/500 of a second is recommended. By using a slower shutter speed you can capture wing motion. In the photo of the osprey, I tracked him as he circled above me. Every time he would come around he would look at me.

Use Your Yard

An easy; inexpensive way to get started in bird photography is set bird feeders and a birdbath in your yard. Choose an open area where the birds will get direct sunlight, showing off their magnificent colors. For the best bird photography, you will want the sun in back of you.

Try Using Props

Occasionally, I will place a stick where I think a bird might land, giving me a desired photo. Birds will often land on a stick or post near a suet or seed feeder before going to the feeder. For the chickadee shot, I placed a stick near a feeder. The background was just an out-of-focus fence, but you can use anything you want for a background, and then wait for a bird to perch. The birds coming to your feeder will get used to you, and you can often just sit nearby and wait for a good shot.

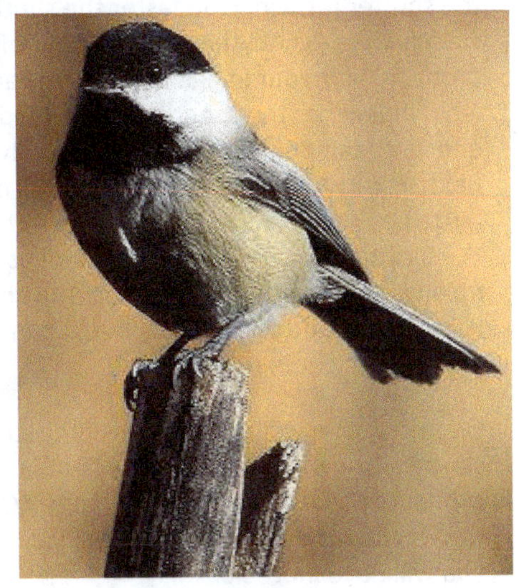

Photography Equipment

When I started photography, the only choice was film. You would take your pictures, and until you had the film developed you weren't really sure what you had. I fought the transition to digital, but what won me over was the instant gratification of seeing my pictures on my computer right away.

Photographers today have a dizzying array of cameras and equipment to choose from.

Since you will probably be shooting in a variety of situations, I highly recommend you get a camera that has interchangeable lenses.

Most of the photos on in this book were taken with a Canon EOS 40D and a 70 to 300 IS zoom lens. I like the camera size and the controls are easy to use. The 300 allows me to get close-ups of small songbirds without getting so close they are spooked. I often take a 500 mm with me, but the 300 is usually on my camera. The longer the lens, the farther you can be from the bird, but there are other considerations. Long telephoto lenses are expensive.

You also need to consider the aperture. A smaller aperture lets in less light than a larger one. The aperture will be shown on the lens barrel in f-stop numbers such as f 8 or f 16. If you let less light in because of the aperture, you need to use a slower speed to compensate so you can get the correct exposure. The shutter speed is the amount of time the shutter is open. The faster the shutter speed is the more motion you can freeze. Anything below 1/60 of a second on a normal lens will probably blur your image because of camera shake. The longer the lens, the higher the speed you will need to use in order to reduce the effects of camera shake. A larger aperture gives you a larger depth of field. For instance, an aperture of f-16 may put everything from the bird's beak to its tail in focus, while with a small aperture of f-2.8, only the bird's beak and eye may be in focus. Basically when you move up an f-stop or speed you double the amount of light hitting your light sensor, and when you move down one stop or speed you cut the amount of light in half.

Good cameras will also have an ISO setting. ISO determines how sensitive the image sensor is to light, and it is the third ingredient for proper exposure. If you set a higher ISO setting you can you can use higher speeds but the image quality suffers because at the higher ISO you will have more noise.

Zoom lenses with image stabilization are quite a bit more expensive; however, if you can afford the extra money, they are worth it. IS will reduce camera shake usually by a couple of f-stops. For instance if you are shooting at 1/250th of a second, the IS lens will let you shoot the same shot at 1/60th of a second.

Most professionals use a tripod so they can reduce camera shake allowing them to use slower shutter speeds or smaller apertures. You will get higher quality pictures with a 12-megabyte camera than a 5-megabyte camera because 12 megabytes means you have higher resolution or more pixels.

Habitats

Many birders like to learn the habitats and range of different birds. Habits
are complex and constantly changing. Many bird species will live in a certain
habitat because it provides things they need, such as food, water and
protection. They may live in a certain habitat during certain times of the year.
Ecotones, or edge areas where two types of habitat come together are likely to
have a higher number of species in them.

Try to think about where birds you are looking for might be in a given habitat.
For example hawks may be seen soaring high in the sky. Kingbirds and
flycatchers may be found in higher tree branches. In the lower branches you
could see wrens and grosbeaks, while towhees and juncos like to hope around
in the undergrowth.

**Here are some examples of habitat types and the kinds of birds that might be
found in each.**

Woodlands

- Boreal Forests: Chickadees, Northern hawk owl, grosbeaks, Pine siskin,
  thrushes, finches, sparrows, warblers, Yellow-bellied sapsucker
- Woodland edges: American Goldfinch, Brown thrasher, cowbird,
  flycatchers, grosbeaks, hummingbirds, juncos, kinglets, nuthatches,
  sparrows, warblers,
- Clearings: Bluebirds, quail, flickers, robins, swallows, flycatchers,
  kestrels, woodcocks
- Wooded waterways: Bullocks oriole, crows, herons, red-shouldered
  hawks, flycatchers, kingbirds, magpies, vireos, towhees, warblers,
  wood ducks
- Medium trees with underbrush: Buntings, cowbird, Juncos, Gray
  catbirds, goldfinches, Northern cardinals, sparrows, towhees,
  thrashers, warblers
- Forests of mixed conifers and deciduous trees: flycatchers, grosbeaks,
  Hairy woodpecker, Pileated woodpecker, Northern goshawk, Scarlet
  tanager, White throated sparrow, Winter wren, warblers

Grasslands

- Prairies - fields - plains: American crow, bobolink, Chestnut-collard
  longspur, sparrows, lark buntings, kestrel, meadowlark, Northern
  cardinal, Red-tailed hawk, Ring-necked pheasant, sandpipers,
  mountain plovers, eagles, short-eared owls
- Farm fields: blackbirds, cow-bird, crows, House wren, Retailed hawk,
  killdeer, plovers, redpolls, swallows, sparrows, goldfinches, kestrels,
  warblers

Wetlands

- Lakes and ponds: American Coot, ducks, loons, Belted kingfisher, Bank swallow, Canada goose, Great blue heron, osprey, warblers

- Freshwater Marshes: American bittern, blackbirds, Common yellowthroat, dowitchers, gulls, herons, egrets, Red-winged blackbird, terns, swallows, rails, Swamp sparrows, shorebirds such as plovers, stilts, wrens

Coastal

- Beaches: Black skimmer, grackles, dowitchers, egrets, gulls, herons, pelicans, plovers, sanderling, sandpipers, spoonbills, terns, willets

- Rocky shorelines: Bald eagles, gulls, Harlequin ducks, cormorants, eiders, loons, grebes, oystercatchers, osprey, pelicans, puffin, sandpipers, terns

- Sea cliffs: auks, cormorants, gannets, gulls, guillemots, kittiwakes, murres, puffins, peregrine falcons

Deserts

- Shrub lands: Flycatchers, thrasher, gnatcatchers, buntings, Black-throated sparrows

- Canyon and cliffs: Golden eagles, falcons, hawks, Rock wrens, swallows, White-throated swifts

Favorite Birds

American Kestrel

Identification

(*Falco sparverius*)

American Kestrels, also called Sparrow hawks, are very colorful small falcons about 9 to 12 inches, with long, narrow, pointed wings. They have short necks, and the head is crowned blue-gray with some orange. They have a short, dark, hooked beak, and there are two dark mustache marks on the face. The large talon-tipped feet are ideal for hunting. They have a rufous brown tail with a dark tip and a rufous brown back. The tail 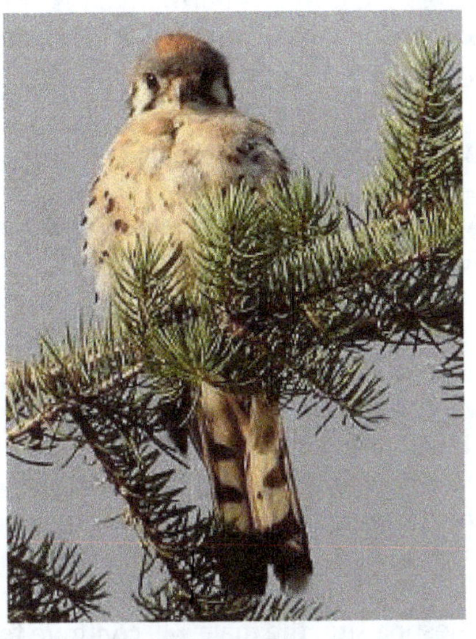 is white underneath with a few black bars. Their under parts are pale buff to orange, with black spots. The males have blue-gray wings with black spots. Both sexes have a white face with two black vertical bars. Females are slightly larger than males. The back of the female's wings and tail are rusty brown with fine dark bars. Young birds have a lot of barring on their back, and a buffy chest with streaking.

They like to sit on treetops, fence posts, or wires in an erect position. They may be seen hovering in one spot, with rapid beating wings, like a kingfisher.

Kestrel sound

The kestrel's sound is sharp metallic notes like klee-klee-klee. This is given during courtship and when alarmed. Both sexes also make whining calls during mating and feeding.

Preferred Habitat

Kestrels are the most common falcon in North America. They can be found across Canada in the summer, and are year-round residents across the U.S. The northern birds are migratory. They like the edges of wooded areas, farmland, and residential areas. They need to have open ground for hunting.

Breeding and Nesting

After the male establishes a territory, a female will start doing activities such as hunting with him. The pair will usually bond for life. Kestrels breed in the spring from April to early June in open habitats such as grasslands, meadows, deserts, and agricultural fields. They nest in cavities in trees, cliffs, or in a nest box. Falcons do not build nests and will use cavities excavated by flickers and other large woodpeckers. They do not add nesting materials to the cavity. Since they need a large hole and they can't make their own nesting sites are always in short supply. On rare occasions they have been known to nest in an old bird nest such as a Magpie nest. Like many birds, the male brings the female morsels of food during courtship. After they have chosen a nesting site, the male will continue to bring her food while she lays 4 to 5 whitish eggs with brown dots on them. The female does most of the incubation for around 30 days. After about 11 weeks the young will take short flights from the nest waiting in trees for the parents to feed them.

Food

Kestrels eat insects, small birds, and small animals like mice. They are able to catch small birds and for this reason was once call a Sparrow hawk.

Kestrels may nest in boxes placed on your property.

Bald Eagle U.S. national bird

Identification

(Haliaeetus leucocephalus)

The bald Eagle, the majestic national bird of the U.S., is 30 to 43 inches with a wingspan of 6 to 8 feet. The white head and the white tail stand out against the dark body. The large, powerful, yellow beak, and large taloned feet are typical of birds of prey that eat animals and tear meat. They have piercing, bright, yellow eyes. Males and females are identical in plumage, but the females are quite a bit larger than males.

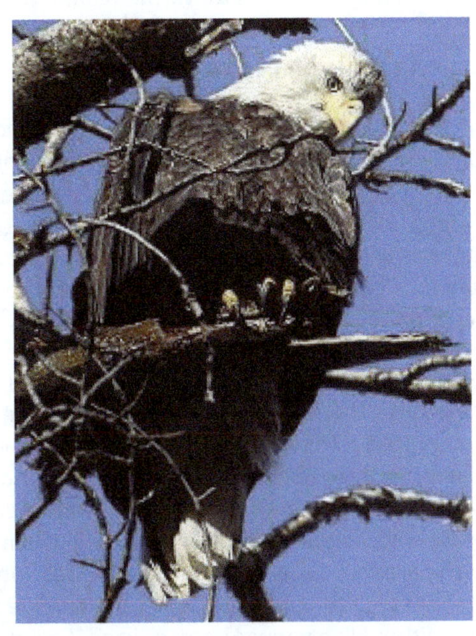

Young birds are often mistaken for Golden Eagles, which have mottled brown plumage speckled with white, white on the belly, and yellow feet. Bald eagles do not get the white head, and tail of the adults until the 4th or 5th year. The Bald Eagle's average life span is 20 years in the wild, but they may live 30 or more years. The birds are very powerful flyers, flying with deep strokes and often soaring with flattened wings on thermal convection currents.

Bald Eagle Sound

The eagle's call consists of weak chirping whistles. The voice is a sharp high-pitched cackle like kleek-kik-ik-ik or a lower kak-kak.

Preferred Habitat

Bald Eagles can be found across Canada and the U.S. They live along rivers, coasts, lakes, in the mountains, and open country. They prefer to stay away from humans. The availability of a food supply determines if they migrate or not.

If their territory gives access to water with fish year round they will
stay all year. If the water freezes over, and they can't get enough food,
they will migrate south to warmer country.

Breeding and Nesting

Bald Eagles mate for life. Their courtship involves elaborate calls and
flight displays. During this flight they do swoops and chase each other
through rapid turns and dives. In a cartwheel flight, the birds will
fly high, lock talons, and free fall, tumbling toward the ground and
separating just before they reach the ground. They need old-growth
stands of coniferous or hardwood trees for perching, roosting, and
nesting.

Both birds together will build a nest of sticks, lined with fine wood
materials. The nest may be on a cliff or the ground but is usually in
a large tree.   The nest, which can be 8 feet wide, is the largest nest
of any North American bird. They will normally use the same nest
each year, adding more sticks each year. The female will lay 1 to 3
white eggs and both birds will incubate them for around 35 days.
Both parents will care for the young birds, which may not fledge for
12 weeks. Often only one eaglet will survive because an older sibling
may either kill a younger one or keep it from getting food. The eagles
will fiercely defend the eggs and young from predators such as crows,
raccoons, and magpies.

Food

Bald Eagles hunt for fish in rivers, lakes, and other bodies of water.
They hunt fish by swooping down and snatching the fish out of the
water with their talons. They are opportunistic and will kill other
animals and birds for food as well as feed on carrion. They will also
steal food from other birds, and mammals. Sometimes Bald Eagles
hunt cooperatively; with one bird flushing prey out while the other
attacks it.

Baltimore Oriole

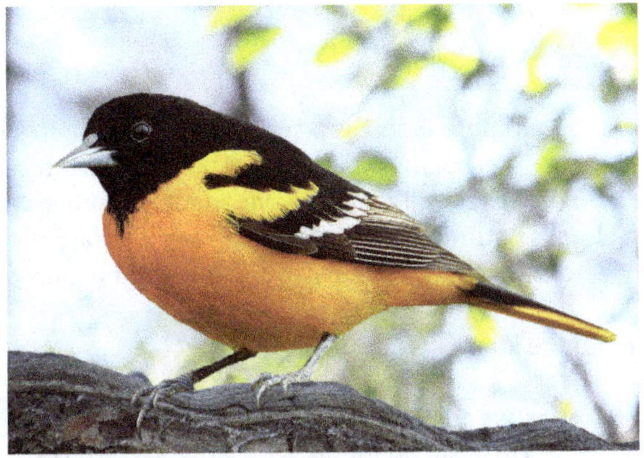

Baltimore Orioles are another favorite of bird watchers.

Just like the robin, the oriole is a sign of spring and summer for many in the United States and Canada. Orioles are one of the most colorful and vocal of the birds that visit our backyard feeders and gardens.

Identification
(Classification: Icterus Galbula)

Baltimore Orioles are 7 to 8 inches.

Male orioles are flaming orange or yellow with a black hood that extends to the back. The tail and wings are black with white wing bars. The female and young are olive brown above and burnt orange below. Some females will have a black hood but it is not as pronounced as the male.

Bullock's Oriole has slightly different colors than the Baltimore oriole. Bullock's has yellow cheeks, a black eye band, and a large white wing patch.

There is also an **Orchard Oriole**. The under parts are a darker orange than the others, and the male is much darker. The white on the wings is not as vivid as it is in the other.

The **Spot breasted oriole** looks like the Baltimore except for an orange head, a black bib, and spots on the sides of the breast.

There are various hybrid orioles where the ranges of the two types overlap.

Song and Sound of the Oriole

The song of the Baltimore Oriole is a sequence of rich piping whistled notes, sometimes with harsh raspy notes. There is also a tee-dee-dee or hoo-lee sound. Males will tend to have an identifiable pattern. The female song is less patterned than the male. Loud nasal calls that sound like dee-dee-dee are made by young birds or fledglings.

Habitat and Range

Orioles prefer open woods, shade trees, orchards, parks, and gardens with shade trees. They can be found across the Eastern U.S. and Canada. They winter in Florida, the Gulf Coast, and Central and South America.

Nesting and Breeding

In courtship the male will face the female and bow with his wings and tail spread. Baltimore Orioles like to breed in thickets with scattered tall trees near a forest edge or close to water. The nest built mostly by the female will often be in a tree or shrub 5 to 15 feet high; however, they do put them much higher. They make a deep pouch or sock-like nest that is bound at the top to branches. It is made of twigs, bark fibers, string, grasses, and other materials. The nest is lined with moss, plant down, or fine grasses.

The female will incubate 3 to 5 eggs. The eggs are smooth and glossy. The color is grayish or bluish-white or with a purple tint. They can be marked with black or blackish-purple, usually around the large end.

The young are fed by both parents and can fly in around two weeks.

Food and Feeding

Natural foods are caterpillars, other insects, blossoms, fruit and berries. They are easily attracted to bird feeders with fruit, jellies, peanut butter, or suet.

Baltimore orioles will visit birdbaths to bathe and drink.

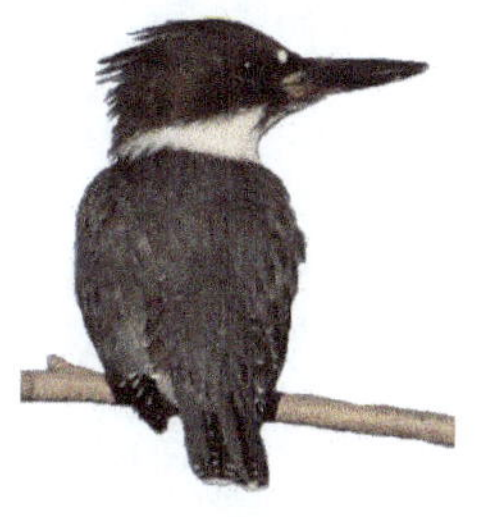

Belted Kingfisher

Identification (Megaceryle alcyon)

Belted Kingfishers are easy to identify with their large head, bushy crest, and large black bill. They are stocky, noisy fishing birds, 11 to 14 1/2 inches. Their plumage is blue gray above with a large white collar, a broad gray breast band, and white under parts. They have a small white spot by each eye.

 Females have rusty a band that goes across the breast and down the sides, making Kingfishers one of the few birds where the female is more colorful than the male. Juvenile males will have a mottled rusty band and young females have a rusty band that is not as pronounced as it is in the adults.

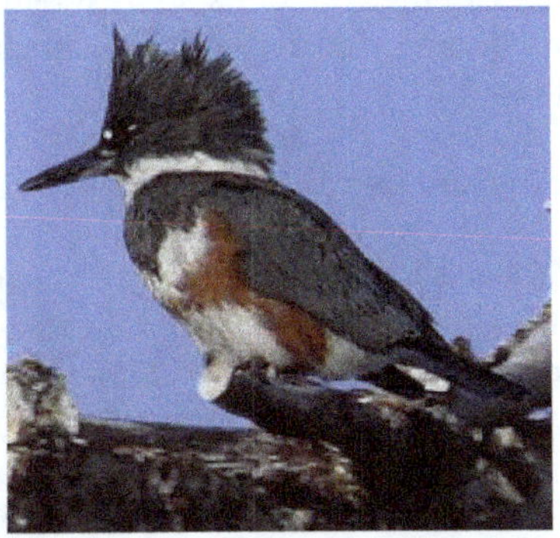

They are often seen hovering in the air with rapid beating wings, as they prepare to dive into the water for a fish. They can be recognized in flight by their deep uneven wing beats.

Sound

The voice of the Kingfisher is a loud high rattle. They often give this as they take off or prepare to dive into water.

Preferred Habitat

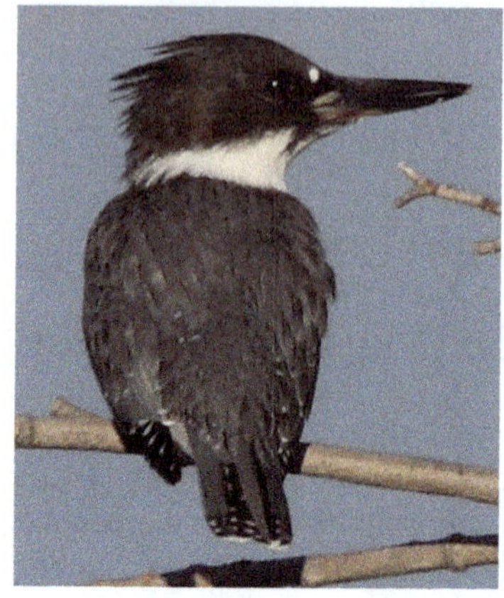

Belted Kingfishers range extends across North America. Northern populations migrate south. In warmer climates the birds are resident all year. They can be found around bodies of water such as rivers, streams, ponds, lakes or coastline.

Breeding and Nesting

After the male establishes a territory, he sings mewing songs to attract a mate. During courtship he will catch fish to feed her. Pairs once formed are monogamous. A typical nest is a burrow in a riverbank excavated by both sexes. In addition to their large bill, two of kingfisher's toes that are fused together aid in their digging, providing the birds with a built-in shovel. During excavation the two birds will constantly rattle to each other. The burrow will slope up hill, leaving an air pocket for the young incase of flooding. Females usually lay 5 to 8 white eggs, which are incubated by both birds for about 3 weeks. Both adults will take care of the young birds, which will fledge in about 4 weeks. The young birds will stay with and be fed by the parents for about 3 more weeks.

Food

The Kingfishers' diet mainly consists of fish; however, they also eat other aquatic life such as frogs, crayfish, snails, tadpoles, and insects. They like to perch above clear water so they can dive when they see their prey. Often they will hover in the air with rapidly beating wings, plunging into the water when they see a fish.

In 1986 Canada ran the Birds of Canada series on their currency. The Kingfisher was on the 5-dollar bill.

Great Blue Heron

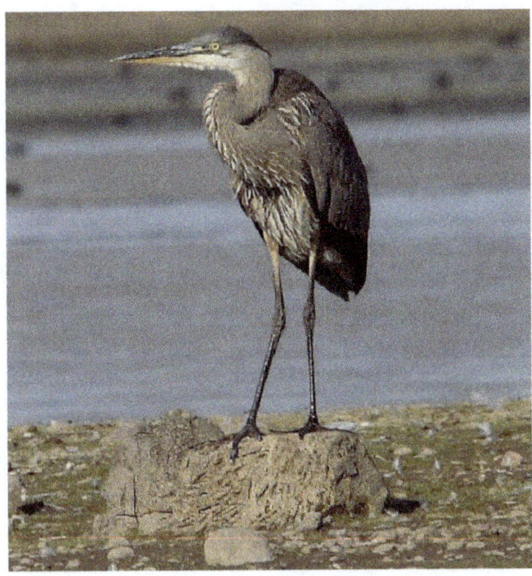

Identification (*Ardea herodias*)

The Great Blue Heron is a lean, blue-gray bird with chestnut on the thighs it stands 4 feet tall, and is 42 to 45 inches. It is the largest heron in North America. Their long legs, long neck, and long, sharp, orange bill are all well suited to their habit of wading and fishing. The adults have a shaggy ruff on their neck, and show white around the head. In breeding plumage they may have plumes. They have a 6-foot wingspan and fly with their neck folded in an s shape, and the legs trailing behind. The sexes look similar. Young birds are duller in color and have a dark gray crown. Herons are often seen standing motionless with the head either erect or between the shoulders.

Although they may stand 4 feet tall, they usually only weigh around 5 pounds because they have hollow bones. These birds are often mistaken for cranes.

Sound

The Great Blue Heron's voice is a deep harsh croak.

Preferred Habitat

Great Blue Herons range across most of North America. They can be found near water sources such as swamps, lakes, rivers, shorelines, and tidal flats. Northern populations may be migratory while birds in others areas are year round residents.

Breeding and Nesting

At the beginning of the nesting season the male chooses a territory and performs displays to attract a female. Herons usually nest in large colonies called heronries, but may nest as lone pairs. For a nest they build a stick platform lined with moss, grass, bark strips, and twigs usually in a tree or bushes, but sometimes on a cliff edge or in reeds. The female lays 3 to 6 bluish eggs. The parents will take turns incubating the eggs for around 30 days. Both adults will feed and care for the young birds, which will fledge in about 2 months. The young birds will return to the nest to be fed for an additional week. A pair only raises one brood each year.

Food

Herons feed mostly on fish but also eat things like frogs, salamanders, small mammals, birds, crabs, crayfish, and insects. They have two methods of foraging. In one method they stand still until they see their prey, then they strike swiftly with their dagger-like beak, grabbing or impaling it. They also stock their prey, wading slowly until they are in striking distance. They fish both night, and day however they are more active during mornings and dusk because these are the best fishing times.

Blue Jay

Identification (Cyanocitta cristata)

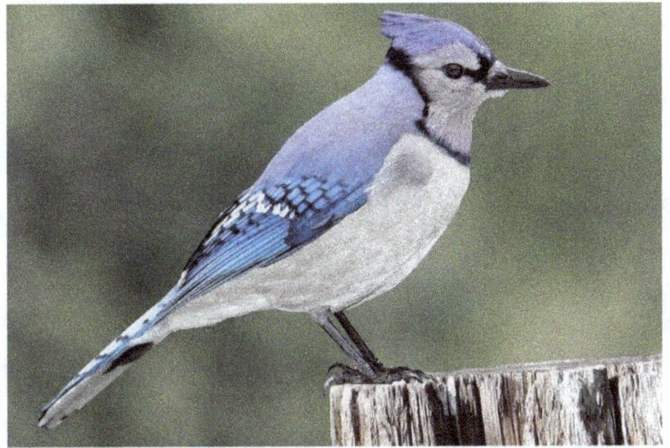

Blue Jays are a very attractive bird, a little larger than an American Robin, about 11 to 12 inches. Both male and female are blue above with a crest and a black necklace. The wings and tail have spotted

white and black markings. They are dull gray to whitish below.

They can be found in woodlands, parks, and your backyard feeders across central, and eastern U.S., and southern Canada year round. They have a wide expanding range in the western U.S. and much of southern Canada.

Breeding and Nesting

Breeding season is April to May. They breed in mixed wooded areas usually near open space. They like oaks and pinewoods as well as gardens.

Nests are built in trees or shrubs, sometimes in a tree cavity. Both adults will build a nest with twigs, grass, strips of bark, feathers, rags, and even paper. Mud may be used as mortar. Blue Jays can have more than one brood in a season. The female will incubate 4 to 6 eggs. Eggs are smooth and glossy. They can be pinkish, green, bluish, or pale olive. They are specked with brown, olive or purple.

The young birds are attended by both adults and can leave the nest in around 3 weeks.

The Blue Jay's Song

The Blue Jay is a very noisy bird with a harsh jay, or a musical wheeedlee or too-lool. Soft nasal notes are given when the birds are close. Blue jays will often mimic the call of hawks.

Food and Feeders

Along with Goldfinches, Juncos, Tree Sparrows, and others, Blue Jays will visit your backyard feeders.

Some people would just as soon not have Blue Jays at their feeders because they consider them bullies. It seems that in some areas they have these aggressive traits, and in others they don't.

Bluebirds

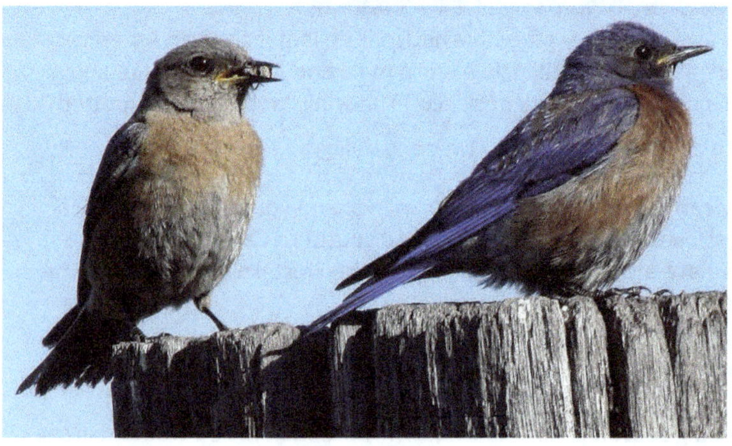

Bluebirds are a favorite of mine, and in fact of most birders. They are not as common as they once were, and there is a concerted effort by many birders to change this. The establishment of bluebird trails is increasing their number. A bluebird trail is a series of nest boxes in appropriate habitats. Even putting up a single nest box helps the cause.

Identification

Bluebird Types

Bluebirds are a member of the Thrush family. They are related to the American robin. There are three types living in North America.

Western Bluebirds (*Sialia mexicana*) are a little larger than a sparrow, around 6 to 7 inches. The head, wings, and tail are blue. The belly is white, the breast, and back are rusty red. In some birds the back will be partially blue.

Eastern Bluebirds (*Sialia sialis*) look the same as Western Bluebirds except they have a rusty throat.

The **Mountain Bluebird** (*Sialia currocoides*) is almost all blue with a whitish belly. The females in all types have duller colors. In the Mountain Bluebird it is dull brownish with a touch of blue on the wings, rump, and tail.

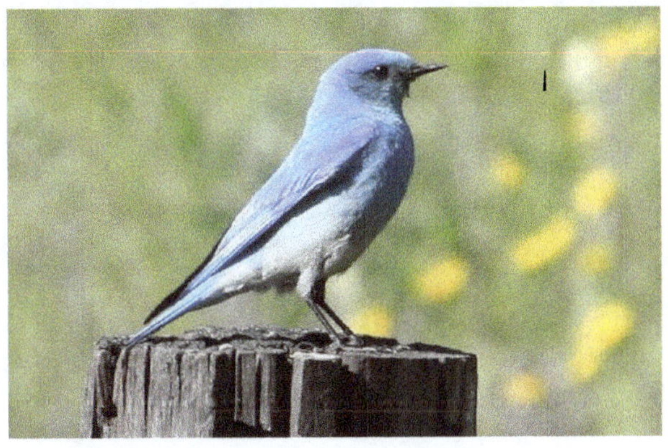

The Bluebird's Song

The Eastern Bluebird makes a note that sounds like *tru-ly*, and the song is soft gurgling notes.

The Western bluebird sounds like *pew.*

Mountain Bluebirds have a chru sound and a song that is a low warble.

Bluebird Trail and Nest Boxes

Below are some tips for starting your own Bluebird trail or attracting these little birds to you backyard.

I will sometimes use "birdhouse" and other times use "nest box" to mean the same thing.

Location - Location

Bluebirds like open spaces with short vegetation and lots of insects. This could be gulf courses, parks or a field on the edge of a wooded area. A large lawn is fine. They nest naturally in dead tree cavities, and abandoned woodpecker holes. The birds do not make their own nest cavities. They rely on natural or manmade cavities such as birdhouses to build nests in. Try placing your birdhouses where there are some nearby trees or shrubs for them to perch on. They are tolerant of humans and do not mind nesting around them.

Many bluebird trails will go on for miles. The boxes are generally spaced around 300 feet apart. The reason for the spacing is bluebirds are territorial when breeding. You can also put up a house or two in your backyard to attract them.

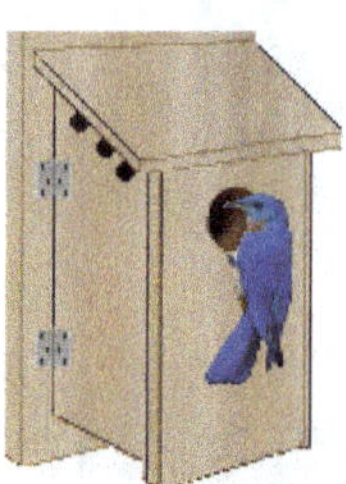

Placement & Mounting

You can place your nest boxes on a pole, fence post or attach it to a tree. Keep in mind that there are many predators. Cats, dogs, squirrel, and snakes all pose a danger.

Try to place your boxes where nesting materials such as soft grasses and pine needles are available. Some people put out containers with these materials for the birds.

Mount your house so the hole faces away from the prevailing wind, preferably out of the direct sun, about five feet above the ground is good. For more about birdhouses see the Birdhouses & Nest Boxes section.

Other Visitors

Do not be surprised to find other birds such as Chickadees or Wrens in your birdhouse. Sparrows can be a problem for Bluebirds. They may destroy the eggs and kill the young. If you see Sparrows building a nest you can remove the material before they finish.

Bluebird Territory

Males will establish a territory of two to five acres. In early March or April the male will try to attract a female with his sweet song. In courtship he will raise and quiver one or both wings and often feed her morsels of food. After she chooses the nesting spot she will lay one egg a day until there are 3 to 5 in the clutch. In 12 to 14 days the eggs will hatch and both adults will feed the young ones. They will fledge or develop the feathers to fly in 15 to 20 days.

Monitoring and cleaning

It's a good idea to check birdhouses once a week. Many people keep records such as the date eggs were laid and hatched. The number for a season, as well as the date and number of young birds can be recorded. The adults will return after you examine the nest. After the nestlings have fledged, remove the old nest so the birds will start over. After breeding season you should bag the nest and throw it away. Check to see if the nest has insects. If you find insects get rotenone powder to dust the box with. If the birds start building a new nest before you remove the old one just leave it alone.

Create a Habitat in Your Backyard

Two things that will attract birds to your backyard are food and plenty of water. You can also plant fruit and berry trees. Add herbaceous flowerbeds to this and you will have an attractive habitat.

Bird Feeders

A bluebird's main diet is insects. They also eat berries, sunflower seeds, nutmeats, and other foods. There are many styles of bird feeders. Use feeders that will not attract larger birds, and do not put them too close to the nest box. Like other birds that eat insects, bluebirds are attracted to suet feeders.

Brown Thrashers

Identification

Sometimes know as the Brown Thrush, these birds are around 10 inches. The upper parts are light brownish red. They have a striking yellow eye and grayish face.

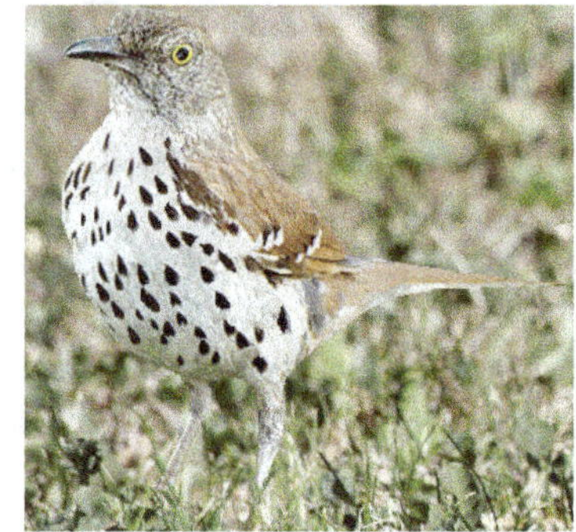

 The wings are crossed by two faint, buff or white bars, and have dark or black tips on secondary coverts. Lower parts are yellowish white, with dark brown spots or streaking on the breast and sides. Their long downward curved bill is useful when probing for insects. The tail is long and fans out.

The scientific name (*Toxostoma rufum*) is a combination of two Greek words, *toxon* (a bow) and *stoma* (mouth). It comes from the curved bill of the Brown Thrasher. The last part of the name (*rufum*) is Latin for reddish, and comes from the body color.

Females look roughly the same as males but are smaller.

Thrashers are the official state bird of Georgia.

Song and Calls

The song includes various phrases repeated two or three times.

Habitat and Range

Thrashers prefer low trees and shrubs with dense vegetation. They can be seen in fields, wood edges, and residential areas throughout most of the United States, and parts of Canada.

Breeding and Nesting

Breeding season is March through July. Both birds build a large, coarse, cup-shaped nest of twigs, dead leaves, and other vegetation. Fine grass lines the inside of the nest, which will be located in shrubs or bushes on near the ground.

Both birds will incubate 2 to 6 smooth and glossy eggs for 11 to 14 days. The egg color is white to pale blue or greenish-blue with reddish-brown speckles. The young will fledge in just less than 2 weeks. The two adults will care for them until they fledge, and for a short period after that.

Food, Feeding, and Water

Natural foods are insects, invertebrates, fruits, berries, nuts, and seeds. Brown Thrashers like to feed on the ground using their long curved bill to search leaf and ground debris for food.

You can attract them to your backyard with seed and suet feeders. They will come for corn, mixed seeds, suet, fruit, and bakery goods. They will find crumbled bits of suet or puddings spread on the ground. The birds will gratefully use a water source such as a birdbath to drink and bathe in.

Brewer's Blackbird

Identification

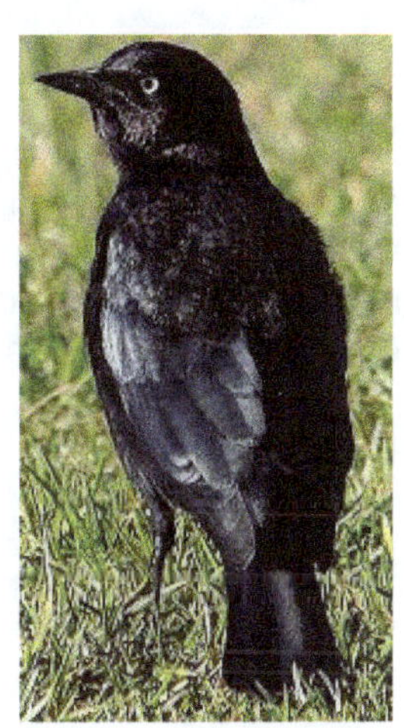

(Euphagus cyanocephalus)

Brewer's Blackbirds are named after ornithologist Thomas Mayo Brewer. They are all black with yellowish eyes and about 8 to 10 inches. They have a pointed bill, long legs, and a long tail. In strong sunlight they have iridescent, purplish reflections on the head and neck, and metallic green on the body. In the winter they may have rusty barring. The females are brownish gray with a dark eye. They are often mistaken for European Starlings, which have a much shorter tail.

Songs and calls

The song is a harsh que-ee sound, like a rusty hinge. They also have a sharp check call.

Range and Habitat

Brewers range across much of North America, although they are rare in the east. Birds in the west may stay year round, but those in the north will fly south for the winter. They may be found in a large variety of habitats, such as prairies, open fields, woodlands, marshes, and towns. They have adapted well to humans, and may be seen in farmlands, parks, golf courses, lawns, and parking lots.

Breeding and Nesting

They are very social birds that nest in loose colonies of up to a hundred birds. The males will guard colonies from perches. If predators such as hawks are spotted, they will give an alarm call, and often dive at them to make them leave. The first females to arrive in the nesting area will choose their nest sites, and others will find sites around them. The nest is built of twigs, course grass, and mud, and lined with fine grass, and hair. It may be on the ground, in a bush, or in a tree. The female will lay 4 to 6 heavily spotted eggs, which will vary in color and pattern. She will incubate them for 12 to 14 days.

Food and Feeding

Natural foods are seeds, grains, insects, spiders, and fruits. Most foraging is on the ground, but they will all catch insects in the air. When foraging on the ground, they may flip over stones to look for insects. They do some damage to fruit in orchards, but they make up for this by eating large a large amount of harmful insects.

Bullock's Oriole

Identification

(Classification: Icterus bullockii)

Bullock's Orioles are 7 to 8 1/2 inches,
with a pointed bill and a long tail. The
male is a striking bird, with bright
yellow, or orange and black plumage.
The head has a black crown, there is a
black line through the eye, the throat,
back, and the wings are black, with
white wing bars. Their legs and feet are
gray.

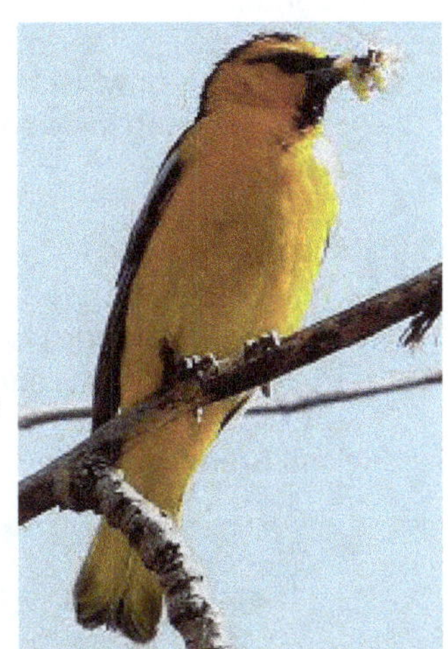

The females and young are olive-gray
to yellow above with
yellow on the throat,
and tail, and the belly
is paler. The wings are
brown or grayish with 2
wing bars.

Young males look like
the female but have a
black throat and a black
line through the eye.

Baltimore Oriole's colors
are a little different,
having more black than
Bullock's oriole.

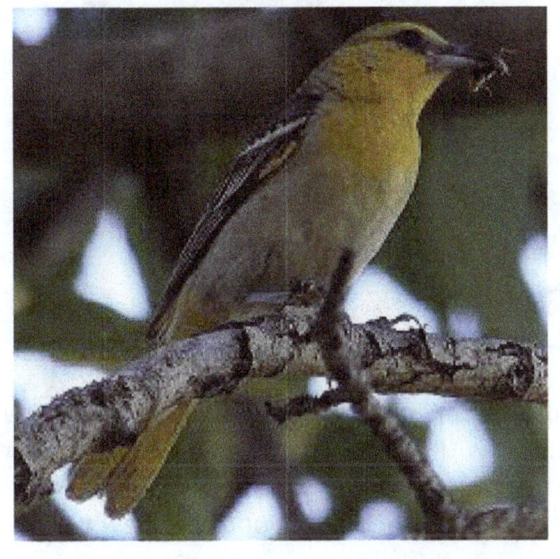

Orchard Orioles, similar birds, look more like the Baltimore oriole but
has darker under parts.

The **Spot breasted Oriole** looks like the Baltimore except for an orange
head, a black bib and spots on the sides of the breast.

The Baltimore and Bullock's Oriole were once considered to be one species, the Northern oriole. There are various hybrid oriels where their ranges overlap.

Song and Sound

The song is a series of whistled notes and rattles. Their call is chatter with a low chirp. Both male and female sing similar songs but her song has a harsher ending.

Habitat and Range

Their summer range is western U.S. and Canada, and they migrate to Mexico and Central America for winter. They can be found in open woods, trees along streams and rivers, and residential areas.

Nesting and Breeding

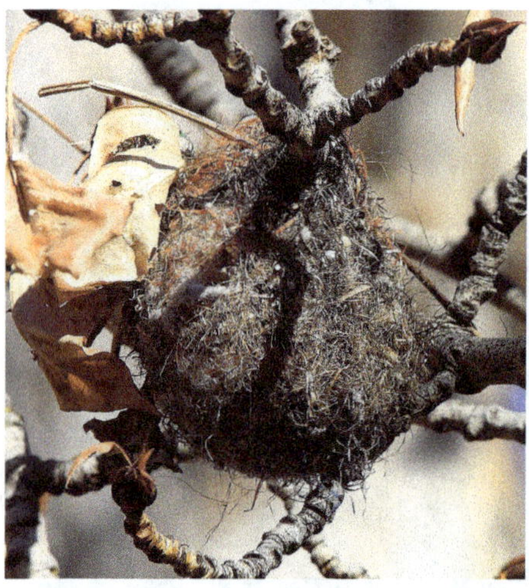

During courting the male will rise up then bow repeatedly to the female with his wings and tail raised. The nest is a pouch hung from a branch, made with grass, hair, twine, and wool, and lined with feathers and cotton from cottonwood or willow trees.

The female will lay 3 to 6 blue or grayish white eggs, scrolled with purple or brownish lines. She will incubate the eggs for about 2 weeks and the young birds will fledge in 2 more weeks. Both parents feed the young.

Food and Feeding

Natural foods are insects such as caterpillars and ants, spiders, blossoms, fruit, berries, and nectar. Orioles forage in trees and shrubs. They can be attracted to bird feeders with fruit, jellies, peanut butter, or suet. Orange slices are a favorite, and they will also visit hummingbird feeders.

Like other backyard birds, Orioles love water. A good supply of food and a fresh, clean, birdbath, will keep Bullocks' Oriole coming back.

Canada Goose

Identification

(Branta canadensis)

The Canada Goose is a large, gray-brown goose, from 22 to 36 inches, with a long neck, webbed feet, and a wide, flat bill. They have a light tan or cream-colored breast, and a black head and neck, or "stocking." They have a white patch on each side of their head like a chin strap. The tail is black, 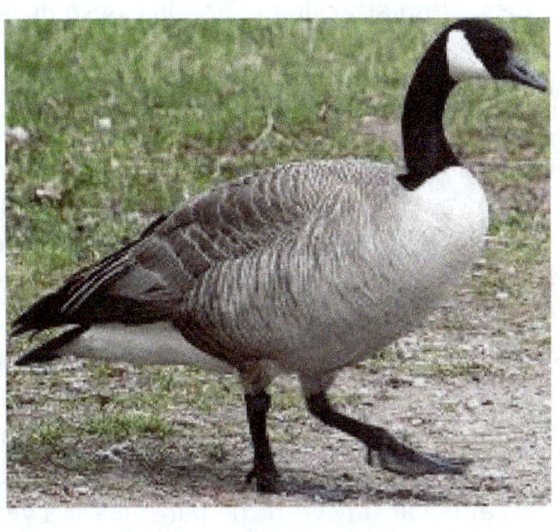 with a white rump band. The bill and legs are black. The bill has teeth-like structures around the outside edges, used for cutting. Male and female birds look the same. Newly hatched birds are covered with a yellow down. The down will be slowly covered with feathers as the birds grow, until they look just like the parents. There are several subspecies, with a large variation in size.

Range and Habitat

Canada Geese—or Canadian Geese—are the most widespread geese in America. They range across Canada in the summer and much of the U.S. for the entire year.

 In winter many northern birds will migrate to the southern U.S. and Mexico. They may be found in lakes, ponds, rivers, marshes, bays, prairies, and grain fields. They are often seen on lawns, golf courses, and in parks. When they travel in flocks, they fly in long V-shaped formations. Often the first indication that they are flying overhead is their honking sound.

Migrating flocks can number in hundreds or thousands of birds. Scientists believe flying in V-formations allows the following birds to use less energy, because they make use of the drag effect from birds in front of them.

Breeding and Nesting

Male geese are very aggressive, and during nesting season they will defend their territories from other geese, predators, and humans. They will lower their heads to the ground, pumping it up and down, and hiss, often attacking. Canada Geese usually breed after their second year and mate for life. They will often nest in the same area that the female's parents did. They breed in a range of habitats, but most nest sites will be near water, such as ponds or lakes. The nest is made of grass, moss, and reeds, and is lined with down. Breeding is timed so that the plants the young birds will feed on will be plentiful. The female will incubate 5 to 7 whitish eggs for around 28 days, while the male stands guard. The young birds, called goslings, start communicating with their parents while they are still in the egg, with distress calls, greeting peeps, and calls of contentment. They use an egg tooth at the top of their bills to break out of the shell. Canada Geese have very strong family bonds. After hatching the goslings will follow the parents everywhere. They will be able to fly in up to 9 weeks, and will stay with the parents for a year after hatching.

Sound

They have a variety of calls, but are best known for their deep honking, which sounds like ka-ronk.

Food and Feeding

Canada Geese feed on grass, leaves, stems, roots, flowers, seeds, and berries. They forage mostly on land. Other foods are insects, crustaceans, and small fish. They will also forage in water, sticking their head, and upper body below the surface, stretching their long necks, and using their bills to scoop food from the mud, and silt on the bottom. In winter they will feed in fields of crops such as corn, wheat, rice or oats. Fights over food occur in which the birds will grab each other's breasts or throats with their bills and hit each other with their wings.

Gray Catbird

Identification and Pictures
(*Dumetella carolinensis*)

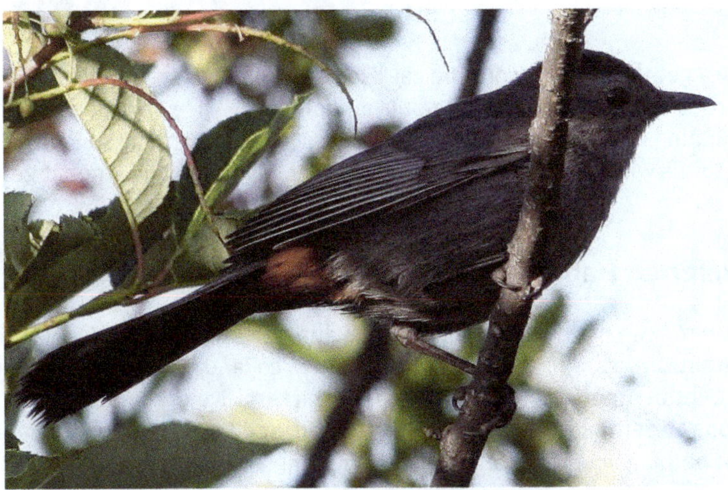

 Gray Catbirds are slate gray songbirds 8 to 9 1/4 inches. They have a black cap, dark slender bill, black legs, and a long black tail. The under tail coverts are chestnut, and are not often seen. Males, females, and juveniles have similar plumage. They are always flipping their tail.

Catbirds are known by other names such as Black Mockingbird, Cat Flycatcher, and Black-capped Thrush.

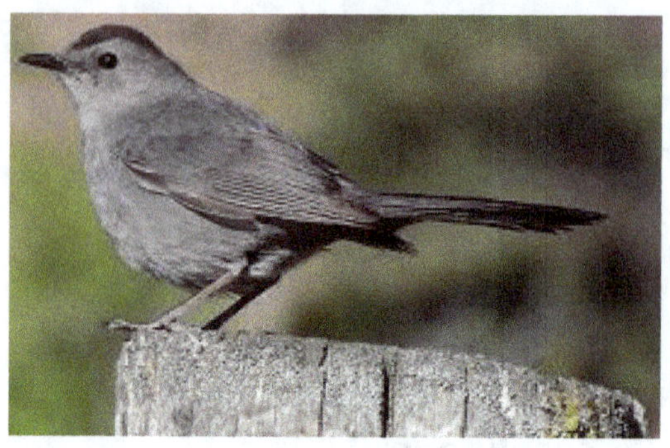

Catbird sound

They get their name from the cat-like meowing note they make. Their song is a series of disjointed notes and phrases. They are good at imitating other birds such as jays, hawks, quails, and many songbirds. Catbirds will start singing before dawn and still be singing when it gets dark.

Preferred Habitat

Catbirds can be found throughout Canada and much of the U.S. Most Catbirds migrate to the southern U.S., Mexico, and Catbirds winter in Central America. They prefer dense thickets, like the undergrowth along stream sides, wet, dense-vegetation, and bushes in bogs. They like bathing and can often be seen splashing around the edges of small ponds.

Breeding and Nesting

Catbirds breed from April through August. Males arrive on the nesting grounds a few days before the females and begin singing. During nesting season the male will spend much time singing and defending his territory from anything that gets close. During courtship the two birds can be seen in chases, dashing in and out of shrubbery. The birds normally mate for life. The nest is cup of twigs, weeds, leaves, and grass lined with finer material such as pine needles and hair. Their nests are usually well hidden in thick shrubbery. Both birds may gather nesting material, but the female will build the nest to her liking. When the male brings material, he will give it to her for construction. The female will incubate 3 to 6 blue-green eggs for 12 to 15 days. Both parents feed the young birds.

The young leave the nest in 10 to 15 days, and the parents will continue to feed them for around 12 days. It is common for the birds to have more than one brood in a season. They are often victims of Cowbirds, which lay their eggs in the nests of other birds. Catbirds are better at detecting the Cowbird eggs than many other songbirds, and often eject them.

Food

They eat berries, fruit, seeds, and insects. They often forage on the ground, flipping leaves over with their bills for insects such as beetles, caterpillars, grasshoppers, and ants. They will visit feeders for things like nuts and berries.

Black-Capped Chickadee

Chickadees will visit your yard if you have feeders and water.

Identification   *(Parus atricapillus)*

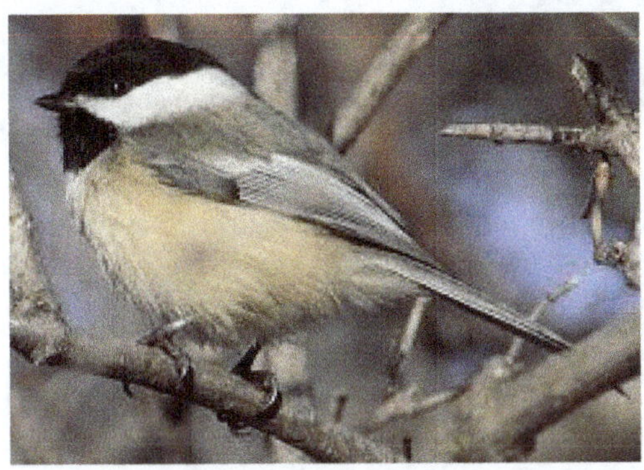

These are small fluffy round birds 4 to 5 ½ inches. They have a black cap and bib with white cheeks. Their upper parts are gray with lighter under parts, which may have a bit of yellow. The sides are a buff color with white feathers on the wings.

Some say this bird is fun to watch because of its acrobatic actions as it hangs upside down or forages through branches.

Determining male from female is difficult, as indicated in this poem by a Wisconsin bird bander:

"Here's to the little chickadee;
The sexes are alike, you see.
It's hard to tell the she from he;
But he can tell ... and so can she!"
Harold Wilson

Range and Habitat

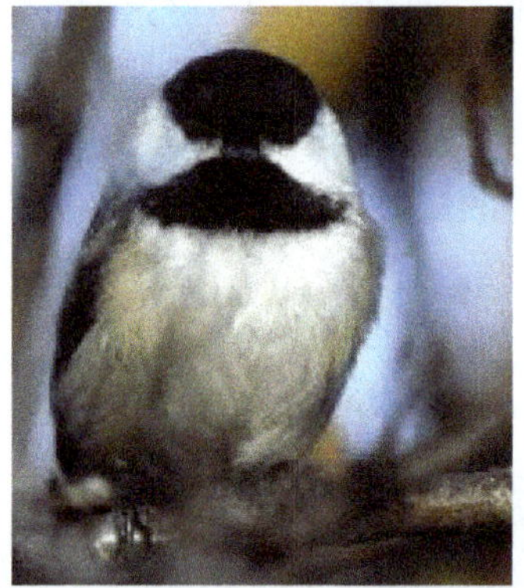

There are 10 chickadee species in North America and Black-capped Chickadees are the most familiar in our backyards. They can be found throughout the northern U.S., Canada, and Alaska. They like open woods, willow thickets, groves, parks with shade trees, farmlands, and backyards with trees, and shrubs. Chickadees may be seen in your yard all year long. In winter they will form in foraging flocks with nuthatches, titmice, and even woodpeckers. In late winter, as the males become territorial, these flocks will break up.

Breeding and Nesting

Breeding season is early April to mid May depending on the area. During courtship chickadees do what is called mate feeding. Females will solicit this behavior. The male will fly to the female with an insect or seed. With a high call and quivering wings she will take the offering.

They breed in forests and open areas with scattered trees. Both birds will excavate a nest cavity in a stump or tree. The cavity will be around 9 inches deep and have moss or plant down in the base. They sometimes use an old woodpecker hole or a nest box.

If you have birdhouses in your yard there is a good chance these entertaining little birds will move it.

The female alone will usually incubate 6 to 8 eggs. The eggs are smooth, white, or creamy, with fine purplish or reddish-brown speckles. Both parents tend the young birds for around two weeks, at which point the young can leave the nest. The young will remain with the parents for 3 to 4 weeks.

Song and Call

When chickadees are around, there is a constant chatter of clear chick-a-dee-dee-dee. This is often given during flocking. The male's song of fee-bee-bee is a clear whistle that sounds like "feed me feed me" to many people. The calls are used to warn and to recruit other birds to harass, or mob the predator and chase it away.   Recent studies at the University of Washington by Christopher Templeton show that nuthatches understand the warning calls of chickadees.

Food and Feeding

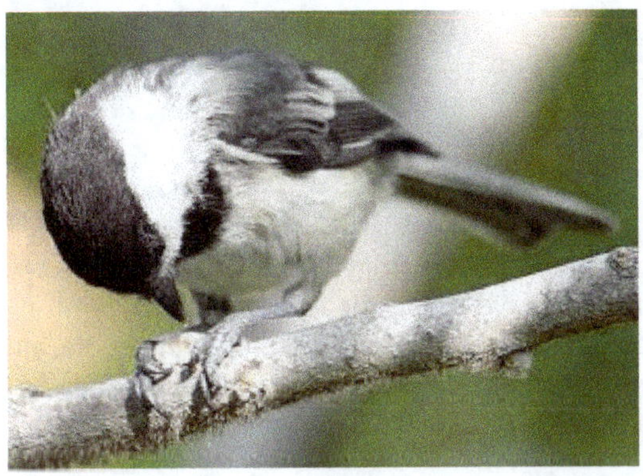

Natural foods are insects and seeds. Most foraging is done by hopping from branch to branch, often hanging upside down to feed on the underside of a branch. They will come to both suet and feeders with sunflower and other seeds. They are a very curious and trusting little bird and will often be quite tame. Many people get them to eat out of their hands.
Chickadees like to grab a sunflower seed from a feeder and fly to a nearby tree to crack it open and eat it. They hold the seed with their feet while cracking it open with a few quick thrusts of their bill. It can be fun to watch them flying back and forth from tree to feeder and back again.

Many people are surprised to find out that birds such as chickadees will eat out of your hand. If chickadees are visiting your feeder, it often does not take much to entice them to eat out of your hand. Let them get used to seeing you stand by the feeder. Soon they will take seeds from the feeder when you are there. Now put some seeds in your hand and hold it out. Make sure you stand still. After a while they will start landing on your hand to grab the seeds. Other birds that will eat from your hand are nuthatches, and hummingbirds will eat out of a small dish of sugar water held in your hand.

Common Loon

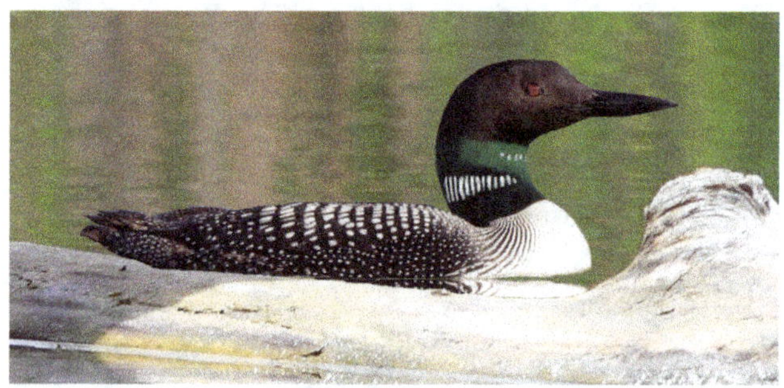

Identification

(Gavia immer)

Common Loons are long bodied ducks from 24 to 32 inches, that swim low in the water. They have a black head and long dagger shaped black bill. They have dark backs with rows of white spots, and a necklace of white lines or spots. Under parts are whitish. In my opinion a very attractive bird.

Preferred Habitat

They like bodies of water such as lakes, bays, or the sea.

Food

Loons eat small fish and other aquatic life.

Loon's sound

They have a long wail, usually heard in breeding season. They also do a yodel like call and a sound like mechanical laughter.

Breeding and Nesting

Loons are monogamous. The pair will defend a territory and come on land to breed. During courtship they will swim in circles and make dives together. After the male chooses the site, the two birds build a nest of dead plant materials, on the edge of a pond or lake. The female usually lays 2 to 3 brown spotted eggs. She will sit on the eggs for around 30 days. The chicks are covered in dark down. They can be seen riding on the mothers back for around the first 10 days. At around 12 weeks they can fly and will become independent.

Cooper's Hawk

Identification

(Accipiter cooperii)

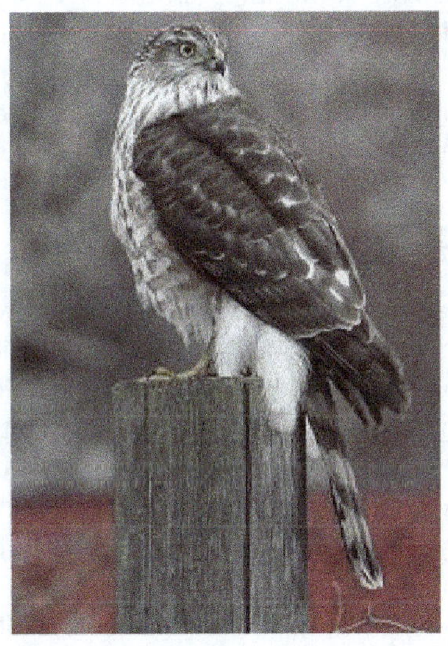

Cooper's Hawk, a raptor named after the naturalist William Cooper, is 14 to 20 inches with a wingspan of 2 1/4 to 3 feet. They have short wings and a long, rounded tail with gray and black bands, and a white band at the tip. Adults have blue-gray backs, white under parts with fine, thin, reddish bars, red eyes, and a black cap. The sexes look alike but females are about a third larger than the males. Younger birds are brown and streaked below and the eyes are yellow. They fly with stiff, strong wing beats.

They are often confused with the much smaller Sharp-Shined Hawk. Cooper's Hawks have a whiter more finely streaked breast, the legs are thicker, the head is larger, and younger birds have a reddish hue on the side of their heads and nape. The Sharp-Shined Hawk's tail is square.

Cooper's Hawk sound

Their voice is a rapid kek-kek-kek, which sounds much like a flicker, as well as a mewing like a Sapsucker.

Preferred Habitat

Some Cooper's Hawks have a summer range from Southern Canada through Northern U.S. The hawk can be found in most of the U.S. the entire year. The Northern hawks migrate for the winter. They like woodlands, riversides, and canyons, and can often be seen soaring over head.

Breeding and Nesting

During courtship the male may feed the female for up to a month. A pair will mate for life. Their nest, built mostly by the male in a large tree is built with sticks and lined with bark, needles and down. They have been known to take over an old crow's nest or even build on a squirrel's nest. The female will lay 3 to 5 pale blue to white eggs, which are sometimes spotted. The eggs will be incubated by both birds for around a month, and hatchlings will be covered with white down. The male will bring food while the female cares for the young until they fledge in 25 to 35 days. The young birds will return to the nest for feeding for 4 weeks after fledging.

Food

These hawks eat small birds such as robins, sparrows, starlings, flickers, chickadees, and many more. They will often perch in a tree or on post to pluck the feathers off their prey. They also eat mammals such as chipmunks, squirrels, mice and rabbits. The hawks also eat insects, and reptiles such as frogs, snakes, and lizards. When they hunt they move quietly through the woods getting close enough to capture their prey with a burst of speed. They are quick and agile with the ability to navigate through dense brush at high speeds. They kill their prey by squeezing it with their talons, but have been known to hold them under water until they drown. Smaller birds at backyard feeders may attract Cooper's hawks. The hawks will swoop down from a nearby tree and catch one of the birds in flight as they scatter.

The hawks were once called Chicken or Hen Hawks and hunted because they preyed on chickens. It is now known that the number of chickens they take is insignificant.

American Coot

Identification *(Fulica americana)*

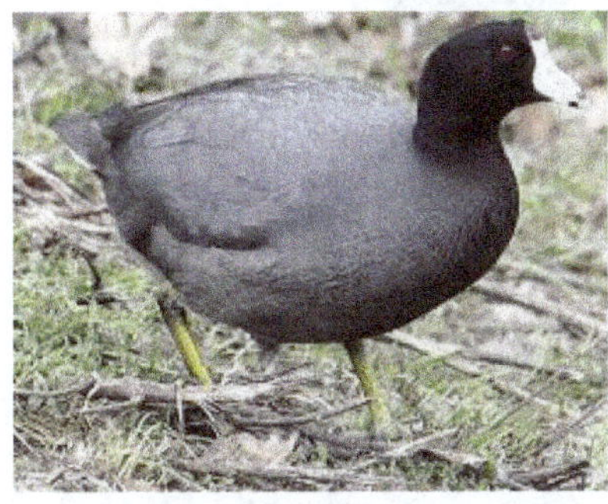

American Coots are a duck-like bird with short wings and a short tail, about 13 to 16 inches. They have a slate gray body, white chicken-like bill with dark red ring near the tip, and black head and neck with a red-orange eye. There is a dark shield on the top of the bill where it meets the forehead. Under the tail is a divided white patch. They have yellow legs and big lobbed feet. A white border can be seen on wings when in flight.

They pump their head and neck back and forth while swimming. When they take off they run across the water with their wings flapping to get airborne.

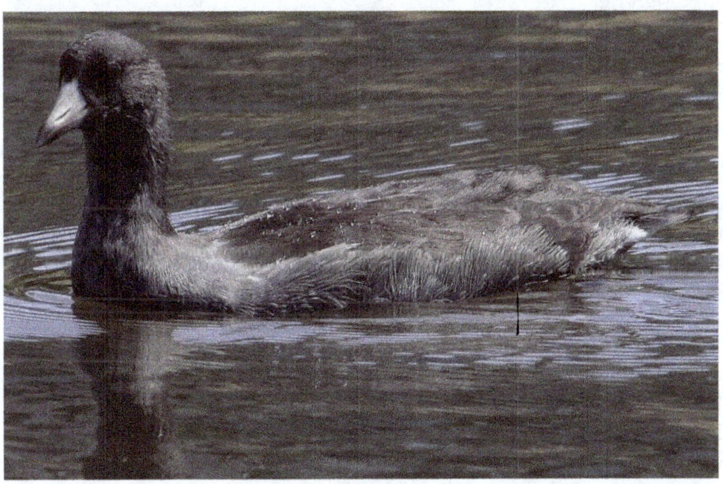

The sexes are similar. Younger birds are paler and chicks have a hairy orange-red head and shoulders.

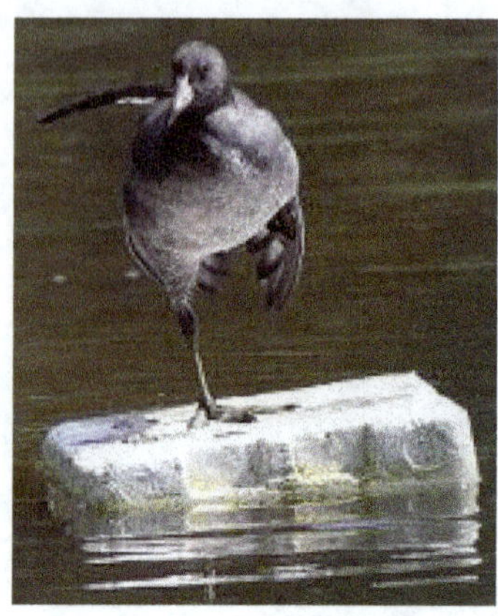

I guess this is where the term "Crazy as a Coot" comes from.

This Coot would flap his wings to get the box moving, he would then stand on one leg until it stopped. I watched for some time as he kept repeating this.

The Coot's sound

The Coot's sounds are Ka-ha ka-ha, short cackling sounds, and a grating kuk-kuk-kuk-kuk.

Preferred Habitat

The Coot's summer range is across much of Canada and Northern U.S. They will migrate south in the winter but are year-round residents in much of the Western and Southern U.S. as long as they have access to open water. They are found in ponds, marshes, and lakes. In winter they can be seen in coastal bays, inlets, and fields.

Breeding and Nesting

Mating season is around May or June, and both sexes will perform displays to attract each other. During these displays they will splash around while calling to each other. Coots usually nest on the edges of ponds. Both birds build a nest of stems, and leaves on a floating platform. It will be hidden in the vegetation and anchored to reeds. The female will lay 8 to 12 buff eggs with brown spots. Both birds will care for the eggs as well as the roles of feeding the young and teaching them to dive.

The young may be divided up each parent taking responsibility for half of them. The eggs hatch in around 23 days. Shortly after hatching, the young begin to swim and follow the parents to be fed. They will be able to fly in 5 to 6 weeks.

Food

Coot's diet is mostly plant material but they also feed on insects, worms, small fish, and tadpoles. They feed sometimes in small flocks on the shore, on lawns, and on the water. They will dive for food with an upward jump before plunging beneath the water. They will bring up plants from the bottom then go through them to pick out anything edible.

Brown Headed Cowbird

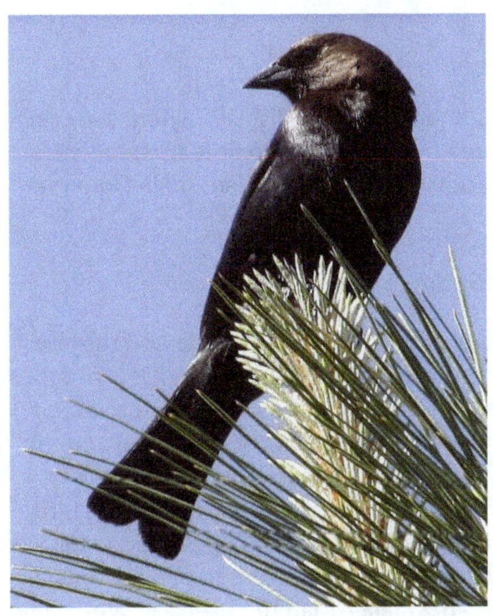

Identification (Molothrus ater)

Brown-headed Cowbirds are stocky, glossy black birds with brown heads, 6 to 8 inches. They have a short tail, long, pointed wings, and a thick head with a short conical bill like fiches. The females are brownish gray. The females may be mistaken for Rusty blackbird females but the Cowbird's bill is much smaller. Juveniles are paler than females and have soft breast streaks.

Young birds are often seen being fed by smaller birds of another species.

Brown-Headed Cowbird Sound

The male's song is a bubbly sound like glug-glug-glee, given while he leans forward in his dance. While he sings, the female will give a series of liquid chatters. They have a flight call that sounds like pee-see-see.

Preferred Habitat

Brown-headed Cowbirds can be found year-round in the western U.S. and much of eastern U.S. Their summer range extends up into Canada. They like riversides, wood edges, fields, pastures, and suburbs. In winter, Brown-headed cowbirds may join large flocks with several blackbird species.

Breeding and Nesting

Males gather in small flocks to do courtship displays where they sing with their wings and tail spread while fluffing their feathers to attract females. The females will usually pick the dominant male from the group.

The Mafia Bird

Cowbirds are brood parasites. They do not build nests and they do not take care of their young. They lay their eggs in the nests of other birds. Their eggs are white, light blue, or green with red, brown, or purple speckles. Amazingly, their strategy is very successful and the host birds often raise the young cowbird as one of their own. It is believed cowbirds lay their eggs in the nests of as many of 220 bird species. Female cowbirds may lay as many as 40 eggs in a season. The female will watch the activities of other birds to find one building a nest. They prefer birds that are smaller than themselves. When a nest is discovered she will return to lay her egg. She will remove one of the host's eggs from the nest in around 60 to 70 percent of the time. Cowbirds' eggs hatch sooner and grow faster than many other birds, giving the young Cowbirds the advantage of more food. They will often pitch the host bird's eggs and young out of the nest. Catbirds are better than other birds at detecting and removing the unwanted egg. Yellow Warblers will often build a new nest over the top of the Cowbird egg.

Cowbirds have been labeled Mafia Birds because recent studies have shown that if a host bird removes the Cowbird egg, the parent routinely comes back and destroys the nest and eggs in it. It is thought that as a result of this behavior the host birds learn they are better off leaving the unwanted egg.

Food

Cowbirds eat seeds, grains, and insects. They often forage on the ground. They received their name from the habit of foraging for insects in herds of grazing animals. They will often eat eggs removed from a nest they have laid an egg in. They also eat snails, giving them the much-needed calcium they need to lay large numbers of eggs.

American Crow

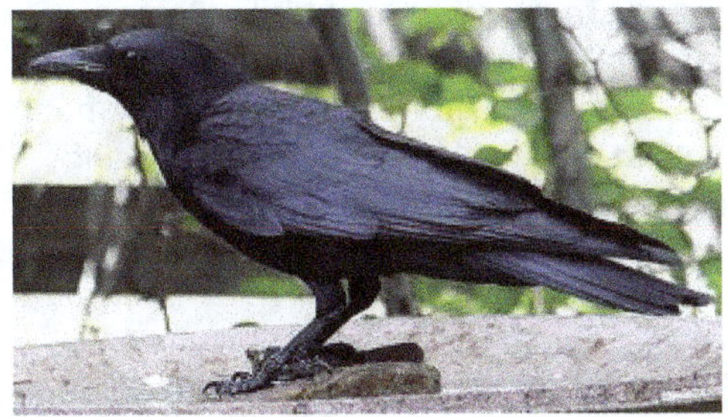

Identification

(Corvus brachyrhynchos)

The American Crow or Common Crow is a large, chunky, all black bird, about 17 to 21 inches. The feathers have a glossy shine to them, and in strong sunlight they can have a purplish hue. They have a large, thick, black bill, and strong, black legs and feet. The wings are broad and rounded, and they have a short rounded tail. Their flight is a slow deliberate wing beat. Both sexes look similar. Young birds look like the adults but have blue eyes. Crows are fairly intelligent and sometimes mischievous birds, which are very good at problem solving. They are able to recognize, and remember individual people, and pick them out of a crowd.

Sound

They have a number of calls they use for communication. Their most notable call is a loud caw-caw, given as they thrust their heads up and down. Sometimes family members will do coordinated duets. They are also able to mimic the sounds of other animals

Preferred Habitat

They range across Canada in summer and most of the U.S. all year long. They can be found in woodlands, river groves, farms, fields, and shores. They do well around people and are often found in towns, around parks, cemeteries, lawns, garbage dumps, and parking lots. They are often seen in treetops, on telephone poles, and along roadsides. Crows are very social birds and are often found in large groups, sometimes numbering into the thousands. In winter communal roosting groups may be in the millions of birds. Some roosting groups have been forming in the same areas for hundreds of years. Crows may establish year-round territories for their family, but will also leave this territory to join with the large groups for foraging and roosting. Foraging flocks may post sentries to watch for and warn the others of predators.

Breeding and Nesting

Most crows do not breed until they are at least 4 years old. A pair will form a family with young birds from 5 years back. Both birds in a pair will build a nest together, often with the help of young from previous years. The nest is a well-made bowl of sticks; lined with pine needles, bark, and animal hair, build in a tree. They are very aggressive, and will loudly mob any animal that comes near their nest, often chasing away birds such as hawks. All members of a family will help defend the territory. The female will incubate 4 to 6 greenish spotted eggs for around 18 days, and the young will fledge in around 35 days after hatching. Previous offspring will often help a pair raise their young. During breeding season some birds will also join floater flocks, of up to 50 birds. These flocks have not been thoroughly studied, but it is thought this gives individual birds a chance to find a mate while still staying with their family.

Food

They eat insects, earthworms, seeds, fruit, small animals, fish, aquatic life, carrion, and garbage. Most foraging is on the ground, but they often raid garbage cans. Crows also hunt for mice, frogs, and other small animals. They sometimes steal food from other animals. One or more crows may distract the animal so others can steal the food. They have also been known to make and use tools such as a sharpened stick used to probe for food. They will follow songbirds to find their nest and eat the eggs and nestlings. Some crows have developed an interesting technique for cracking nuts. They will place the nut in traffic. After a car runs over and cracks the nut they will retrieve it.

Dipper

Dippers or (Water Ouzels) are usually seen along fast moving creeks or rivers.

Identification

(*Cinclus mexicanus*)

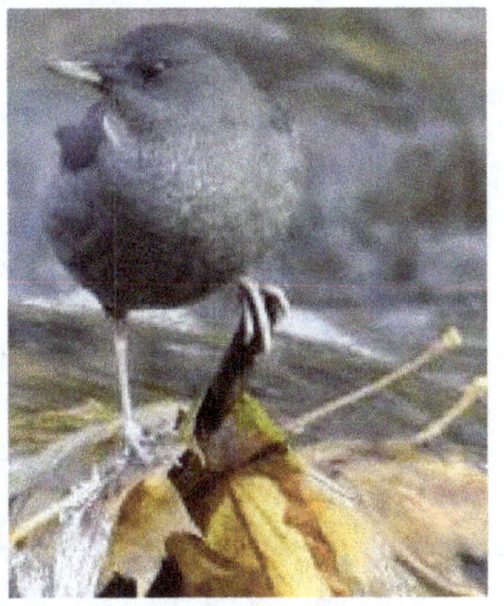

American Dippers are songbirds that swim. They are shaped somewhat like a large wren with a stubby tail. They have a slate-gray body, dark eyes, and beak, long gray legs, and may have a brownish head. The eyes appear to flash white when the bird blinks because of white feathers on the eyelids. These birds are around 7 to 8 1/2 inches. Males and females look alike. Young birds look like the adults but may have white tips on their feathers. They get their name from their constant dipping motion as they bend and straighten their knees.

Dippers have dense waterproof feathers down below. They waterproof the feathers using oil from a large preen gland. Their blood can store more oxygen than most passerine birds. These adaptations plus a flap that covers the nostrils and a clear membrane called a "nictitating membrane" which can cover the eye, allow dippers to dive and search for food under water. They also have strong toes, which allow them to grasp rocks on a stream bottom. Their average dive is 5 seconds, but they can stay down longer.

Dipper sound

Both male and female sing all year with loud, repeated whistles. They often give a high zeet sound. During flight they give a rattling call.

Preferred Habitat

Dippers will inhabit stream and riverbeds in the mountainous regions of western North America, where they can be seen diving and swimming under water for aquatic insects and small fish. You may see a dipper dive from a bolder and bob back to the surface a few seconds later with an insect. Unfortunately their habit of swimming sometimes makes them prey for large fish. Unless their stream ices over they will remain in an area all year.

Breeding and Nesting

A pair of dippers will defend a territory along a streambed from March through July. They will approach intruders in a high posture with their bills pointed into the air and may chase them. This dispute often ends when one bird submits, and the victor pecks it or even forces it under water. During courtship the birds will strut and sing in front of each other with their bills pointed up and their wings drooping. American Dippers build a bulky nest of moss, grass, and leaves, with an opening on the side. The nest will be close to water, possibly on the bank of a stream or river, on a rock ledge, or under a bridge. The female will choose the nest site and both birds will build the nest together. They will often reuse or build over an old nest. The female will lay 3 to 6 white eggs, which she will incubate for around 13 to 17 days. Both adult birds will feed the young, which will fledge in around 20 to 25 days, and can swim and dive as soon as they leave the nest.

After nesting they will molt, but unlike most songbirds dippers loose all their feathers at once so they are unable to fly for a short time. When molting is done dippers may move downstream to avoid the ice buildup as winter comes.

Food

Dippers feed by wading, diving, and swimming in water for aquatic insects, small fish and fish eggs. They also catch flying insects out of the air.

Downy Woodpecker

The drumming of Downy Woodpeckers is a sign that winter is coming
to an end. They can be attracted to your backyard with suet and seed
feeders, water, and a little landscaping.

Identification

(Picoides pubescens)

They are the smallest and most
common backyard woodpeckers in
North America, about 6 ½ inches.
The top of the head is black, and they
have a fairly small bill. The sides of
the head are white with a black mask
that extends from the eye to the
back of the head.

They have a white back and belly.
The wings and inner tail feathers
are black with white patches. The
outer tail feathers are white with
black patches. Males have a red nape
patch.

Downy Woodpeckers can easily
be mistaken for the larger Hairy
Woodpecker, which is closer to 9 ½
inches. The two birds can be distinguished by bill size compared to
their heads. The Downy Woodpecker's bill is about half the width of
the head, and the Hairy woodpecker's bill is about the same as the
width of the head.

There are others, such as Ladder-backed or Nuttall's Woodpecker, that
look similar. Two other woodpeckers that look similar but are easier
to distinguish from the Downy are the Three-Toed and Black-backed
Woodpeckers.

Song and Call

The Downy uses drumming as a call. Both sexes drum on wood. They also give a high-pitched descending whinny of notes as well as a sharp pick. During courtship they make a queek-queek sound.

Pecking

There are three types of pecking. Loud rapid drumming on hollow trees can be used to define a territory, keep track of a mate, or to search for a mate. Softer pecking is usually for searching for food, during which they will chip away at trees. The third kind of pecking is cavity excavation, and is usually done in soft or partially rotted wood.

Habitat and Range

The Downy can be found year-round throughout most of the U.S. and Canada. Their preferred habitat is open forests, orchard, river groves, and backyards with trees, and shrubbery.

Nesting and Breeding

Downy Woodpeckers breed in woodlands, orchards, and parks with scattered trees from April to July.

Members of a pair will have separate overlapping territories until late winter. At this time they will begin to coordinate activities, drumming on trees. Courtship and defending of a territory begin in spring with behavior such as chasing in flight and up trees, bill waving, and loud calls.

Both birds work together to excavate a cavity 10 to 15 inches deep with an entrance hole of about 2 ½ inches. The nest hole will usually be in a tree trunk or limb, often on the underside of a limb.

Both birds will incubate 3 to 6 small white glossy eggs for around two weeks. They only have one brood but will replace lost clutches of eggs. Both adults will feed the young, which will climb to the entrance around 17 days after hatching and leave the nest in 30 days. The young will rely on the adults for another two weeks. Downy woodpeckers are generally year-round residents.

Food and Feeding

About 75 percent of their diet is animal matter, mostly of harmful insects such as beetles, caterpillars, ants, and weevils. These friendly birds are likely to forage for insects in trees next to your house. They also eat fruits, seeds, and nuts. They can be attracted to both suet and seed feeders. Beef suet is preferred, but they will also come for cracked corn, sunflower seeds, doughnuts, and fruit.
Like most birds that visit backyards, food, cover, and water will attract them. Downy Woodpeckers do not drink at birdbaths as often as other birds, so food and cover are a priority.

Eastern Kingbird

Identification

(Tyrannus tyrannus)

Kingbirds are about 8 to 9 inches. The attractive Eastern Kingbird is gray-black above and white below, with a white band at the tip of its tail. Its crown has a small patch of red feathers that is not often seen. They received their name because they are very aggressive in protecting their territory. This member of the flycatcher family will attack any bird that dares get near the nest, swooping down with screaming cries. Even large birds like hawks and crows will be attacked if they get near the nest.

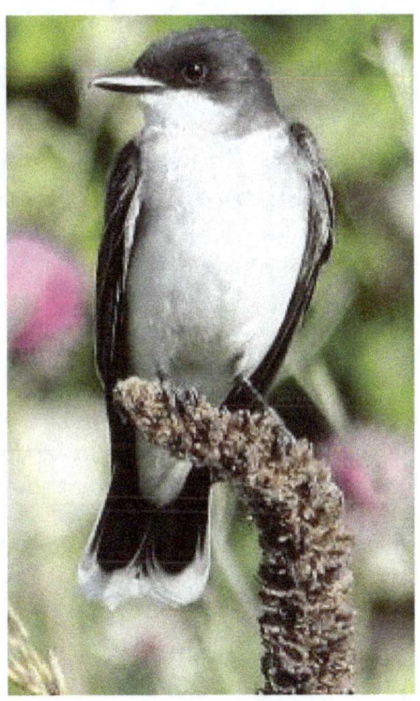

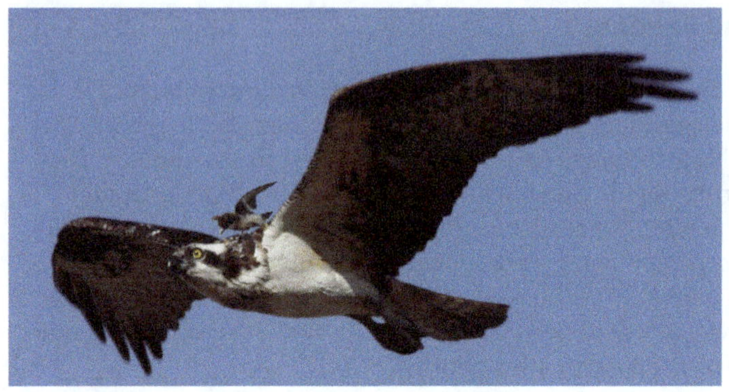

In these attacks they will even ride on the back of a larger bird and peck at its head.

The two sexes look much the same; juveniles are similar to adults but a bit paler, and the wings have a buff edge. The male crown feathers will more often show a crest. Like other birds in the flycatcher family, the male sits with an upright posture. The female does not usually show her crest and tends sit more horizontally on a perch.

Western Kingbirds (Regulus satrapa) look much the same but have yellow below.

Sound of Eastern Kingbird

Eastern kingbirds make sharp dzee-dzee or tzeet and a rapid kit-kit kitter-kitter calls.

Preferred Habitat

The Eastern Kingbird can be found from Canada to the Gulf of Mexico. Eastern kingbirds like to forage in agricultural areas with shrubs, lightly wooded areas, river edges, and meadows.

They will often perch on a treetop, cattail or fence post where they can get a clear view of the surrounding area.

Breeding and Nesting

They prefer to breed in wooded areas near rivers, streams, or wetlands. As with many birds, during courtship the males perform elaborate displays in the air, including backward somersaults and zigzags.

A pair of kingbirds will flutter their wings and call noisily in a greeting display whenever they meet. The female builds a large nest of weeds, twigs, and bark lined with feathers and plant down. The nest can be in a shrub, low tree near water, or even on a man-made structure such as a fence post or telephone pole. The female lays 2 to 5 creamy white or pale pink eggs with dark blotches. She incubates the eggs for 14 to 17 days.

Brown-headed Cowbirds will often lay their eggs in the nests of kingbirds. Kingbirds will often destroy these eggs if they are put in the nest before their own are laid but are more likely to leave them after theirs are laid.

Both parents will feed the young birds until they start to fly in around 17 days, and the adults will continue to feed them for up to five weeks after this. The young tend to remain with the parents until the birds gather in flocks for migration.

Migration

Eastern Kingbird's will gather in large flocks much like waxwings do, during migration, wintering mostly in South America.

Food

Kingbirds feed on insects in spring and summer, and like fruit and berries when they become available. They will sit on a perch and fly out to grab insects out of the air. The birds also feed on the ground, especially in winter.

Evening Grosbeak

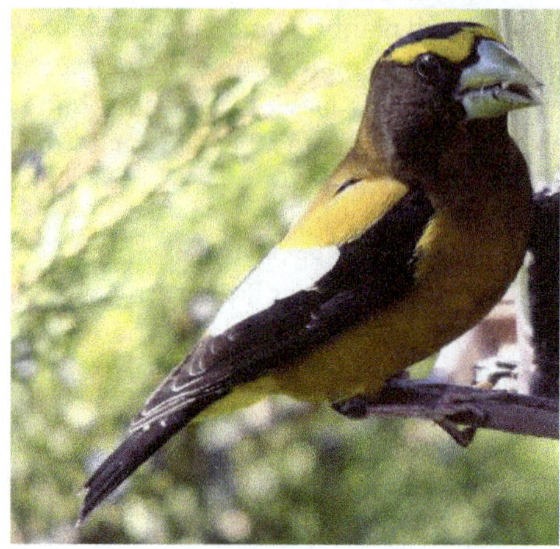

When I think of my favorite birds, grosbeaks are near the top. Where I grew up in Montana, we would see huge flocks of these colorful birds. We had quite a few fruit, berry, and maple trees, and the birds could not resist them. They seem to especially like the Mountain Ash berries.

Identification (*Coccothraustes Vespertinus*)

Evening Grosbeaks are stocky short tailed birds about 8 inches, and look much like an overgrown goldfinch. They are members of the finch family, which is the largest bird family in North America. Others in this family are buntings, cardinals, crossbills, finches, juncos, redpolls, siskin, sparrows, and towhees.

Males are dull yellow with a dark head and yellow stripe above the eye. The wings and tail are black, and there is a large white wing patch.
The female is mostly silver-gray with touches of yellow. The wings and tail are black with white patches that are not as pronounced as the mail.
Their large conical bill tells us they feed mainly on seeds.
The bill is a whitish or greenish color in the summer and turns to pale yellow in the winter.

Song and Call

Grosbeaks have a ringing *chirp* or *cleer* sound, and a loud *cleep* call. They also have a short warble song.

Range and Habitat

Grosbeaks can be found year-round in northwestern U.S. and southern Canada. They range from the Rocky Mountain region south to northern Mexico. They winter in Mexico and most of the U.S.

There are a number of different grosbeaks, with varied ranges. Others are the Blue, Rose-breasted, Black-headed, and Pine Grosbeaks.

Grosbeaks like mixed forests. They prefer conifer and spruce forests. They also like fruit and berry trees, or shrubs and maples. In winter they can be found in open areas with trees and shrubs, or at your feeders.

Breeding and Nesting

Breeding in open woodlands begins in mid-May in the South, and mid-June in the North. The male will court a female by dancing in front of her with drooped, vibrating wings.

The nest, built mostly by the female, is constructed loosely from sticks, moss, lichen, and rootlets. The inside can have hair and plant fibers.

The female will incubate 2 to 5 smooth glossy eggs. They are light blue or greenish blue. Eggs are spotted with blotches of purplish to olive brown or purplish-gray, mostly at the large end. The young are fed by both parents and can leave the nest in about 2 weeks.

Food and Feeding

The grosbeak's natural foods are seeds, buds, insects, berries, and fruit. Favorite foods are pine and box elder seeds. Grosbeaks forage in trees, shrubs, and on the ground.

You can attract grosbeaks to feeders with sunflower seeds. Large flocks can descend on your feeders and eat all the sunflower seeds you have. Some years you may see these flocks at feeders, while in other years they stay in the North and are not seen in their winter range. Large southern movements called irruptions are thought to be caused by periodic food shortages.

Golden Eagle

Golden Eagles are the national bird of Mexico.

Identification

(Aquila chrysaetos)

Golden Eagles are large birds of prey about 30 to 41 inches. Their wingspan is 6 to 7 feet. They are dark brownish, becoming a little lighter at the base of the tail. There is a bit of gold on the back of the neck and head. They have a large hooked bill, good for tearing meat. Their tail and long wings are broad. The legs are feathered all the way to the toes. The sexes are similar. Young birds have a white tail, and white at the

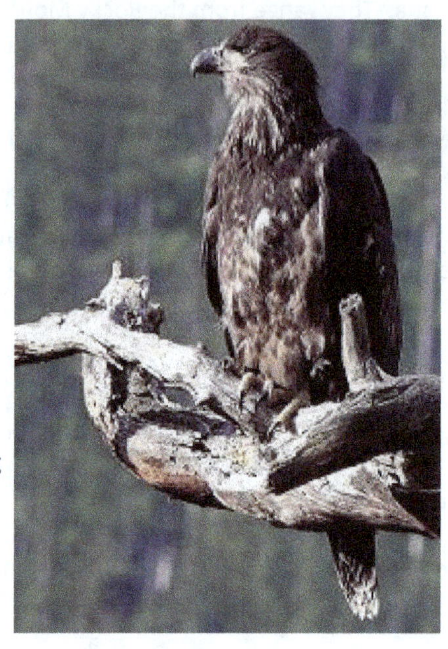

base of the wing primaries that can be seen when they fly. Young Bald Eagles are often mistaken for Golden Eagles. Golden Eagles fly with slow wing beats, often soaring on thermal currents.

The Golden Eagle's Sound

Golden Eagles are not often heard. They have a high scream and yelping bark.

Preferred Habitat

Golden Eagles range throughout most of the Northern Hemisphere. They can be found throughout the western part of North America, but they are not common in the east. They like open mountains, canyons, plains, and foothills.

Breeding and Nesting

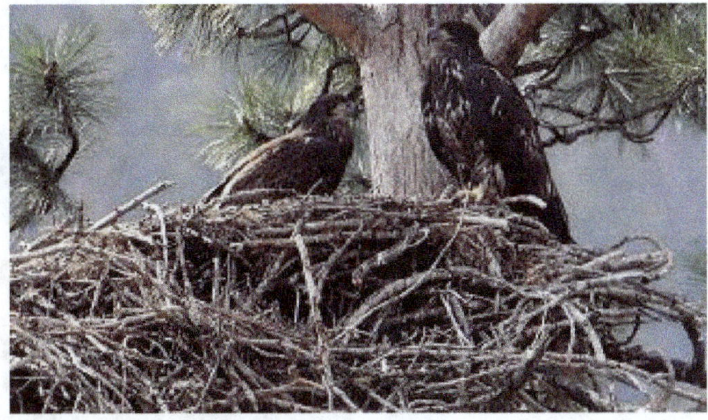

Golden Eagles mate at around 4 years, and pair off for life. During courtship they will dive at each other while circling high in the air. Both birds will build a nest of sticks, lined with fine wood materials on a cliff or large tree. They will normally return to the same nest each year; however, they may have other sites, and alternate between them. The female lays 1 to 4 creamy white eggs with small brown blotches. Normally the female alone will incubate the eggs for 41 to 45 days. While she is incubating, the male will bring her food. Both parents will care for the young birds. The young birds will stay in the nest for around 10 weeks before fledging. The availability of food determines whether the Eagles will migrate or not.

Food

Being powerful flyers, Golden Eagles often hunt from the air. The main diet of Golden Eagles consists of rabbits, hares, groundhogs, marmots, foxes, and squirrels, but the birds can and do feed on much larger animals such as mountain sheep and caribou. They may have a hunting territory of 60 square miles or more.

Golden Eagles are protected in the United States. Possession of a feather or other body part is a felony with a fine of up to $10,000 and/ or 10 years in prison. Native Americans are exempt from this because it is part of their native culture.

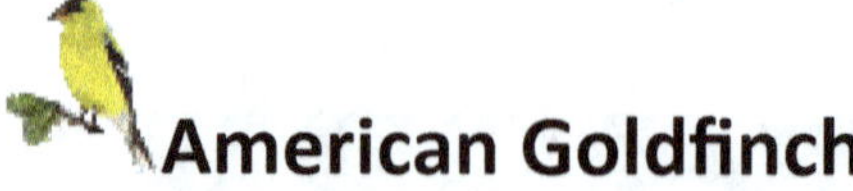

American Goldfinch

Identification

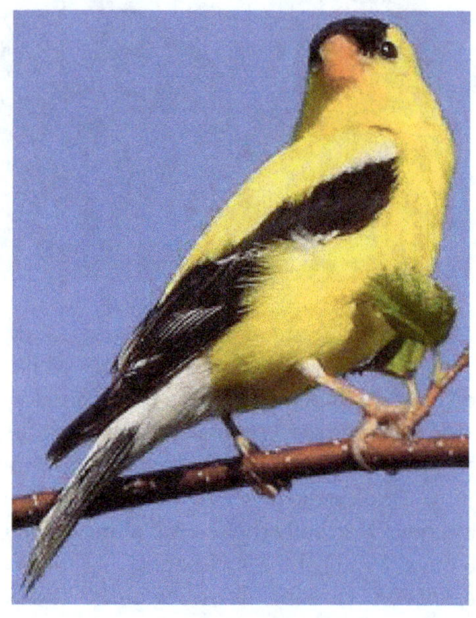

(Carduelis tristis)

The American Goldfinch is a small finch of about 5 inches. Its thick conical bill is good for eating seeds. In summer the male is bright yellow, with black wings, tail, and forehead patch. The female is a duller olive-yellow with black wings.

In the winter they both look more like the summer female, but a little duller. Its flight is undulating, often with a chirp with each dip.

Song of American Goldfinch

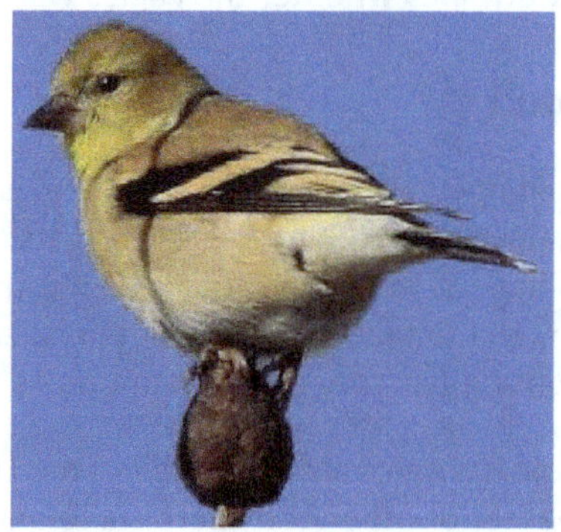

In spring and summer during nesting, males can be heard giving their high pitched canary-like song. Their song is a series of random sounds, clear and light, like per-chek-oree. Some say it sounds like pot-tato-chip. As they fly, each dip in their undulating flight is punctuated by tee-dee-de-dee.

American Goldfinch Habitat

Their natural habitat is woodland edges, thickets, and weedy patches.
They can be seen in open woods, on lawns, and on roadsides. They
forage in large flocks. It is fun to watch flocks fly with their roller
coaster manner. They range from south Canada through the U.S. to
north Mexico

Breeding and Nesting

Breeding season begins in April or May in the southwest to mid June in
the east. Goldfinches like to breed in areas with openings among trees
and shrubs. The female usually builds a well-made nest in high weeds
or in a tree or shrub, often near water. The nest is firm and compact,
made of strips of bark, catkins, plant down, cotton, spider webs, and
wood. The male will feed the female while she incubates 4 to 6 eggs.
The eggs are smooth and pale blue, or greenish-blue, slightly glossy.
Young birds are tended by both parents, and will leave the nest in 10
to 17 days.

Food and Feeders
Goldfinches eat mostly seeds. They also eat insects, tree buds, and
maple syrup. They are active foragers, climbing around in weeds, trees
and shrubs. Feeders with thistle and other seeds will attract them.
Make sure you also provide water.

Hairy Woodpecker

Identification

(Picoides villosus)

Hairy Woodpeckers are a medium sized woodpecker about 8 1/2 to 10 1/2 inches. They have a white back and under parts. The wings are black with white spots. Their inner tail feathers are black, and the outer tail feathers are white. They have a black and white striped head with a large bill, useful for probing bark for insects and excavating cavities for nesting. The males have a red patch on the back of their head. The females look like the males but do not have the red patch. Juvenile birds have red feathers in their crown. They launch into short, rapid flights as they move from tree to tree in search of insects.

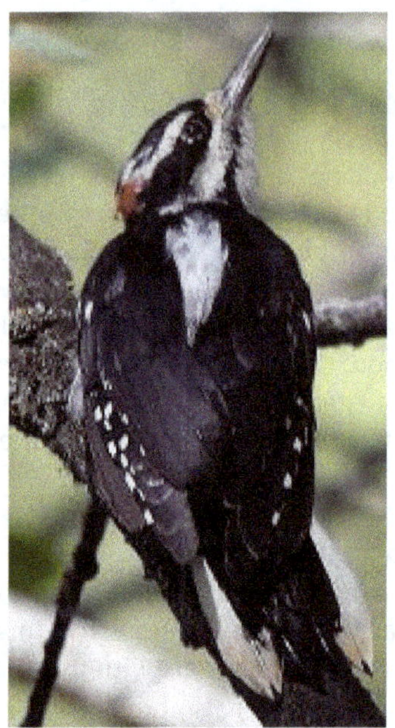

Hairy Woodpeckers are often confused with Downy Woodpeckers. The Downy is smaller and the bill is much smaller in relation to the head.

Sound

The voice is a high rattle, and the call is sharp peek. During conflicts they will make shrill cries while holding their wings over their heads.

Preferred Habitat

Hairy Woodpeckers can be found year-round across much of North America. They like wooded lands, mountain forests, and river groves, both coniferous and deciduous forests. You may also see the birds in parks or your backyard.

Breeding and Nesting

Female Hairy Woodpeckers choose the territory and attract a mate by drumming. During courting the birds bob their heads from side to side, stretch out their necks with their bills pointed high in the air, and circle a tree trunk while flicking their wings. They will also perform drumming duets. They form pairs in late winter. The two birds will excavate holes for nesting and roosting in a tree. They like to nest in deciduous trees even though they prefer to spend more time in coniferous trees. The inside of the nest is usually bare except for wood chips at the bottom. The female will lay 3 to 6 glossy white eggs and both parents will incubate them for about 14 days. The female incubates the eggs during the day, and the male incubates them at night. Both birds will feed the young, which will leave the nest in about 30 days. The young birds will stay with the parents for a couple more weeks. The pair will normally raise one brood a year.

Food

The Hairy Woodpecker's main diet consists of insects, but they also eat fruits, berries, nuts, and sap from Sapsucker holes. They forage for insects by probing the bark on tree trunks, and branches with their sharp beaks. They can hear insects under the barks as well as feel their vibrations. Their long tongues are covered with a sticky substance that insects stick to. They will visit backyard seed and suet feeders.

Hammond's Flycatcher

Identification

(Empidonax hammondii)

Hammond's Flycatchers are small active songbirds, about 5 1/2 inches. They have an olive-brown back, pale yellow belly and gray breast. They have a small pointed bill, almost like a kinglet, long wings with two white wing-bars, whitish under tail coverts, and a whitish eye ring that is not visible in all birds. Their legs and feet are black. These birds flick their wings and tail constantly. This is one bird that gives ornithologists a headache since Hammond's and Dusky Flycatchers are extremely 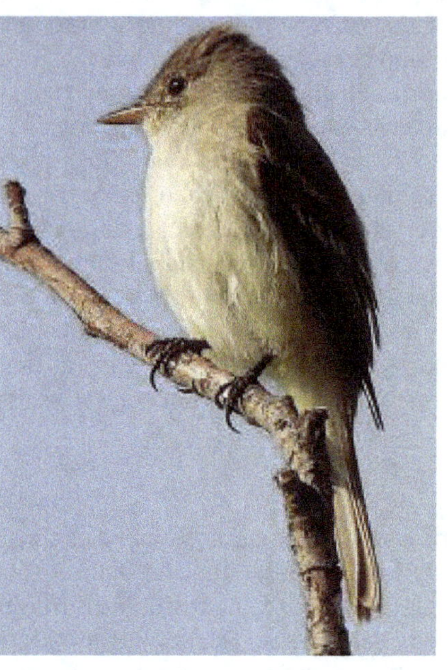 difficult to tell apart. Dusky Flycatchers have a slightly longer tail, there is less contrast between the chest, and belly, and the under parts are not quite as yellow. Hammond's Flycatchers have a weak fluttering flight with shallow wing beats.

Sound

The song of Hammond's Flycatcher is in 3 parts, something like sel-ip, twur, tree, and they have a call that is a sharp pic.

Preferred Habitat

In summer they can be found from Alaska down through Western Canada, and the U.S. They prefer coniferous woodlands or mixed forests, usually staying high in the canopy. They migrate south to Mexico and Central America for winter.

Breeding and Nesting

Like most songbirds the male sings to defend his territory and attract a mate. In early breeding season the males sometimes become locked in mid-air as they fight. The nest is a cup built by the female with grass, plant fiber, pine needles, and twigs. It is lined with feathers and other soft material, set on a high tree limb, away from the trunk. Females incubate 3 to 4 white eggs that are sometimes spotted for around 15 days. Both parents will feed the young birds, which will fledge in 16 to 18 days. The fledglings will usually stay with the parents for another week.

Food

The flycatcher's main diet consists of insects such as beetles, flies, bees, moths, and caterpillars. They are aerial feeders, usually foraging high in the trees where they perch on an open branch and fly out to capture their prey. They sometimes forage in lower vegetation or even on the ground.

House Finch

House Finches originally were a resident of Southwestern U.S. In the 1940s they were being sold illegally as pets with the name Hollywood Finches. To avoid prosecution venders and owners released them into the wild and the birds quickly spread across the country.

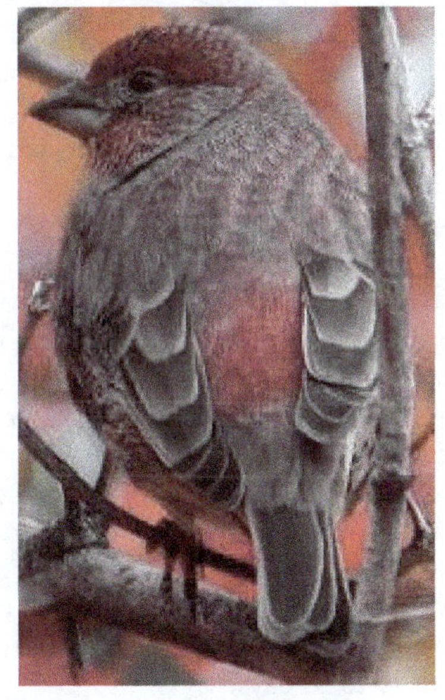

Identification

(Carpodacus mexicanus)

House Finches are about 5 to 6 inches and have brown or grayish streaked backs and wings. The breast is usually streaked with brown and white. They have two white wing bars and a short thick bill good for cracking seeds.

Males will have pink, red, or sometimes yellow on the head, necks, shoulders, and rump.
The male's color will vary depending on their present diet. Females prefer to mate with the reddest male they can find as this indicates he could be a good provider for the nestlings.

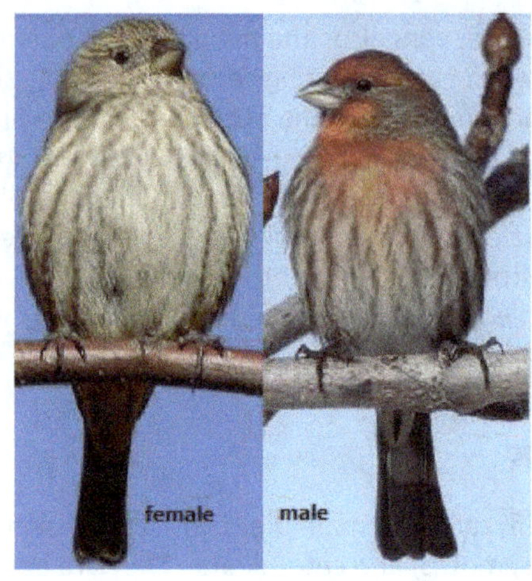

Sound of House Finch

Their song is a lengthy cheerful series of notes like "chee-wee" that shifts rapidly from low to high notes, often ending in a nasal "che-urr." They will call a single sharp "cheep" or "che-urr." The birds will sing while they are in flight as well as from perches.   Males have a longer song then the female.

Preferred Habitat

House Finches can be found from Southern Canada through the U.S. and Mexico. They like deserts, orchards, and wooded areas, as well as cities and residential areas. They are a common bird at feeders all year long, often mixed in with other birds such as sparrows or chickadees.

Breeding and Nesting

During courtship is when you will most often hear the male's lovely warbling song. Male finches will bring bits of food to the female during courtship. He may also feed her during incubation. Female House Finches build a cup-shaped nest of twigs and other vegetation. It can be in areas such as vines on the side of a build or in a tree cavity. If you have birdhouses they may nest in them. The nest will often be used again the next year. From February through August the female will lay and incubate 2 to 6 smooth, pale bluish-green eggs with black spots on them. There are often two or more broods in a year. In around 2 weeks the eggs will hatch. Both parents may feed the young from 11 to 20 days.

Food and Feeding

House Finches eat mostly seeds and berries but will also eat insects. They forage through vegetation and on the ground but are also a common visitor at bird feeders throughout the year. They are often mixed in flocks of birds that come to feeders with sunflower and other seeds.

Chipping Sparrow

Identification

(Spizella passerina)

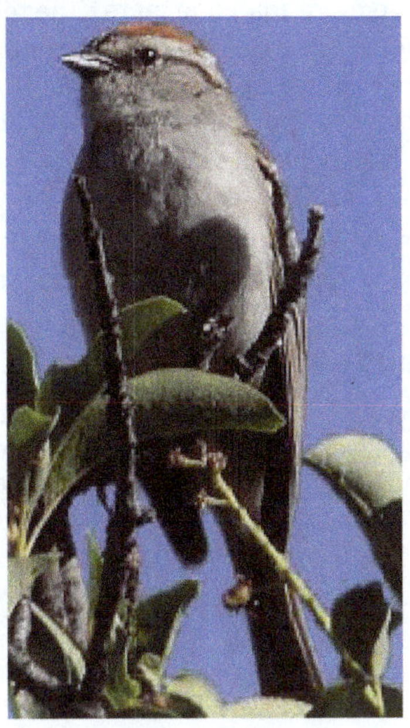

Chipping Sparrows are about 5 inches and are small, slim and gray with long, slightly notched tails. They have a bright rufous cap, a streaked brown back, streaked wings with two white wing bars, a black line through the eye, and a white line over the eye. A gray band runs across the nape of its neck. They have a dark conical bill. In winter the adults are browner, the breast is not quite as gray, the eyebrow line is duller, and the bill turns pinkish. Younger birds are buffer, have a light stripe through the crown, and have light streaks on the breast. In early days in the U.S., it was called the hair bird because of its use of horse hair in its nests.

Song and Call

Chipping Sparrows were named for their song, which is a series of chipping sounds that can sound like long trill. They like to sing this from a high perch. Call notes are a short *chip* and *seet* sound.

Range and Habitat

Chipping Sparrows range across most of Canada and the U.S. in summer, migrating south, usually in flocks, to the southern U.S. and Mexico for the winter. They like open woodlands, conifer forests, towns, farms, and grassy areas such as residential yards.

Breeding and Nesting

Chipping Sparrows are usually monogamous; however, males may have more than one mate. The males arrive to breeding areas before the females and establish territories. The pair will choose a nesting site in a tree or bush together. The female builds a loose cup nest of weeds, grass, and rootlets, lined with hair. The male will feed the female while she incubates 3 to 5 light blue speckled eggs for 10 to 12 days. After hatching, both adults will feed the young birds until they leave the nest in 9 to 12 days, and another 3 weeks after that. They usually only have one brood per season.

Food and Feeding

Chipping Sparrows eat mostly seeds, but they also eat insects. They usually forage in open areas, on or near the ground, running, hopping, and stopping to scratch the ground with their feet. Outside of breeding season they forage in flocks. They will visit backyard seed feeders.

House Sparrow

Identification

(Passer Domesticus)

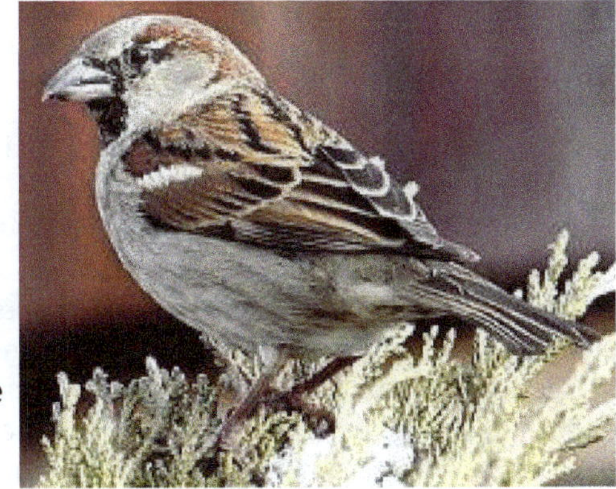

House Sparrows are stocky sparrows with large heads and short tails, about 5 3/4 to 6 3/4 inches. Males have a chestnut back and head, and a black throat. The cheeks, crown, and under parts are pale gray. The nape is a chestnut or brown color. In the summer the bill is blue-black and in the winter it is brownish.

Females and the young do not have the black throat and they are a grayish color below.

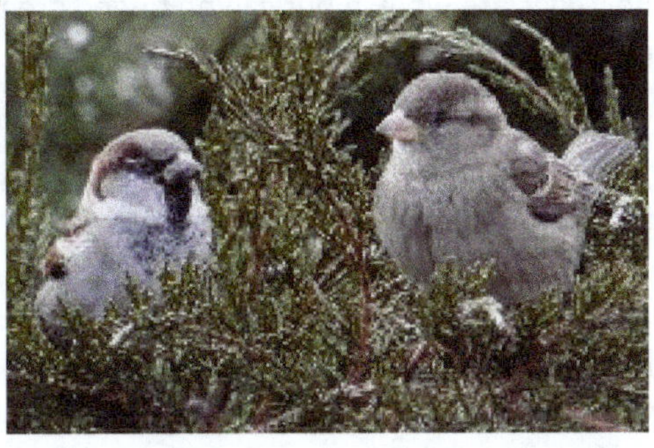

House Sparrows are often seen in large flocks that will roost in evergreens or other bushes. The flocks will often include house finches, especially in autumn or winter.

There are many varieties of sparrows. Most people in North America are familiar with House Sparrows, Song Sparrows, and White-crowned Sparrows. House Sparrows were imported from England in the 1850s. Many people dislike them because they can take over nesting sites other songbirds might use.

Range and Habitat

House Sparrows range across North America and can be found in cities, farmlands, or in the country, forming large flocks. They live mostly where humans live. It is estimated that the population is around 150,000,000 birds. The numbers diminish each year.

Breeding and Nesting

House Sparrows are usually monogamous. Males will sit on a perch outside the nesting site, singing their nest-site call, trying to attract the female. If she comes near, he will quiver his wings and call louder. He will then go in and out of the nest cavity. If she goes in, the two will probably pair off. Generally they build cup-shaped nests in trees, bushes, under eves and in other places. The nest is built with grass, twigs, and leaves, and lined with feathers. Because they tend to take over birdhouses meant for other birds, some people resort to trapping them in an attempt to get rid of them. Unlike most birds in the U.S., the law does not protect sparrows. They nest in colonies, but both sexes will choose and defend a small territory. Females lay 5 to 6 speckled or spotted eggs. The spots can be brown, purple, or black. Their eggs are whitish but can be tinged greenish or blue-gray. The eggs are incubated for around 10 to 14 days. Both parents will feed the young, which will leave the nest in about 2 weeks. The young birds will stay around the parents for another 7 to 10 days and then join flocks of other juveniles. They may have 2 to 3 broods in season.

Song and Call

The chir-up and twittering song of the House Sparrow can be heard all year long. Both sexes sing.

Food and Feeding

Natural foods for sparrows are insects, seeds, and berries. They are frequent visitors to backyard feeders. There will often be more birds than there is room for, but they are happy to scratch the ground for seeds falling from the feeders. Like most birds that come to feeders, they are also attracted to water.

Song Sparrow

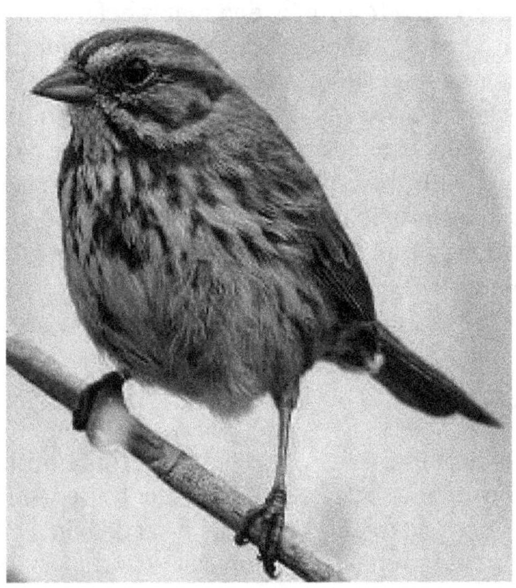

Identification

(Melospiza melodia)

Song Sparrows are 5 to 7 inches. They have a light brown head with a white streak that runs from the beak over the top of the eye to the back of the head. The bill is short for a sparrow. The adults have a streaked breast with a black spot in the center. They have a long, rounded tail, which they hold cocked up, and pump up and down, as they dart around with their short fluttering flight.

Young birds have finer streaks, and may not have the spot. There are many subspecies with variations from one area to another.

Range and Habitat

Song Sparrows range across North America. Birds in northern ranges may migrate to southern U.S., and Mexico, others are resident year round. They like open areas, marshes, thickets, shrubs around field edges, and backyards. They may be seen flitting through low branches and vegetation or hopping and running on the ground. Song Sparrows are solitary birds during breeding season, but they may be found in small flocks with other birds such as House sparrows in winter.

Breeding and Nesting

Song Sparrows are very territorial, and males defend their territories with chases and fights. Although Song sparrows are territorial they often build their nests in close proximity to each other. They are usually monogamous. They build their nest on the ground, in a bush, or in grass. The female builds the nest of grass, leaves, weeds, and bark, and lines it with grass, hair, and rootlets. She will incubate 3 to 5 greenish white eggs with dark marks for 10 to 14 days. Both parents will feed the young a diet of mostly insects. The young birds will leave the nest within 2 weeks, but they will stay around the parents for 3 more weeks. The birds may have several broods in a year.

Song and Call

Song Sparrows sing a series of notes that vary from musical to a buzzy sound. Males may have up to 10 different songs, repeating one several times before switching to another. They will perch in a bush or tree as they sing. A high tic sound is an alarm call.

Food and Feeding

Natural foods for Song Sparrows are insects, seeds and berries, which they forage for in shrubs, and on the ground.

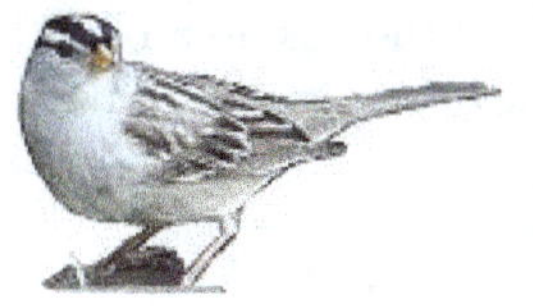

White-Crowned Sparrow

Identification

(Zonotrichia leucophrys)

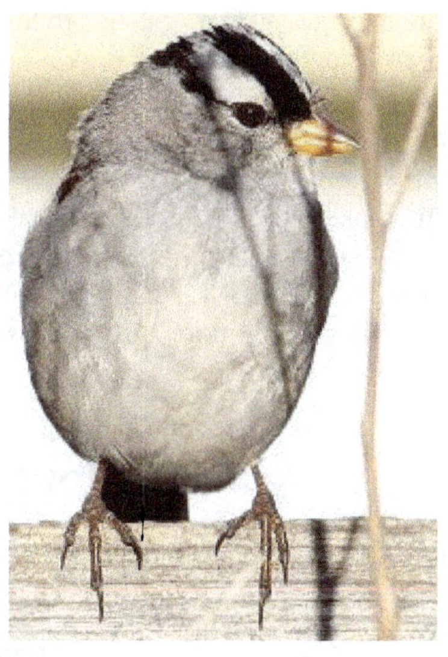

White-crowned Sparrows are about 5 1/2 to 7 inches. A white stripe from the bill to the back of the head, and another over the eye, identifies this attractive bird. Their bill is either pink or yellow and often has a dusky tip. They have a long tail and 2 white bars on the wings. The crown has a puffy look to it. Their breast is gray. In younger birds the head stripe is more of a brown color. Both sexes are similar.

There are 5 subspecies, with variations from one area to another, and telling them apart can be difficult.

Range and Habitat

White-crowned Sparrows range through Alaska, Canada and western U.S. Northern populations may migrate for the winter to southern U.S. and Mexico. They can be found in towns, the country, and along roadsides. Their preferred habitat is low brush, thickets and forest edges. Outside of breeding season they may be seen in flocks with other birds.

Breeding and Nesting

Male White-crowned Sparrows usually arrive in the breeding area before females and sing to protect their territory and attract a mate. The birds are usually monogamous. The female builds a cup nest of grass, pine needles, twigs, and bark strips, lined with fine grass, hair, and feathers on or near the ground. She will incubate 3 to 5 bluish green, pale, spotted eggs for 11 to 14 days.

Both parents feed the young birds, which will leave the nest in around 10 days. They will be able to fly and find their own food in 7 to 10 days after leaving the nest.

Song and Call

Their song is a clear whistles followed by husky trills. A call often heard is a loud pink-pink-pink.

Food and Feeding

The main diet of White-crowned Sparrows is seeds from grass and weeds. In summer they also eat insects such as beetles and caterpillars. They will also eat grains and fruit such as berries. They will visit seed feeders, but prefer to eat seeds dropped on the ground by other birds.

House Wren

Identification

(*Troglodytes aedon*)

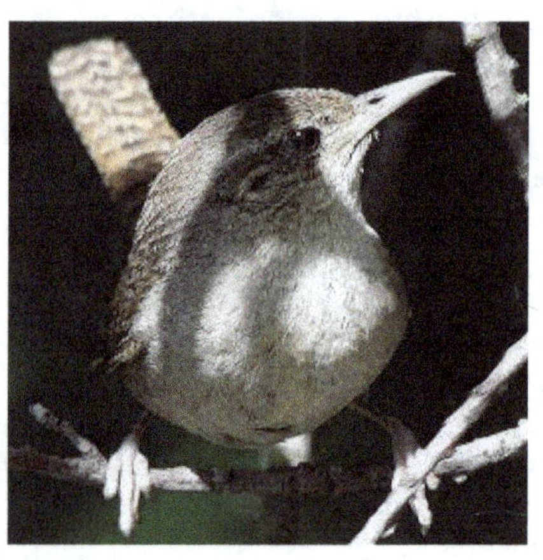

House Wrens are about 4 1/2 to 5 1/4 inches. This is a small stubby, brownish gray wren with darker barring on the wings, and tail. They have pinkish legs, a light eye ring, and the beak is curved slightly downward. They are very energetic, often cocking their tail over their back.

Males and females are similar. There are varying subspecies.

Song

The House Wren's song is a quick gurgling, rising and then falling at the end, heard during nesting season. It calls a rapid prrr, and a harsh cheh cheh. If you get too near their nest, this pugnacious little bird will scold you with their beak open and their body trembling.

Habitat

House Wrens can be found from
southern Canada across most of the U.S.
in summer. They winter in southern U.S.
and Mexico and are resident year-round
in southern California, southern Mexico,
and South America. They like open
woods woodland edges, brushy areas,
orchards, and backyards.

Nesting and Breeding

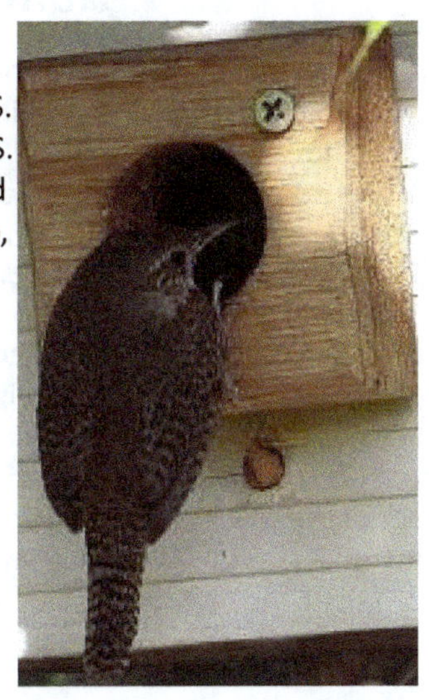

Male Wrens will build several
nests for the female to choose
from. When a female arrives, he
sings excitedly, with trembling wings
and will lead her to the nests for her
inspection. She will inspect each nest and after she picks one, she
may rebuild parts or all of it. They build a cup nest of sticks and grass
in a cavity and line it with feathers and other material.   The normal
nest site is a natural cavity or possibly one made by a woodpecker,
but they will build in almost anything that has a cavity. They often
nest in birdhouses and having several around may make an area more
attractive. During nesting season they are loud, bold, and very active,
becoming quiet and reclusive in winter. Females will incubate 5-8
white or pinkish eggs, speckled with brown for 12 to 15 days. The
young birds are fed by both parents and will fledge in 15 to 18 days.
The birds may have more than one brood per year.

Food

House Wrens feed almost entirely on insects, many of which are
harmful to man. They may also feed at suet feeders. House wrens can
be attracted with food and water. If you have trees and shrubs they
may nest in your yard.

Hummingbirds

Hummingbirds are the jewels of the bird world, with brilliant, flashing colors, hovering in mid air, and darting from flower to flower with acrobatic style. They are fascinating to watch with their iridescent colors.

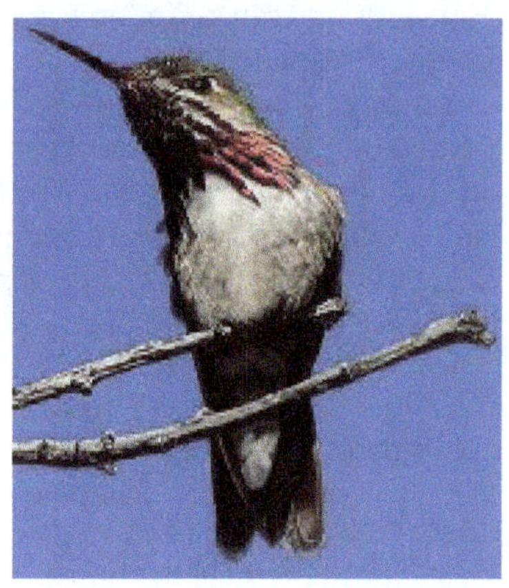

Early Spanish explorers to America aptly named them Flying Jewels. They got the name Hummingbird from early colonists because of the buzz of their fast moving wings. The scientific name Trochilidae comes from the Greek word Trochilos, which means small bird.

Hummingbird Song and Wing Sound

Most Hummingbird songs sound like high-pitched squeaks or chirps to the human ear because they are vocalized so fast. The birds also have a distinctive wing noise from their fast beating wings. Expert birders can identify different species form the wing sound.

Hummingbird Plumage

Plumage is the first thing that makes these little birds stand out. Brilliant colors let them blend in with the flowers they frequent, giving them some protection from predators.

This color, along with their acrobatics and swift flying, makes them poor targets for large birds of prey. Even while sitting on a nest the greenish color on the back of most females hides them from predators above.

While their small feathers do have color, most of the color we see comes from iridescence caused by their feather structure. This iridescence is a result of how light strikes platelets. Platelets are air and melanin filled feathers that reflect light, creating iridescence. When light hits these cells, it is broken apart, causing some wavelengths to be intensified. The result is the shimmering colors we see. The colors can be seen only when the light is hitting the feathers at precisely the right angle.

Different angles will produce different colors causing the shimmering effect.

Male & Female Plumage

Hummingbirds get their specific names from the brilliant plumage in the gorget, or throat area, of the male. Blue throated, Ruby throated, Magnificent, Black-chinned, Mexican pink, and others are all named for the gorget.

Just like other feathers, those of the gorget change color depending on how the light strikes it. The color can go from its main colors of say red to blue, green, and back to the original. Sometimes it will be almost black. In some species the males will also have colorful crests, and streamers that attract the females.

In most birds the male is more colorful then the female, but female hummingbirds, while not as bright as the male, also have colorful plumage. The females do not have the brilliant gorget of the male. With females it is harder determine the species. North American females are usually whitish gray below. Females also have white tips on the ends of their tail feathers.

Nesting and Breeding

Many male hummingbirds do dramatic aerial displays to attract a mate. After mating the female does all the work from incubating the eggs to feeding the young. Because females are not as bright as the male, it is harder for predators to see them as they sit on their nests. The greenish back of North American hummingbird females also helps them blend in.

The females build nests that are well camouflaged to blend in well with surroundings. The 1/2-inch eggs will incubate for about 15 days.

Wings and Flight

These acrobats of the air have combined the skills of both birds and insects. The wings of hummingbirds move in a figure-eight pattern, allowing the birds to hover and fly in all directions. It is a wonder to see them hover in one spot or dive bomb. Their wings are 25 to 30 percent of their body weight and beat at up to 80 beats per second. The normal speed is 25 to 30 mile per hour, but some reach 65 miles per hour. They fly long distances.

The Ruby Throat flies across the Gulf of Mexico each year.

Hummingbird Bills

The bill varies depending on the species. In general they are long, slender tube shaped. They are usually straight or with a slight down curve. They are perfect for probing flowers for nectar or catching insects. The birds also use them as weapons and threaten each other with them.

Torpor

Because they are so small, and have little insulation, hummingbirds lose body heat rapidly, even while sleeping. To survive cold nights hummingbirds go into a state called torpor. In this state they will use 50 times less energy by reducing their metabolic rate by up to 95 percent.

Number of Species

There are 340 different species. 21 of these reach the U.S. and 16 of them breed in the United States. The well-known Ruby Hummingbird covers the widest range and flies across the Gulf of Mexico during migration.

Food

They eat insects for protein. Their tongue has grooves on the sides, making it easier to catch insects. Flower nectar is a favorite and gives them much needed energy. They have an extremely high metabolism and need as much energy as they can get. They need to drink almost twice their weight in nectar each day. In exchange for this, they help pollinate the flowers.

How does that saying go? If you build it they will come. Many people create flower gardens designed specifically for Hummingbirds and even butterflies. If you spread feeders around your yard, hummingbirds will likely visit. Because they have excellent memories, they will often return to the same flowers or feeders each year.

Hand Feeding

Hummingbirds are very friendly and will eat from a feeder in your hand. Hang around your feeder while they are feeding until they get used to you. Once they are used to you, hold a feeder with sugar water in your hand. You will have better luck if it has red on it. Sometimes it helps to temporarily remove your other feeders. It may take a while for them to start landing so be patient.

Indigo Bunting

Identification *(Passerina cyanea)*

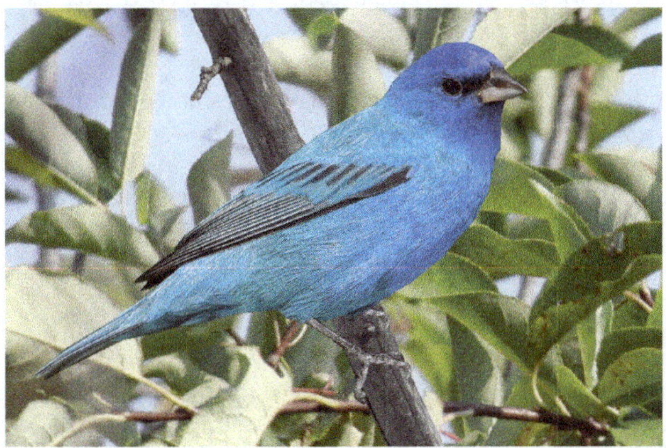

These are small finches, about 5 ½ inches. Their small conical bill is useful for both insects and seeds. When they are in breeding plumage, adult males are all blue, possibly with blackish wings and tail with blue edges. The iridescent blue color is not a result of pigmentation. The structure of the feathers causes light to scatter or reflect often giving the feathers a bright blue coloration. The blue color changes with different lighting.

Young males have black feathers that will turn bluer with each year. The female and young are dull brown with small amounts of blue in the tail and shoulders and blurred wing bars. After breeding season the males lose their brilliant plumage and look more like the females.

Indigo Buntings are often mistaken for Blue grosbeak or bluebirds.

Songs and Calls

From perches throughout his territory, you can hear the constant melody of the male. Its song is a fast warble of paired phrases, sounding like "sweet-sweet, cheer cheer, seeit-seeit." They also have a flight song, usually sung at dawn and twilight that sounds like "tsick." In poor light you may only have its song and its silhouette for identification.

Range, Habitat and Migration

Indigo Buntings prefer thick brushy areas with a few tall trees near woodland edges. They can be found in open brushy fields, and farmlands, forest clearings, along roadsides, and in yards with bushes or shrubbery.

The birds are found in most of eastern North America and in southern Canada during the breeding season.

Most Indigo Buntings migrate to central Mexico, Central America, and northern South America in the winter. Some may stay around all year in warmer areas such as southern Florida.

Breeding and Nesting

They like to breed in brushy and weedy areas. Clearings, swamps, open fields, and woodlands are all used. In April to mid May older male buntings arrive on their North American breeding grounds. By the time the females arrive a couple weeks later the males will have their territories. The female will pick her mate, and the two birds will have 2 to 3 broods.

The female builds a small sturdy nest of twigs, leaves, and plant fibers. The lining includes feathers, fine grasses, cloth, and other materials. The nest is generally hidden in heavy cover close to the ground. The female will incubate 2 to 6 white or bluish-white eggs for around 2 weeks.

Females do most of the feeding of the young until they fledge in around 10 days. After they fledge the male may take care of them while the female gets ready for a second brood. Until the eggs hatch the male stays away from the nest. He does defend it, and increases defense after the eggs hatch.

Both birds may mate with other partners. Indigo buntings will sometimes cross breed with Lazuli Buntings.

They will group together in large flocks from August to November for their long southern migration.

Food, Water, and Feeding

Natural foods are mostly insects, and spiders along with seeds, buds, berries, and fruit. They will come to yards with seed feeders, water, and some shrubbery.

Dark-eyed Junco

Identification *Junco hyemalis*

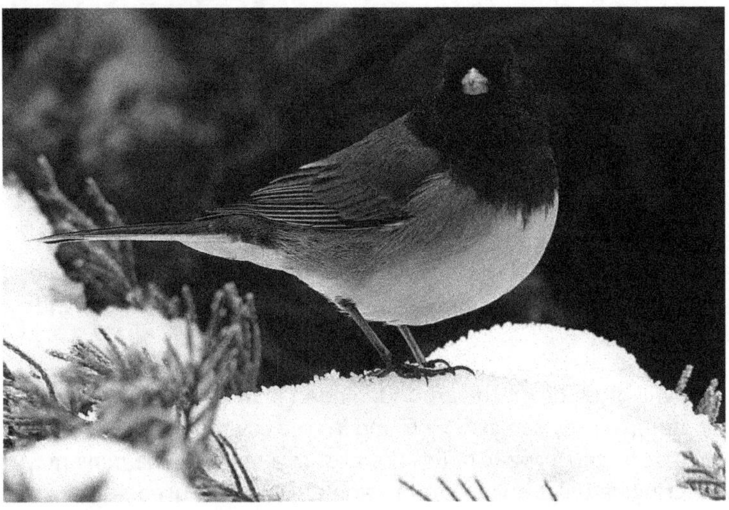

The Dark-eyed Junco is a small 5 to 6 1/2 inch bird. There are several forms of juncos. Four North American species were separate until the 1970s when they were all lumped together under Junco Hyemales.

Slate colored juncos are gray with white outer feathers that will flash during flight. The male has a dark grey or blackish hood on slate gray, with a whitish belly. Female and young ones are duller. The young may have streaks on the breast. Most have a pale pink bill.

Oregon Junco

Oregon Juncos have rusty-colored sides and pink beaks. Males have a black hood with a rusty back. Females have grayer hoods with pink or browns sides. The rusty back is not as pronounced in females. Younger birds are streaked below and grayish.

Pink-sided Juncos have a darker gray hood with pink sides.

Sound of Dark-eyed Junco

The male's song is a musical trill with a sharp tic and twittering notes, said to sound like a ringing telephone. Calls include a nasal *kew-kew*, a *buzy zeet*, and a *tick* when the nest is threatened.

Preferred Habitat

Dark-eyed Juncos like cool forests of mixed wood, and can be seen in undergrowth, brush or along the road. They range from Alaska, Canada, and U.S. They winter in much of the U.S., and North Mexico. In winter Juncos can be seen in small flocks.

Breeding and Nesting

Breeding begins in mid-March to May with double or triple broods. Breeding areas for Dark-eyed Juncos are open woodland, forest edges, bogs, and mountainous regions. They winter in woodland edges and bushy areas.

The nest will often be on the ground, hidden in brush, or behind a rock or stump. They can also be found in tree cavities, or on building ledges. The female usually builds the nest in a hollow. The male may help by bringing twigs and other materials. Materials used are twigs, stems, fine grass, and hair.

Eggs
There are usually 3 to 5 eggs incubated by the female for around 13 days. Egg color is white, greenish or gray with speckles or blotches. The speckles can be red-brown or purplish brown. The young are tended by both adult birds and are able to leave the nest in 10 to 14 days.

Food and Feeding

They like to feed on the ground, hopping around to search for seeds or insects. They will come to seed feeders.

Killdeer

Killdeers are shorebirds that have become comfortable living in agricultural and suburban areas, making them the most common plover in North America.

Identification

(*Charadrius vociferus*)

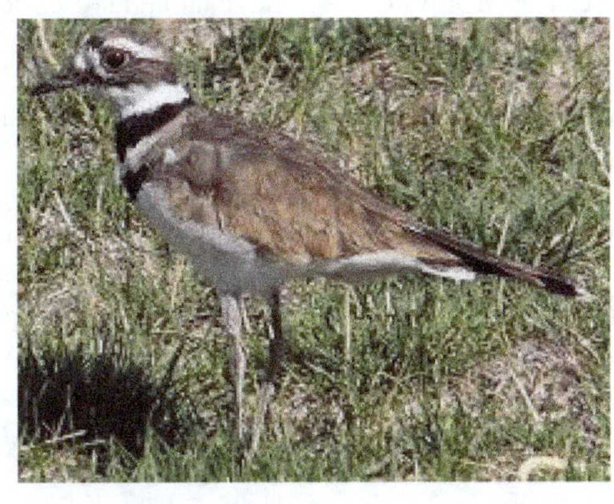

Killdeers are plovers about 9 to 11 inches. Both sexes are brown above, and white below with a reddish brown rump. They have two black bands around the neck, and an orange eye ring. They have a white forehead, and the top of the head is brown. They have long, pointed brown wings and tail. When they fly they show a golden-red rump and white wing strips. Male and female killdeer look similar in appearance. The young birds look like the parents but only have one neck band, and they have buffy tips on their back and wing feathers.

Killdeer sound

These are very noisy birds and are often heard at night. In spring the male can be heard singing kill-deer kill-deer as he circles his territory. An alarm call is a nasal deet-deet-deet. They also have a low trill. In the fall small flocks will fly around and around calling kill-deer.

Preferred Habitat

They are year-round residents of the western U.S. In the summer they range from southern Canada and Alaska to Northern U.S. They winter in Mexico and Central America. They like agricultural areas; fields, lawns, airports, riverbanks, shores, mudflats, and open fields with gravel, and little vegetation.

They have adapted well to humans. Even though they are shorebirds that prefer shorelines, they may live and nest almost anywhere, even if there is no body of water nearby.

Breeding and Nesting

Killdeer normally breed in early spring, starting with the male flying in big circles around the female, calling, kill-deer over and over. The birds nest on the ground. They do not build a nest but will lay their eggs in a depression in gravel. The nest and speckled eggs blend easily into the background making them hard to see. They will nest almost anywhere and have been known to nest in driveways.

If you get near a nest or babies, the adult killdeers will often play like they are injured with a broken wing. They will act like they can barely walk in an attempt to lead you away from the nest. They are very good at this game and will let you get just about in reach before they scurry away a little farther. If either you or potential predators do not follow them, they will come closer and get louder. When they get you far enough away that they feel the babies are safe the wing will miraculously heal. If you look around you can often spot the little ones hiding in the grass. Another deception they use is acting like they are sitting on a nest. When a predator gets near they move to a new spot to settle.

Both parents take turns incubating 4 buff, speckled eggs for 24 to 28 days. As soon as their downy feathers dry after hatching from the egg, the babies start running around after the parents and looking for food. Killdeer are in a group called precocial birds. These birds are in the egg longer than other birds, so when they hatch out they are more developed. They can't fly yet, and they are a little clumsy but they are ready to go. Songbirds such as bluebirds are altricial and require more care from the parents after hatching. In 20 to 30 days the young killdeers will be self-sufficient.

Food

The main diet of Killdeers consists of insects, and invertebrates.

Kinglet

Identification

Kinglets are tiny birds about 4 to 4 1/2 inches; they are one of the smallest in America. They are constantly moving and flicking their wings, making them difficult to see as they flit from place to place. Ruby-crowned Kinglets and the Golden-crowned Kinglets are the two that are seen in North America.

Ruby-crowned Kinglet (Regulus calendula)

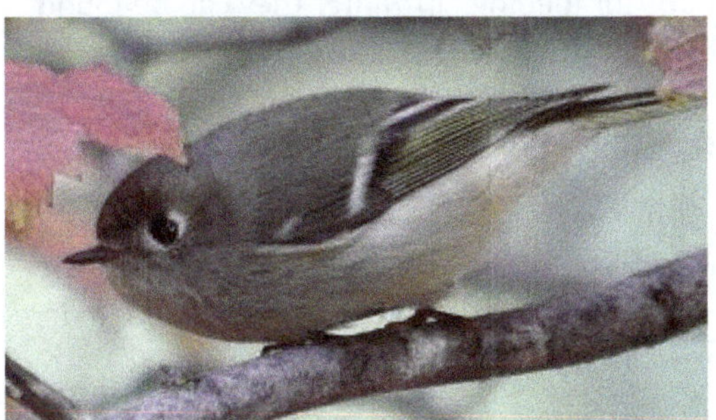

Ruby-crowned Kinglets are olive above and white below. One of the most striking features of this bird is the broken white eye-ring, which gives it the appearance of large eyes. The wings have two white bars. The primary and secondary flight feathers are dark. Wings and tail feathers have a yellow leading edge so flashes of yellow are seen on flight.

The adult male has a bright ruby red crown patch that is usually hidden. The red patch is displayed when the bird is excited.

Golden-crowned Kinglet (Regulus satrapa)

Golden-crowned Kinglets are also olive-gray birds.

The Golden-crowned Kinglets have a bold black and white striped facial pattern with a gold crown patch. The crown patch is yellow in females, and orange to red in males. The adults always show the crown patch with a black border and have a white stripe over the eyes.

Sound of Kinglet

Ruby-crowned Kinglets' call is a single quick di-dit. The song is 3 to 4 high notes, followed by several low notes, and a chant-like (tee tee tee tew tew tew tedatee tedadee tedadee).

Golden-crowned Kinglets' call note is single see see see. The song is a series of high thin notes like the call, which drops down into a chatter.

Preferred Habitat

Kinglets like conifer forests.   Both Ruby and Golden crowned Kinglets will join flocks of other birds for feeding. In winter they can be found in other woodlands and forests.

Breeding and Nesting

Kinglets form new pairs each year for mating. Females build the nests, which are usually in conifers. The nest is usually well hidden. It is a deep nest of grass, lichen, bark strips, twigs, rootlets, needles. Spider webs comprise the outer walls, and feathers, plant down, and hair form a soft lining.

Eggs

Females incubate 7 to 12 whitish eggs with brown or gray spots, for about 2 weeks. The male will bring her food while she sits on the nest. Both parents will feed the young, which will leave the nest in about 15 days. The females may leave the breeding territory but the male will continue to feed the young birds for 10 or so days.

Food and Feeding

Kinglets like to eat small insects. They will often feed in groups of birds such as nuthatches, chickadees, titmice and others. They are always on the move with quick playful movements, hopping about in the branches of trees and bushes in forests or even in backyards.

Lazuli Bunting

Identification

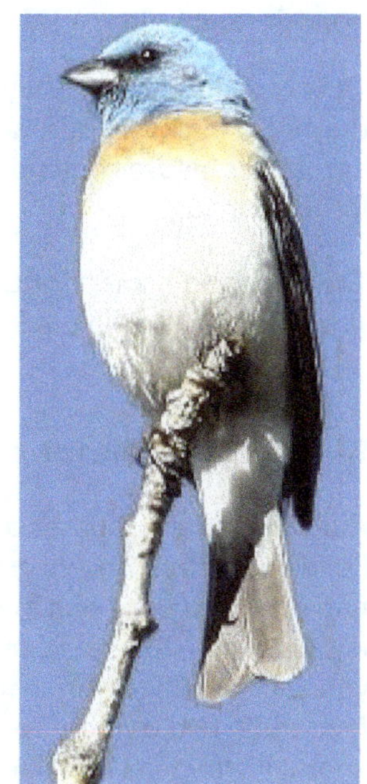

(Passerina amoena)

Lazuli Buntings were named for their gemstone (lapis lazuli) colored head.

They are a small bright blue finch about 5 to 5 1/2 inches. Like other finches, their conical bill is useful for both insects and seeds. The head and upper parts of males in breeding plumage are turquoise blue with black in front of the eyes. The breast and sides have a cinnamon band and the belly is white. They have black tails and wings, with white wing bars. Lazuli Buntings look somewhat like Western Bluebirds, but are smaller.

Young males look like the adults but are paler and have buff feather tips.

Females are brownish with white on the throat and belly and white wing bars.

Songs and Calls

The Lazuli song is a rapid, high warble, similar to that of the Indigo Bunting but longer, and with less repetition.

They sing high phrases at different pitches like see-see, sweet-sweet, cheew cheew, that are usually paired. By the first or second year males will develop their own song, and will sing only that song for the rest of their life. Often they will develop their song by listening to nearby males, so males in a certain area may sound alike. In poor light you may only have its song and its silhouette for identification.

Range, Habitat and Migration

Lazuli Buntings range from British Columbia across Saskatchewan, then south through the western United States.

After breeding season they begin to molt. They will stop molting while they fly in flocks to areas such as southern Arizona and New Mexico for a stopover before continuing on with their migration south to Mexico for the winter.

The preferred habitat for Lazuli Buntings is shrubby areas, brushy slopes, dry hillsides, briars, and streamside. They may also reside in residential gardens.

Breeding and Nesting

After the female chooses a nesting site in low trees or bushes, she will build a cup-sized nest of grass, leaves, and bark. The nest is lined with fine grass, and hair, and may be wrapped in caterpillar silk. She will lay 3 to 4 pale blue eggs and incubate them for around 12 days. The young birds will leave the nest in about 10 days and the parents will feed them two or more weeks after they leave. The female may start another brood in which case the male will do most of the feeding. Lazuli Buntings will sometimes cross breed with Indigo buntings.

Food, Water, and Feeding

Natural foods for Buntings are seeds, grain, berries, and insects. They can be seen foraging on the ground or in bushes, but will also visit feeders, and birdbaths in your backyard or garden area.

Lewis's Woodpecker

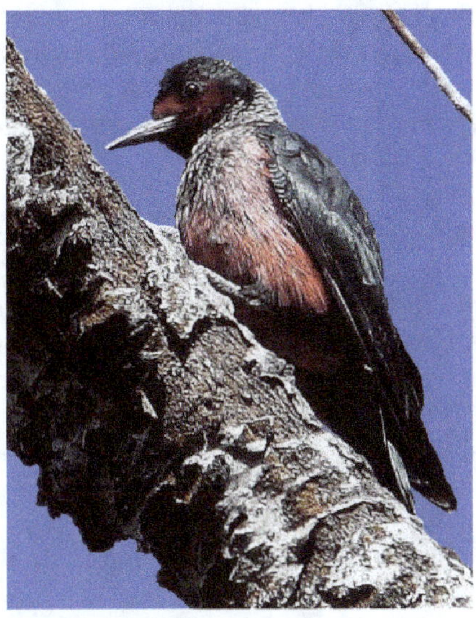

Identification *(Melanerpes lewis)*

Lewis's Woodpecker named for Meriwether Lewis, is a large dark woodpecker, about 10 inches, with a blackish-green back and wings, a pink belly, and a gray collar. The head is black with a red patch on the face. They have a large pointed bill. The sexes are similar. Young birds have a dark back and wings but have brown heads, no red on the faces, no gray collar, and they are mottled brown beneath. The wings are broader than most woodpeckers, and they have a straight flight with slow even strokes like a crow.

Similar birds are the Red-Headed and Acorn woodpeckers

Sound

The call of Lewis's woodpecker is a harsh chee-ur. They also make high ik-ik-ik sound and a dry rattling.

Preferred Habitat

Lewis's Woodpecker is found from British Columbia and southwestern Alberta, through the Western U.S., and into Northern Mexico. They like logged forests and river groves preferring large scattered trees to dense forests. Northern populations may migrate for winter, while southern birds are resident year long.

Breeding and Nesting

Drumming during courtship is a weak roll followed by several taps. To attract a mate, and to warn intruders, the male points his bill and performs a raised wing display, flashing his pink under parts. Lewis's woodpeckers are monogamous and form long-term bonds. The nest is a cavity excavated in a dead tree branch and will usually be reused each season. They may reuse a cavity excavated by other birds. The cavity is lined with wood chips and the female will lay 6 to 8 white eggs. Both birds will incubate them for around 12 days. Both parents feed the young birds, which will leave the nest in 4 to 5 weeks. The fledglings will remain around the nest and be fed by the parents for roughly a week.

Food

Their main diet consists of insects such as ants, bees, grasshoppers, and beetles, but they also eat nuts and berries. In addition to foraging for insects on trees and branches, these birds will sit on top of a tree or poll and fly out to catch insects. They also break up nuts and acorns and store them in holes and cracks in trees and polls for winter. They defend these winter stores aggressively. They will also visit suet feeders.

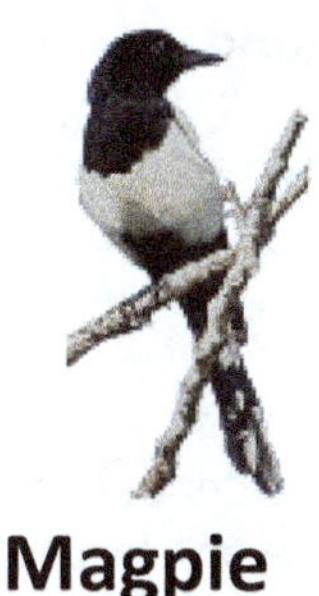

Magpie

Identification

(Pica Pica)

Black-billed Magpies are large, slender, black and white birds about 18 to 19 1/2 inches, with long wedge-shaped tails. The black wings and tail show iridescent blue-green. This is especially evident in their tail as they fly. They have large white patches in the wings. They have long thick black bills. The sexes look alike. Juveniles look similar but are duller.

Magpies are known for their tendency to steal shiny objects and hide them.

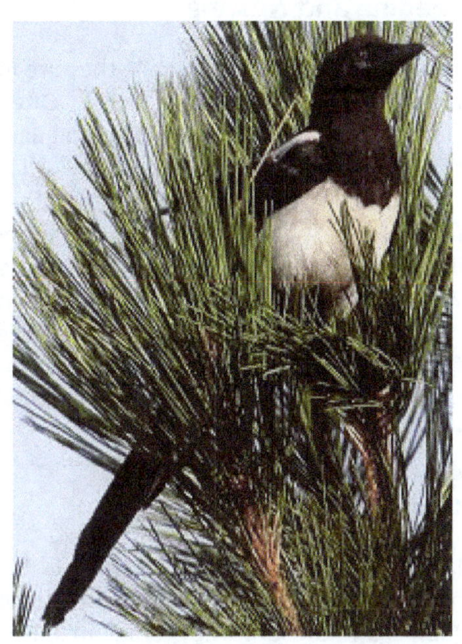

Intelligence

A recent study at Goethe University in Frankfurt showed that magpies can recognize themselves. Helmut Prior place colored dots on the bird's necks. When mirrors were place in front of them they would try to remove the dots, indicating they recognized the image in the mirror.

This is the first time this has been shown in non-mammals.

Black-billed Magpie Sound

Their voice is a harsh wah-wah-wah, as well as variety of squawks and chatters.

Preferred Habitat

Magpies make permanent residence in much of the western U.S., Canada, and Alaska. They like brushy country, forest edges, stream sides, ranches, and farmland. They are often seen in flocks. During winter they will roost in grooves of trees.

Breeding and Nesting

Magpie pairs usually form while they are in wintering flocks. A pair of magpies will stay together for life. Often they will nest in small colonies. Both male and female help build a very large domed canopy of sticks and mud. Inside the canopy will be a cup-shaped nest of mud or manure, lined with grass, hair, and other materials. The nest is built in a tree or bushes and will have an entrance on both sides. Females will incubate 6 to 9 eggs for around 18 days. Their eggs vary in color from blue-green to cream, and have brownish blotches. The male will bring her food while she incubates, and the two of them will take care of the young birds. In 3 to 4 weeks the young birds will leave the nest and join with other broods. The parents will feed their own fledging for another 3 to 4 weeks.

Food

Black-billed Magpies eat mostly insects, but they are opportunists and omnivorous. They also eat berries, nuts, seeds, bird eggs, small rodents, and carrion. They forage mainly on the ground searching for food by using their bill to flip over debris. They will follow predators to clean up after a kill. Magpies are known for preying on the nests of other birds. They are often seen on the backs of large animals such as cattle, where they eat large quantities of ticks.

Mallard Duck

Identification

(Anas platyrhynchos)

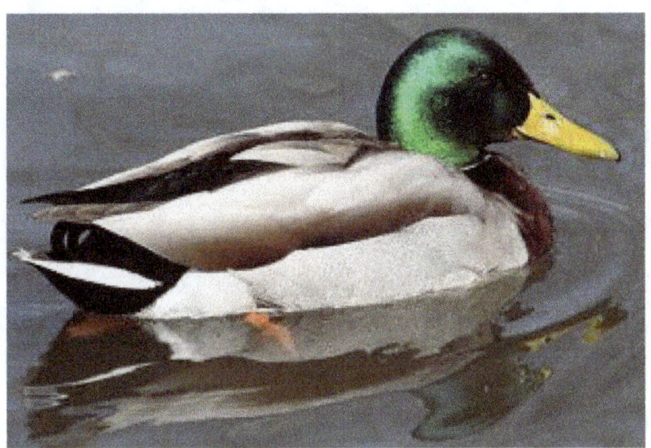

Mallard Ducks are probably the best known of all ducks. In fact they are the ancestors of almost all of our domestic ducks. They grow 18 to 27 inches in length. They are identified by most people by the male, or the drake's iridescent green head, and narrow white collar. Their body is grayish with chestnut breast, and white tail feathers with black central tail feathers that curl up. They have a yellow bill, orange feet, and a purple speculum. Unfortunately like most birds, he will lose his bright colors after breeding season.

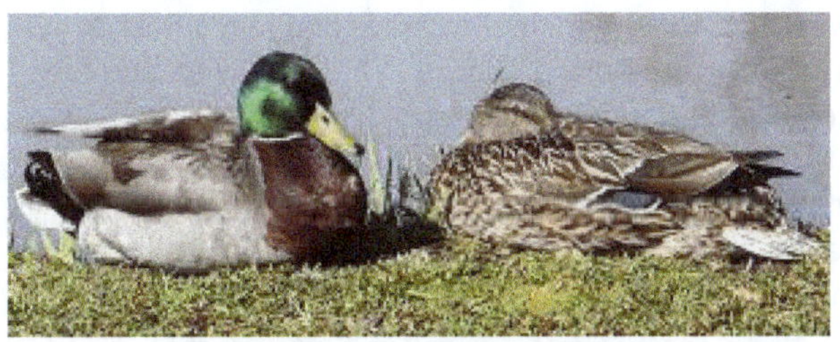

The females are mottled brown with a white tail, and a mottled brown and orange bill. Juveniles are similar to females. Mallards are often seen in small flocks flying in a V formation.

Duck sound

Ducks are noisy birds. The male's call is a low nasal quack. During mating season he makes sharp whistles. The female's voice is quack-quack-quack.

Preferred Habitat

Mallards are found throughout North America. They prefer calm shallow water, but can be found in almost any body of water from marshes, ponds, rivers, lakes and irrigated land. They are often seen in city parks.

Breeding and Nesting

Mallard breeding season starts in the fall, and they will pair up by winter. During courtship the male will whistle and grunt, pump his head, and preen in front of the female. Females will respond with loud calls and posturing. This normally takes place in the water. They will also perform chase flights. If they migrate once paired, they will migrate to the female's territory of origin.

Attended by the male, the female chooses a nesting site. They normally nest in the reeds. The female builds a hollow nest with grass, leaves, and feathers, lined with down. Occasionally they may use the nest of other birds such as a crow or hawk. Females lay and incubate 8 to 15 eggs for about a month. Mallard eggs vary in color from creamy white, pale blue to blue-green, and they have no markings. While she is incubating the eggs, the male may leave and join a flock of other males. Ducklings are born precocial. They can swim and feed themselves shortly after hatching. They will fledge in around 8 weeks, but until then they will follow the mother for protection. While the female is raising the young birds, the male will leave to molt. This takes 2 to 3 weeks, and he will be temporarily flightless. When the molting is complete, the male will look much like the female.

Food

The Mallard's main diet consists of aquatic vegetation, fish, and invertebrates, which they get by dabbling near the water surface. Often they can be seen completely upended as they dip below the surface. They also eat grains and plants on land.

Western Meadowlark

The distinctive black V across the yellow breast of Western Meadowlarks is a common sight along roadsides and in fields across much of North America. It is the state bird of 6 states.

Identification

(Sturnella neglecta)

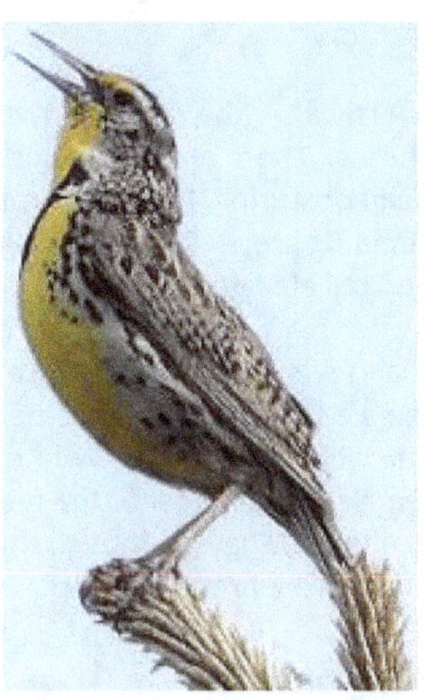

Western Meadowlarks are about 8 1/2 to 11 inches and have a bright yellow throat and a breast crossed with a black V. Their sides and under-tail feathers are a white with dark spots and streaks. Their upper parts are a mix of buffs, browns, and black streaks. A bright yellow line runs over the eye to long slender bill. The birds have a short tail, and long legs. Adult birds have a dark crown with a white stripe. When approached on the ground their white tail feathers will be visible as they run away giving a sharp alarm.

The sexes look similar, but the female is smaller and has less marking. Eastern meadowlarks are similar, but the yellow throat extends farther into the face in Western Meadowlarks.

Range and Habitat

Western Meadowlarks can be found from British Columbia, Manitoba, northern Michigan, and Ohio, south to Missouri, central Texas, and northern Mexico. They like grasslands, and open country with plains, and meadows.

Most will stay within breeding areas in winter but may move into the valleys when deep snow covers their food sources. They will flock in the winter sometimes with other blackbirds. There are some populations that migrate south.

Breeding and Nesting

Male meadowlarks arrive to claim their territory a couple weeks before the females. They will claim about six or seven acres and stand guard, singing from fence posts, and wires. If another male dares to intrude on the territory, it will be attacked. When they fight, they lock feet and peck at each other rolling around on the ground. When one of them escapes and flies away, the victor will pursue it out of the territory.

Shortly after the female arrives, she will initiate a series of aerial chases. These are short flights followed by periods on the ground with male posturing. He struts around the female, puffing his chest, and standing erect. During this dance the female will stand with her bill and tail elevated, and her wings drooped slightly.

Males will mate with more than one female at a time. The nest the female builds is a grass dome concealed in thick grass on the ground. She will incubate 3 to 7 white spotted eggs for around 14 days. The female will do most of the feeding, and the young will leave the nest in about 10 days, although they will not be able to fly yet. The female may have 2 broods a year.

Song and Call

Meadowlarks have many songs and calls, flute-like notes with guttural chatter. Growing up in Montana the two bird songs I remember signaling the arrival of spring were the robin and the loud melody of the meadowlark. Both sexes sing; however, the loud territorial song of the male is the sound most people are familiar with. Western meadowlarks sing continually from treetops and fence posts or utility poles in their territory. A male will have as many as 10 different songs, usually switching songs if another male is present.

Food

Insects are the main diet of meadowlarks in the summer as they forage mostly on the ground, probing the soil with their bills. In fall and winter they eat seeds.

Common Merganser Duck

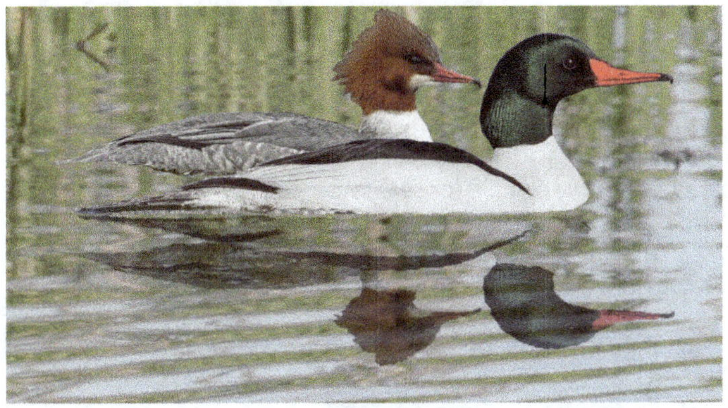

Identification

(Mergus Merganser)

Mergansers, sometimes called goosanders are long-bodied ducks, 24 to 25 inches. The male has a long white body with black on the back and green-black head. The bill has serrated edges and both it and the feet are reddish. The female and young birds are gray with white front and under parts and a rufus crested head and a square white wing patch. Like the male their bill and feet are reddish.

Preferred Habitat

They like bodies of water such as lakes, rivers and ponds. They can be found in most of the U.S. but not often along southeast coastal states.

Food

Mergansers dive and swim to catch fish their main diet, but also eat insects , crustaceans and other aquatic life.

Merganser's sound

The male gives low rasping croaks, and the female low short quacks.

Breeding and Nesting

The male will do courtship displays where he swims in rapid circles while he stretches his neck and gives soft calls. Mergansers usually nest in a tree cavity but sometimes in a hollow on ground lined with down. She will usually lay 6 to 12 pale buff eggs, which she will sit on for 30 to 35 days. The young may leave the nest in a day or two, but will be cared for by the female for several weeks.

Mourning Dove

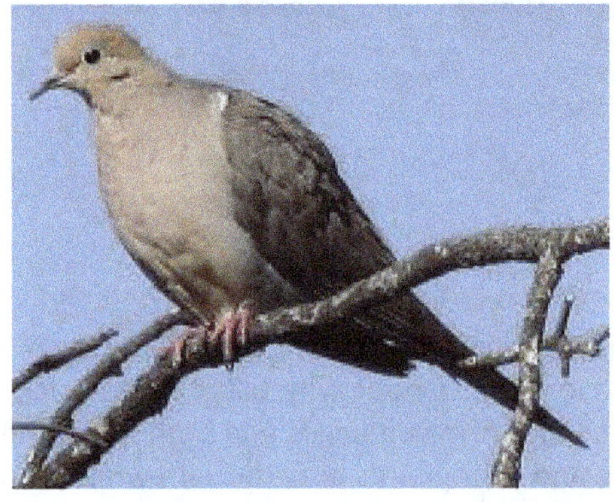

Mourning Doves are one of the most wide spread birds in North America. This makes them not only a popular songbird but a game bird as well.

Identification

(Zenaida Macrouraare)

Mourning Doves are small slim doves, about 12 inches. They are fawn colored with black spots on their backs and pinkish-red feet and legs. Their distinctive long pointed tail with large white outer tail feathers stands out. Males have a slightly bluish crown and nape, with a bit of pink on the breast.

When the birds fly they flap their wings continually creating a whistle as the air passes through the wing feathers. Just like other doves and pigeons, this one jerks its head with each step when it walks.

Calls and Songs

Sometimes mistaken for an owl, the male's courtship and territorial call is a series of cooing notes. It sounds like *coah cooo cooo coo.* Both adults give a shorter call like oowa when near the nest. There is also a whistling twitter when they take off.

Range and Habitat

In late fall mourning doves gather in large flocks across nearly all of the United States, and southern Canada. Many, but not all northern Mourning Doves migrate south in winter. They can be found in grasslands, farmlands, open woods, and roadsides. They are equally at home in backyards with evergreens, fruit trees, and suburban gardens. In fact they are at home in virtually any habitat. When you hear talk of a bird for all seasons this is it.

Breeding and Nesting

Mourning Doves breed in all 50 states, southern Canada, Alaska, Mexico, and into Panama. Breeding starts in March and April.

Courtship starts with the male cooing call while puffing out his throat and bobbing his tail. The Fish and Wild Life Service actually counts them by listening for this call. Another part of the courtship is the flight of the male. He will fly to around 100 feet then glide back down to the female in large sweeping circles. He will also strut and bow repeatedly in front of the female. After mating the male vigorously defends the nesting area. What is unusual is that the Mourning doves will do most of their feeding outside the nesting area.

The nesting site is often on a tree branch 10 to 25 feet up and is chosen by the male. He then gathers sticks and bring them to the female, landing on her while she sits on the partly built nest. Although they seem to take great care, their nest is one of the flimsiest of all bird nests. The eggs can even be seen through the twigs. Often they will just use old nests from other birds such as Robins.

Usually there are two white eggs with both birds taking turns on the nest. Many nests are lost to bad weather. In addition doves have many predators such as squirrels, snakes, and other birds. Both adults will feed the young and they can leave the nest in 10 to 14 days.

They will have as many as six broods of two chicks each during a
season. This fast reproduction allows them to thrive and spread even
with high predation. Young birds leave the nest in around two weeks,
and the parents continue to feed them outside the nest for another
two weeks.

Food and Feeding

Mourning Doves' natural foods consist of a wide variety of wild
seeds, grains, and insects. They often feed on grain in open fields
and croplands. They will be seen at feeders in larger numbers when
the ground is covered in deep snow. Just as with other songbirds,
food, water, and cover will attract them to your backyard. Stock your
feeders with cracked corn, millet, and a variety of other seeds to
attract Mourning doves. Doves are ground feeders, so tray feeders
are best. While many songbirds will scatter when jays or crows arrive,
Mourning doves will just ignore them and keep eating.

Water
Birdbaths will attract them, but running or dripping water will draw
more birds. You are also likely to get more birds if you have trees and
shrubs for cover.

Common Nighthawk

Identification

(Chordeiles minor)

Common Nighthawks, part of the nightjar family, are very acrobatic, slim-winged birds, often seen high in the air. They are gray or gray-brown birds, about 8 1/2 to 10 inches. They have large eyes, short bills, small feet, and long pointed wings with broad white bars. The bill is surrounded by stiff feathers called rictal bristles, which help it catch flying insects. When they are at rest the wing tips extend past the tail. Their dead leaf pattern camouflages them when resting on the ground. The male has a white throat and white bar across the notched tail.

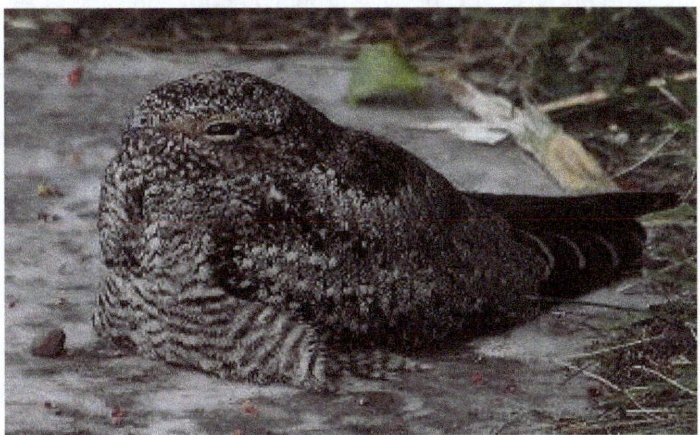

Nighthawks are also called "Mosquito Hawks," "Goatsuckers," "Bull Bats," and "Night Jars". The name "Goatsucker" was given to them in ancient times when goat herders saw the birds flying over their flocks with open mouths. The birds were catching insects but the myth developed that they were sucking milk from the goats.

Sound

Their call is a nasal peer or pee-ick normally heard in flight.

Preferred Habitat

They range across the U.S. in summer. In winter they migrate to South America, often in huge flocks that may contain hundreds or thousands of birds. They are often seen in open country from mountains to lowlands. They like treeless plains and open pine woods. They may be seen sitting on the ground, a roof, or a fence post with their eyes closed, or flying high in the air at mid day, but they prefer dusk. Males perform an aerial display where they dive then swoop up making a deep booming sound with their wings.

Breeding and Nesting

Nighthawks usually nest on the bare ground, laying 2 cream or whitish colored eggs, with purplish-gray or olive-brown markings, in sand, gravel, leaves, or on a rock. In cities they may lay their eggs on a roof. Mostly the female incubates the eggs for 18 to 20 days. Both parents will care for the young, which will fledge in around 20 days. Young birds will be on their own in 25 to 30 days.

Food

Nighthawks catch flying insects such as mosquitoes, flying ants, moths, or beetles out of the air. They prefer feeding at dawn or dusk but will forage at night with a bright moon or streetlight.

Northern Cardinals

Identification *(Richmondena cardinalis),* name changed from Cardinalis cardinalis in 1918.

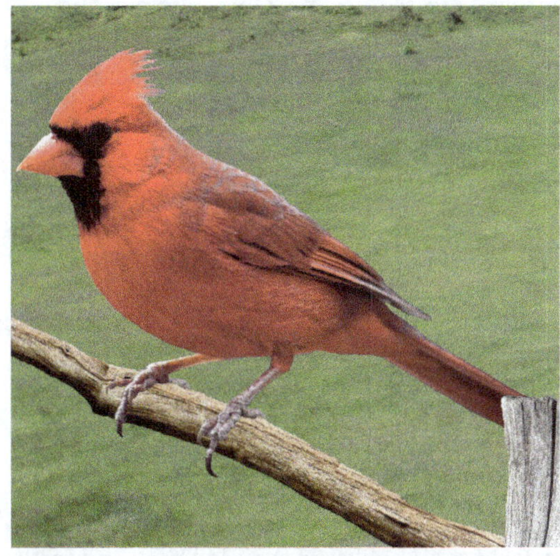

Male Northern Cardinals are all red with the exception of the black patch around their thick triangular or conical bill. Their bright color and the pointed crest make it instantly identifiable by bird enthusiasts. They keep this bright red plumage year round, and it is very striking in snow.

The female is brownish with some red on the wings and tail. Just like the male, the female has a dark face, and heavy red bill, good for eating seeds. Adults are 7 ½ to 9 inches. Young birds look much like the female, with darker bills.

At one time cardinals were kept as caged pets, but the Migratory Bird Treaty Act of 1918 banned the practice In the U.S.

Sound

Cardinals have several variations of repeated whistles (whe-cheer-cheer or whertee-whertee-whertee). A contact or alarm call sounds like chip. Female cardinals sing while they are on their nest. A pair will have song phrases they share.

Range and Habitat

The Northern Cardinal is a year-round resident of the eastern U.S., and continues to spread north. It is so well liked that more states have adopted it as their state bird than any other bird. These states are: Illinois, Indiana, Kentucky, North Carolina, Ohio, Virginia, and West Virginia. They like the edges of wooded areas, river thickets, and gardens. You can find them in areas near people, such as parks and backyards.

Nesting and Breeding

Breeding season begins in late March to early April. Cardinals will breed in a wide variety of areas. Once he develops a territory, the male cardinals aggressively defend it. They have been known to attack their reflections in windows, mistaking themselves for other males.

The male feeds the female during courtship. Cardinals will mate for life and remain together throughout the entire year.

The male usually follows the female as she searches for a nest site. They carry nesting material in their beaks, as they call back and forth to each other. They prefer to build their nest in shrubbery or a thickly branched tree. Males may bring nesting material to the female, who will build a cup-shaped nest in 3 to 9 days. Nesting materials are twigs, weeds, and grasses, bark fibers, dead leaves, moss, rags, and other debris.

The female will lay between two and five white or greenish eggs with dark streaks and spots on them. Usually the female will incubate the eggs for 11 to 13 days. The young will be fed by both parents for around 10 days and will be able to fly well in about 20 days.

Two, three, or four broods may be raised in a breeding season. The male will tend the brood while the female starts the next brood.

Feeders and Food

Natural foods

In the wild, Cardinals eat fruit, seed, and insects. Their heavy conical bills allow them to eat a wider range of seeds than birds with smaller bills such as sparrows or finches.

They search from the ground for food and can be heard foraging in bushes when they are out of sight. As they hop around they will scratch the ground with both feet searching for insects and other food.

Attracting Cardinals to Your Backyard

Because Cardinals are not migratory, you can attract them to your yard all year long with feeders, water, and shrubs. Many kinds of shrubs and trees will attract them to your yard. Some are blueberry, cherry, dogwood, and mulberry.

In addition to eating any fruit these trees may provide, they may nest and raise their young in the dense shrubs.

Feeders
If you put out feeders, they will eat almost any kind of fruit and seeds you offer them. Good food choices are cracked corn, millet, bread, nutmeats, safflower, peanut butter mixes, and suet. A favorite is unhulled black oil sunflower seeds.

If you watch them at the feeder, you will see them touch beaks as they offer each other seeds.

Water
In addition to food, provide a source of water for drinking and bathing. Many birds will come to clean their feathers in a birdbath. Running or dripping water will also attract them. Birds love to bathe in a slow sprinkler.

Northern Flicker

Identification

(Colaptes auratus)

There are two types: both are 12 to 14 inches. The Yellow-shafted Flicker has white under parts with dark spots, a black patch across the upper chest, and a red patch on the nape.

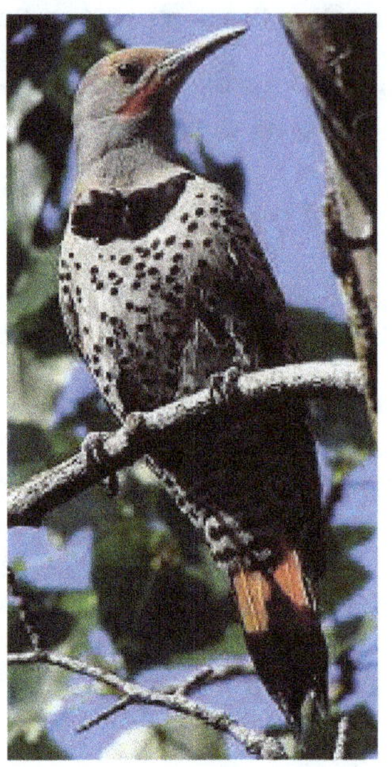

Although there are two main types, there is crossbreeding, resulting in variations.

Males have a black patch or mustache starting just below the bill and moving backward on the neck. The under part of the wings and tail are golden and flash when they fly overhead with its undulating flight. Just like most woodpeckers, they rise with a couple wing beats and then close their wings and fall. This repeated action causes the undulating flight we see.

The Red-shafted Flicker looks the same but salmon red replaces the under part of the wings and tail. They do not have the red patch on the nape, and the patch on the neck is red instead of black. The Yellow-shafted is in the East, and the Red-shafted is in the West. There are of course overlaps in their territories, where they interbreed.

Like all woodpeckers, they have heavy sharp bills, and thick neck muscles for hammering on trees, and getting beneath the bark for insects. They also have sharp curved claws for clinging to trees, and the tail feathers are stiff, allowing the tail to serve as a prop.

Flickers or Yellowhammers, as they are also called, are the Alabama state bird.

Song and Calls

The song is a loud wick wick wick, ki-ki-ki. During aggression and courtship a loud flick-a flicka is heard. Flickers also drum on resonant wood.

Pecking

Woodpeckers do three types of pecking. Loud rapid drumming on hollow trees can be to define a territory, keep track of a mate, or in search of a mate. Softer pecking is usually for searching for food when they will chip away at trees. The third kind of pecking is cavity excavation, and is usually done in soft or partially rotted wood.

Range and Habitat

Flickers cover the U.S. all year and north into Canada and Alaska in summertime. The northern populations migrate and can sometimes be seen in flocks.

They like open forests, groves, orchards, farms, and semi-open country.

Breeding and Nesting

Breeding season can be from March to July, depending on the area. Breeding is in open areas with scattered trees. For both courting and defending their territory, males perform displays in which they spread their wings and tail and swing their head back and forth. Woodpeckers are called primary cavity nesters: they excavate the holes many other birds will use. The male chooses the nest site and both birds excavate the cavity, with the male doing most of the work. The nest hole will be in a tree truck, stump, pole, wooden building, and occasionally even in the ground. They will use nest-boxes. The nest entrance is around 4 inches and the cavity is usually 10 to 18 inches deep.
There are usually 6 to 8 smooth, glossy, white eggs, incubated by both birds. They will only have one clutch, but will replace it if lost. The eggs will hatch in just less than two weeks, and both adults will tend the young. The young birds will climb to the entrance in about 18 days and may leave the nest in 25 to 30 days.

Although they are primary nesters, they will still sometimes use birdhouses of the right size.

One way to attract woodpeckers is to leave dead branches or trees on your property. These snags attract the kind of insects woodpeckers feed on, and they are also used to excavate nest holes. When the woodpeckers are through using the cavity other birds may move in.

Food and Feeding

Natural foods for flickers are insects such as ants, beetles, and larvae. Flickers have the bill for digging these out of wood. They forage on tree trunks and limbs, as well as hopping around on the ground looking for insects.

Flickers also eat fruits, seeds and nuts, which they will store for the winter. They will come to your yard for suet feeders. They will also come for black oil sunflower seeds, mealworms, and other foods.

Northern Mockingbird

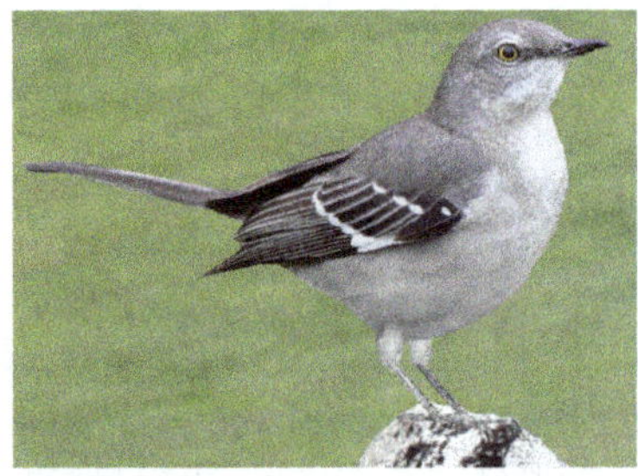

Identification
(Mimus Polyglottos)

Mockingbirds are 9 to 11 inches, about the same size as a Robin, but a bit slimmer. The birds are grayish above with a slight buff color on the under parts. There are white patches on dark wings and tail. The wing patterns are conspicuous in flight and wing displays. Younger birds will be brown with spotted breasts.

Several states claim this as their state bird:
Arkansas, Florida, Mississippi, Tennessee, and Texas.

Song and Call – The Mimic

Northern Mockingbirds received their name because of their well-deserved reputation for imitating the songs and sounds of other birds. The mockingbird sings almost perfect imitations of many other birds. Close to a third of its singing will be imitations, which can include other sounds such as machinery, sirens, frogs, other animals, or a human whistling.

Mockingbirds sing a long succession of notes and phrases, which will be repeated several times, and then changed. The call phrases can be imitations of songs of other birds. Other sounds are a raspy chijjjand a harsh chewk. The male sings in the spring and both birds will sing in the fall. They will often sing long into the night.

Range and Habitat

Mockingbirds can be found throughout most U.S. all year. They like open land, forests, woodland edges, roadsides, thickets, farms, and towns. Thick shrubbery in your backyard will attract them. The birds establish two types of territories. Individual male and female birds will have separate feeding territories that they will defend. During breeding and nesting a pair will claim a territory.

Breeding and Nesting

Breeding season is February to April, depending on the area.
They breed in open woodland and countryside with scattered trees and shrubs.

In the spring the male mockingbird will clam its territory and defend it very aggressively.   He performs a type of aggressive dance, wagging his tail with rising, and lowering of wings. If his wing display doesn't work he will chase intruders. He will also chase females until he chooses his mate.

He does a looping flight to and from a chosen perch and sings to attract the female. Once they build the nest, they will aggressively defend it, dive-bombing any creature that dares to come to close. This includes humans, dogs, cats, and other wild animals.

The female picks the nesting site. The male will then start by putting
nesting material in her chosen location, and then both birds will build
the nest. The nest can be in a tree, shrub, or thicket. They build
a bulky nest made of twigs, weeds, leaves, string, rags, and other
materials. The inside is lined with fine grasses, plant down, moss, and
hair. The female alone will incubate 3 to 5 smooth glossy eggs. Eggs
can be pale blue, greenish blue, or pinkish blue, spotted with reddish
brown, or purple blotches. The markings will usually be more intense
near the large end. The young will be tended by both adult birds, and
can leave the nest within 2 weeks.

Food - Feeding and Water

Natural foods of the mockingbird are all types of insects, fruits, and
berries. They forage on the ground, and will also watch from a perch
and fly down to grab an insect. The best way to attract mockingbirds
to your backyard is to plant trees and shrubs they might nest in, those
with fruits and berries are best. Suggested plants are hackberry,
dogwood, mulberries, cherry, crab apples, and others. They will visit
suet and other feeders with fruit, raisins, breads, and even seeds, such
as sunflower. Just like all songbirds, water for drinking and bathing will
attract them, especially if you have running or dripping water.

Clark's Nutcracker

Clark's Nutcracker was named after William Clark, who observed the bird during the Lewis and Clark expedition in 1805.

Identification

(Nucifraga columbiana)

A member of the crow family, Clark's Nutcracker has the build of a small crow, and is about 12 to 13 inches. It has a light gray body, with white patches in its black wings and tail. Its long, sharp bill is perfect for extracting nuts from pinecones. Juveniles are similar to adults but are buff gray with dull black or brown wings.

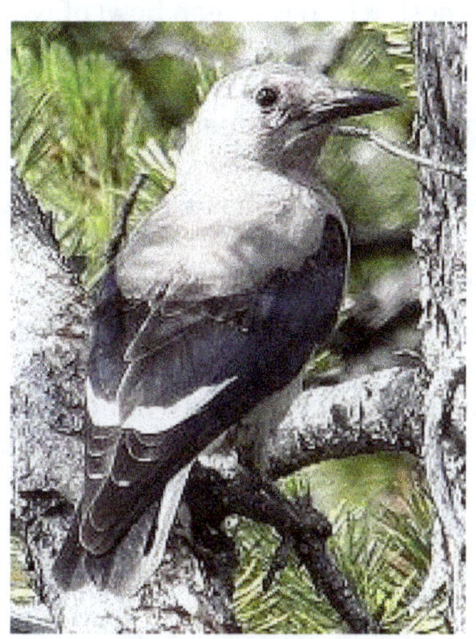

They have a pouch under their tongue that they use to carry pine seeds long distances, where they cache them for later use. Caches are generally buried in the soil on exposed slopes. They will hide thousands of seeds, and studies show the bird will remember where it hides most of them for as long as 9 months.

Clark's Nutcracker is sometimes mistaken for Gray Jays, but the Jay does not have the white wing patches and has a much smaller bill.

Sound of Clark's Nutcracker

They make many different sounds, but the most common call is a grating khaa-khaa-khaa.

Preferred Habitat

Nutcrackers are found in much of the American West, flying in loose groups outside of nesting season. They like to be near the tree line of coniferous forest in the mountains, often seen in mountain resorts.

Breeding and Nesting

Pairs of Nutcrackers form long-term bonds and will stay in their territory yearlong. In late winter they begin nesting.

The nest, which is a deep bowl of twigs, and bark-lined with pine needles, grass, and leaves, is built by both birds in coniferous trees.

Females lay 2 to 6 green spotted eggs. The male helps incubate the eggs for around 18 days and even develops a brood pouch like the female. Both parents help feed the young, which will leave the nest in around 20 days. The young birds will be fed from seeds the parents stashed away earlier. The young will stay with the parents for 3 to 4 months. Storing seeds for the young allows Nutcrackers to stay in high elevations year round and to breed as early as January or February. Clark's Nutcrackers have a symbiotic relationship with pine trees. The trees provide food for the birds, and in return the caches that the birds do not eat produce pine trees.

Food

They feed on nuts, insects, berries, eggs, small mammals, and carrion. They will eat suet and sunflower seeds. These birds are very bold around humans and often come to picnic and camping areas to beg for handouts.

Osprey

Identification

(Pandion haliaetus)

Osprey, also called the Fish or Sea Hawk, is about 23 to 24 1/2 inches. This large majestic hawk dives in the water for fish, becoming completely submerged. The head is mostly white with a white crest, and a black mask through the eyes. It is blackish above and, clear white below. The tail has alternating brown and white bands. The sexes look similar.

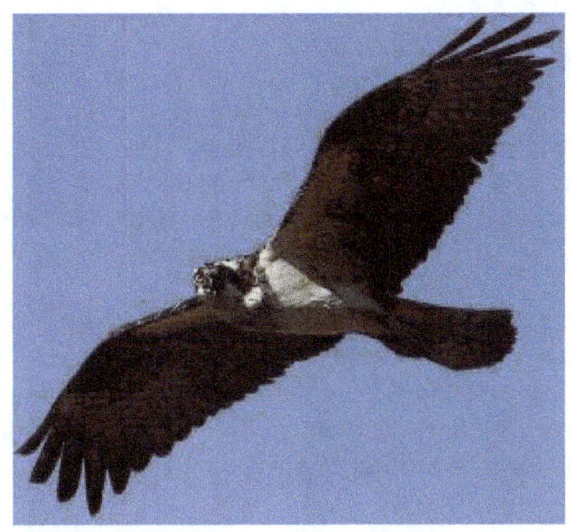

The wingspan is reaches 6 feet. It flies with a crook in its wing showing a black carpal patch contrasting with the mostly whitish underside of its wings.

Their large strong talons are designed for catching and carrying fish. They have four toes. The outer toe can be rotated so that it extends to the rear of the foot allowing them to seize fish with two claws on each side of the fish.

Habitat

This member of the raptor family is found on every continent except Antarctica. The summer range for the American birds extends from Alaska across Canada and parts of the U.S. They migrate south in winter.

They live near bodies of water with fish in them, such as rivers, lakes, reservoirs, and along the coast.

Breeding and Nesting

At the start of mating season they perform air displays where the male repeatedly flies high into the air, hovers for a few seconds, and then dives. The female may participate in this display while pursuing the male. Osprey pairs do courtship feeding while in flight. They usually pair for life.

They build large nests on dead trees, artificial structures such as utility poles, or the many nesting platforms put up for them by man. The nest consists of branches lined with grass, twigs, moss, bark, and other materials such as ropes, cloth, or plastic. Once it is constructed, the nest will usually be used year after year with more branches added each year, often resulting in huge nests.

After the female lays 2 to 4 creamy-white eggs with reddish-brown spots, both birds will incubate them for 32 to 38 days. The female will stay with the newly hatched young while the male brings food. When the young can be left alone, both parents will bring food. Young birds will fledge in around 45 days.

Sound of Osprey

The sound of the Osprey is a chirping sound that is often loud.

Foods

Ospreys hover over the water, and when a fish is spotted, they plunge feet first to grab it. When in flight, they will turn the head of the fish forward allowing for more streamlined transport through the air. Although they feed mostly on fish, they also eat small animals if fish are scarce.

Pileated Woodpecker

Identification

(Dryocopus pileatus)

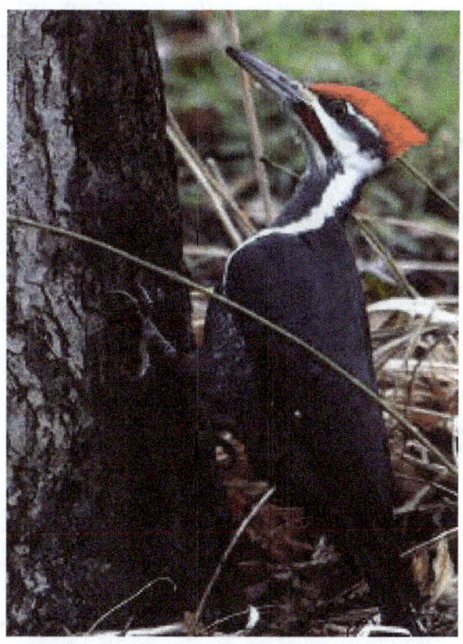

Pileated Woodpeckers are very large woodpeckers, about the size of a crow, 16 to 19 1/2 inches. They are black with a bright red crest from the beak to the back of the head. The face has a red mustache, and a white bar goes across the face, and extends down the neck. Males have a white line over the eyes. They have a long, sharp, black bill, with yellow bristly feathers over their nostrils that help keep out wood chips. Their strong feet allow them to cling on tree trunks. Females have a dark forehead and do not have the red mustache. In flight they can be identified by the white under wing coverts and sweeping wing beats.

You may see a Pileated Woodpecker as it flies from tree to tree searching for insects. When it detects a grub beneath the bark, it will begin its slow methodic hammering. The head swings in a large ark, chips fly as the bill smashes into the tree like a sledgehammer with a force that you might think would break its neck. When the hammering stops he will probe the holes with his pointed, spear-like tongue until he gets his meal. His extremely long tongue ends in a horny, barbed tip, which can be used to impale prey.

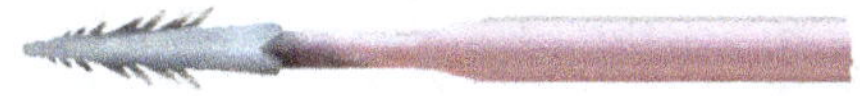

Pileated Woodpecker Sounds

Their call sounds much like the Flicker's call, but louder. They also have a ringing call that rises and falls. In addition to the sound they make digging for insects in trees, they drum on hollow trees to claim territory, making loud drumming sounds that can be heard over long distances. They use this drumming to attract mates, and to define their territories.

Preferred Habitat

Pileated Woodpeckers can be found across Canada, as well as in eastern and western U.S. They usually remain resident and defend their territory year round. They like mature, wooded coniferous and deciduous forests that contain a lot of dead trees. They will also reside in city parks and golf courses.

Breeding and Nesting

During courtship they will do displays, swinging their head back and forth, spreading their wings, and gliding. Pileated Woodpeckers mate for life. For a nest both birds excavate a large cavity in a tree. The nest will often have more than one entrance, giving them an extra escape route in case of predators. They will peck the bark around the hole to get sap running. The sap helps keep predators away from the nest. These woodpeckers excavate a new cavity each year, providing cavities for other birds to use. They also nest in nest boxes. The females lay 3 to 5 white eggs. Both parents incubate the eggs for about 2 weeks, and the young birds fledge in roughly a month. The parents continue to feed and teach the young birds how to forage for several months after they fledge. The young birds leave the parents in the fall and establish their own territories in the spring.

Food

These woodpeckers eat insects such as ants and beetle larvae, as well as nuts and berries. They pull the bark off trees and chip out large holes in trees with their long sharp bill, searching for insects. They have a long sticky tongue that they stick in holes to pull out ants. They also forage on the ground. They will also visit suet feeders in backyards.

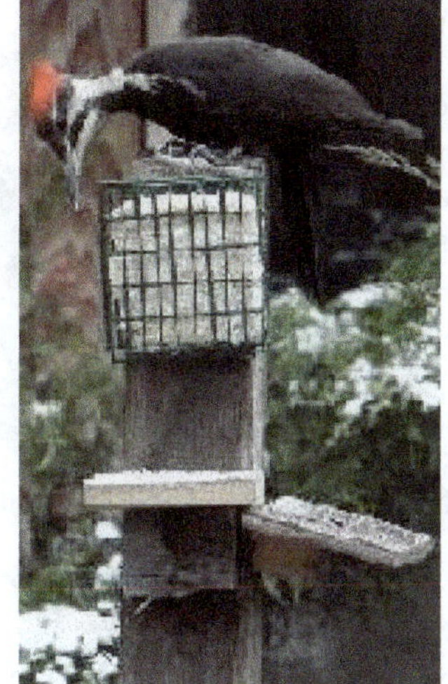

The Pileated woodpecker was the inspiration for the cartoon character Woody Woodpecker.

Pine Siskin

Identification

(Carduelis pinus)

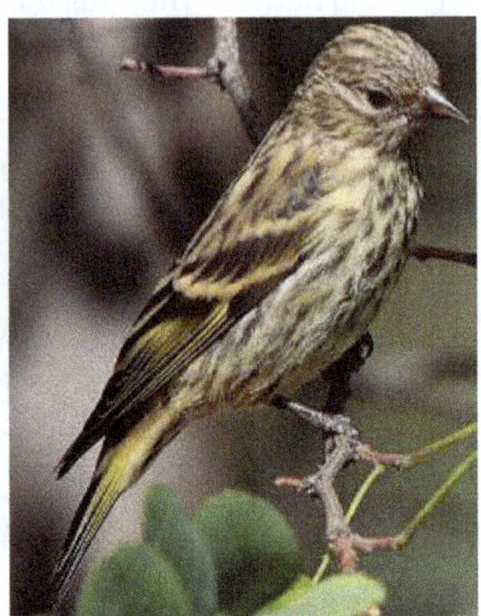

Pine Siskins are small dark finches, about 5 inches. They have pointed conical bills and a deeply notched tail. The wings and tail have yellow patches. Females and young birds appear similar to adult males; however, the males have more yellow. The contact calls as they fly overhead in their undulating flight are often the first sign the birds are around.

Birds similar to Pine Siskins are House Finches and Goldfinches and Common Redpolls.

Sound

The Pine Siskin's call sounds like clee-ip. They also make a zzzz sound, and when in flight, they call tit-i-tit.

Preferred Habitat

Pine Siskin can be found in much of Canada and the U.S. Birds in Southern Canada may migrate south. In much of Northern and Western U.S. they are resident all year. They can be found in conifers, mixed woods, and weedy fields. Pine Siskins are very sociable and form into flocks year round. In winter the flocks are larger and are often mixed with other species. Migration varies and may depend largely on food supply.

Breeding and Nesting

Siskins pair up while in winter flocks, and pairs are monogamous. They may nest as single pairs, or in small colonies where nests are built adjacent to each other. After she chooses a nesting site in conifer trees, the female builds a well-hidden nest of twigs, grass, bark, lichen, and leaves, which is lined with feathers, plant down, moss, and hair.

She lays 3 to 6 pale blue eggs and incubates them for around 13 days. The male brings her food while she incubates the eggs, and both adult birds feed the hatchlings. After the young fledge in about 2 weeks, the parents feed them for around 3 more weeks. A pair of Pine siskin may raise 2 broods in a year.

Food

Pine Siskins forage in trees and shrubbery, often hanging upside down as they climb about. Their diet consists mainly of seeds, but they also eat nuts and insects. They will visit backyard suet and seed feeders, often feeding on the ground under them.

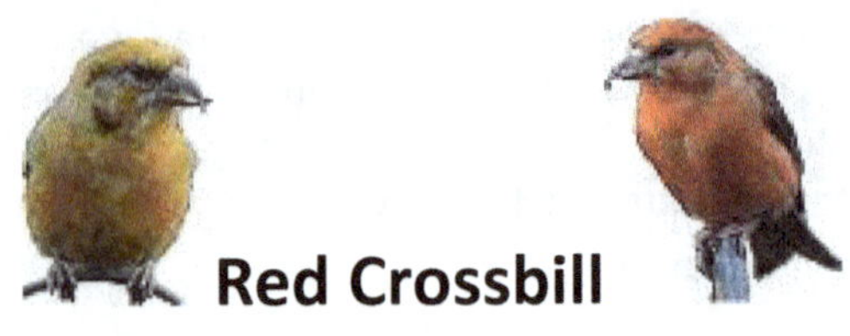

Red Crossbill

Identification

(Loxia curvirostra)

Crossbills are finches that are about the same size as sparrows, 5 1/4 to 6 1/2 inches.

Crossbills get their name from their crossed bills, which do not all cross in the same direction. Their odd bills are useful for removing seeds from cones. They start at the bottom of a cone and spiral upward, opening each scale and removing the seeds with their tongues.

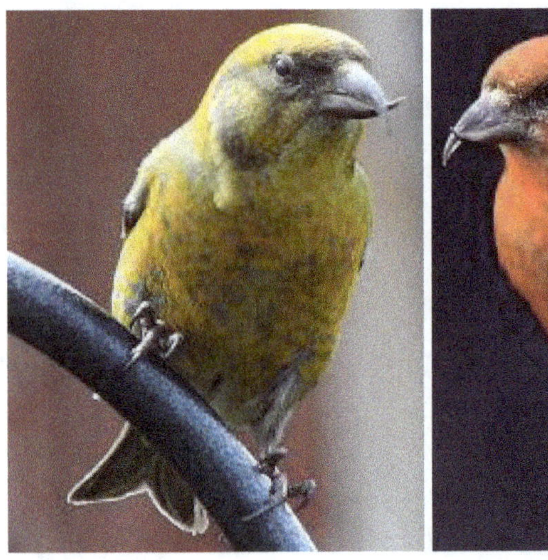
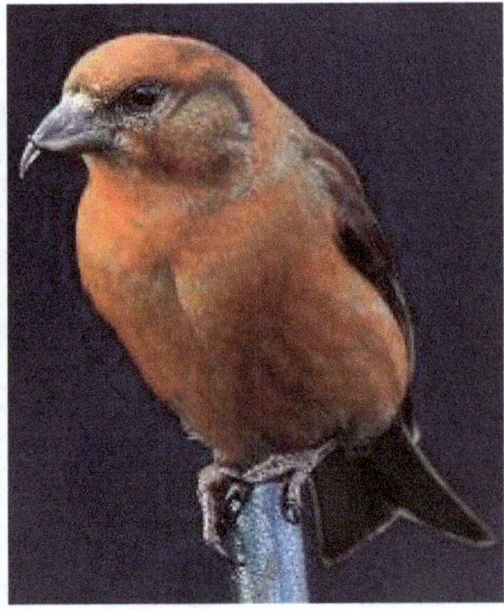

Another distinctive feature is their long pointed wings.

Male crossbills are red with dusky wings and tail. Young males are more orange. The females are greenish-yellow with black wings, and the young are striped.

A similar species, the White-winged Crossbill, has white crossbars on the wings.

Crossbills are often seen hanging from evergreen cones while they feed on the seeds.

When at feeders these birds can be very curious and may come quite close to people. There are 9 species of crossbills. They do not cross-breed, and they specialize in eating different seeds. The bills are different in each species.

When the young birds are learning to extract seeds from a cone the tips of both top and bottom bills begin growing. Because of the pressure from prying and twisting, the upper mandible will curve down, and the lower mandible will curve up.

Song and Calls

The Crossbill's song sounds like jip-jip jeeaa jeeaa.

Range and Habitat

Red Crossbills range across most of North America and congregate in areas with pinecone trees. They are usually in small flocks. They may move to wooded lowlands in winter, but they do not migrate like many songbirds do.

Crossbills like conifer forests where they can be seen using their bills to grab cones and branches as they climb through the branches. Trees they like to feed in are Lodge pole pine, Ponderosa pine, Sitka, and Western hemlock. Each species prefers a certain type of tree.

Breeding and Nesting

Crossbill pairs form within flocks and are monogamous. They can breed at almost any time of year as long as there is sufficient food around.

The female builds a cup-shaped nest of loose grass, twigs, moss, and lichen lined with feathers, and fine grass. The nest will be in pine trees, and the distance from the ground varies. She incubates 3 to 5 pale blue spotted eggs for 12 to 15 days.

The male brings food to the female while she is incubating and to the young for a few days after they hatch. After about 5 days both parents feed the young.

The young birds leave the nest in roughly 20 days, but the parents feed them for about a month while they learn to feed themselves.

Food and Feeding

Crossbills eat mostly conifer seeds; however, they also eat insects, berries and other seeds. These curious birds will come to your feeders for seeds.

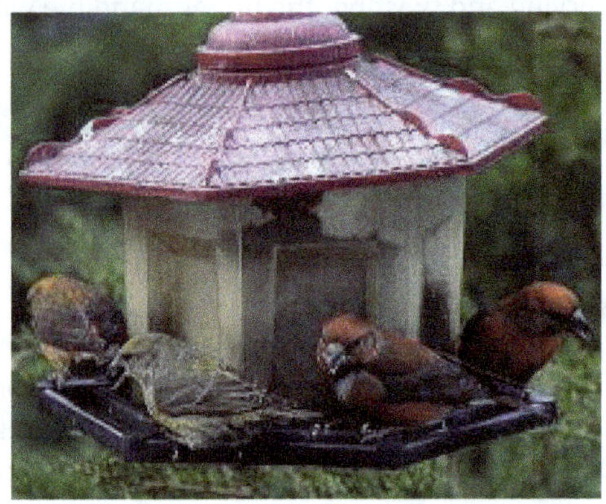

Common Redpoll

Identification

(Acanthis flammea)

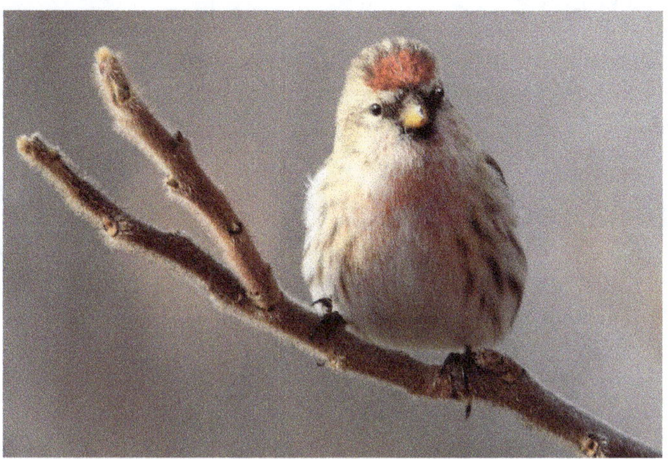

Common Redpolls are around 5 to 6 inches. They are finches that look somewhat like a Pine Siskin, but have a bright red cap on their forehead. Redpolls are a gray-brownish bird with dark stripes on sides and a black chin. Males have pink on their breast. Energetic little birds that will travel in flocks.

Range and Habitat

Redpolls like woodland edges such as birch forests, brush and weedy fields. They breed in northern Canada, and depending on food supply will fly south in winter across north and central U.S. During winter they are know to tunnel into snow the keep warm.

Breeding and Nesting

Redpolls form monogamous pairs and the female chooses a nest site which is in low bushes or on the ground. She will make a nest of grass, twigs and tree moss, where she will lay 2 to 6 pale green spotted eggs which will hatch in around 10 days. After hatching the young will be fed mostly by the female and will leave the nest in around 12 days.

Song and Call

Their call is a rapid chit-chit-chit, often given in flight. Song is a trill followed by the chit-chit-chit.

Food and Feeding

Redpolls like small seeds such as thistle or nyjer seed, and will come to feeders in winter. They have pouches in their throat where they can store seeds.

Red-breasted Nuthatch

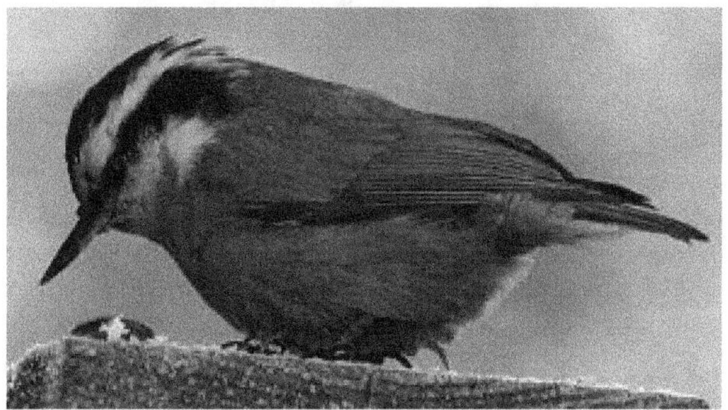

Identification

(Sitta Canadensis)

Red-breasted Nuthatches are very energetic, compact little birds about 4 1/2 to 4 3/4 inches long with stubby tails, thick necks, and long pointed bills. Like all nuthatches they are very agile and you will often see them hopping down a tree trunk headfirst. A distinguishing feature is the broad black line through the eye, with a white line over it. They have a black cap, blue gray back and wings, and are rusty below. Females and young are less colorful then males. They have strong legs and feet enabling them to climb up and down tree trunks. They get the name Nuthatch from wedging nuts into bark crevices to hack at them with their strong bill.

Nuthatch Songs and Calls

Their call of ank ank is higher and more nasal than that of White-breasted Nuthatches. As a pair moves around together they will make soft calls to each other. Their song is a high-pitched wa-wa-wa. Recent studies by Christopher Templeton at the University of Washington show that Nuthatches understand the warning calls of chickadees. Chickadees use different alarm calls to signal the type and size of predators, and to get other small birds to help in mobbing a predator to chase it away.

Range and Habitat

Nuthatches can be found in parts of Canada in summer, and year round in the northwest, north, and northeast U.S. Their winter range is throughout the U.S. They inhabit both coniferous and deciduous forests but prefer coniferous. They will usually be in pairs but may be in mixed flocks.

Breeding and Nesting

Breeding season begins in late April or May. Red-breasted Nuthatches are monogamous. The male will sing from a perch. When a female approaches, he will lift his head and tail, and sway from side to side with drooping wings. The nest is in a cavity excavated by both birds, usually in an old stump or dead tree. They smear pitch around the entrance to deter insects, mammals, and other birds. A piece of bark is often used to spread the pitch. They fly straight into the hole to avoid the pitch. The female lines the inside of the nest with grass, bark fibers, moss, needles, feathers, and hair. They sometimes use birdhouses and old woodpecker holes. The female will incubate 4 to 8 white, cream or pinkish eggs, spotted with light red, reddish-brown or purplish spots. The male feeds her while she incubates the eggs for around 2 weeks. Both parents feed the young birds for 18 to 21 days while they are in the nest, and for another 2 weeks after they fledge. They normally only have one brood.

Food and Feeding

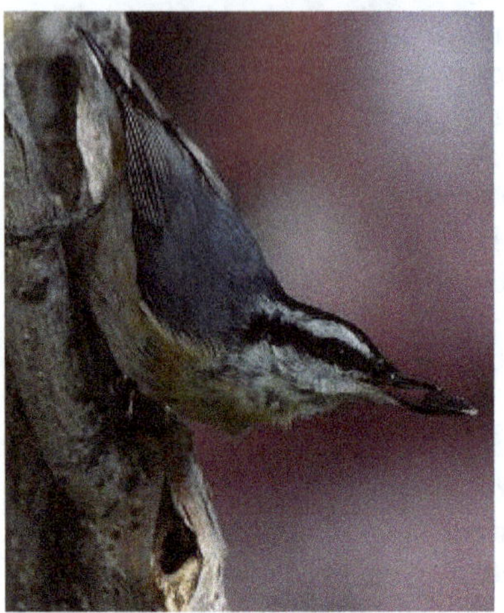

Natural foods are insects such as beetles and caterpillars. They also like nuts and seeds from pinecones. Just like White-breasted Nuthatches, they will work their way down a tree trunk. They will also fly out to catch insects out of the air. Nuthatches will store food in bark crevices and small holes in trees for winter use. They will come to your yard with suet, and feeders with sunflower seeds and nuts.

Nuthatches can be fairly tame and may even take food from your hand. There are even reports that some nuthatches will follow a person they are used to around until they get food from them.

Red tailed Hawk

Identification

(Buteo jamaicensis)

Red-tailed Hawks are very common North American Buteo hawks. Like all Buteos, they are a very large hawk, about 19 to 25 inches. They have broad wings with a wingspan of around 4 feet, and a short wide tail. Typical adult plumage is dark brown above with a white chest with brown streaks on the belly and brown eye. They get their name from the most distinguishing feature in adult birds, their brick-red tail. The females are larger than males.

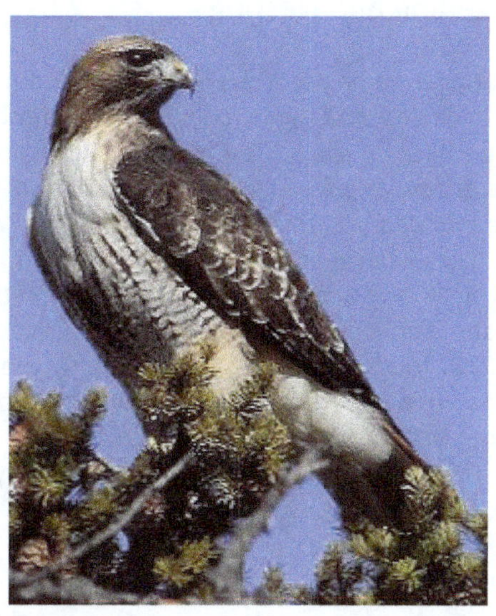

Young birds look much similar but the upper chest is more mottled.

There are a number of subspecies of Red-tailed Hawks, with much variation in the plumage. There are all dark, rufous, and very light phases.

The under wings are mottled dark and light with a dark band on the leading edge, called the patagial markings.

Sound

The voice of the Red-tailed Hawk is a high-pitched descending scream, like kee-eer.

Preferred Habitat

Red-tailed Hawks are found all across North America. They can be seen in a large variety of habitats. They like mountains, open woods, prairies, plains, and agricultural areas.

The hawks are often seen perched on a poll on roadsides. Northern populations may migrate in winter, but most stay in their territories all year.

Breeding and Nesting

 During breeding season they perform dramatic flight displays. They fly in circles until they are very high, and the male will dive and then circle back up again. The two birds lock talons and tumble towards the ground in a free fall, letting go just above the ground. The hawks are monogamous, normally mating for life, and staying in the same territory each year. They may have more than one nest in their territory, and alternate between them. Both sexes help build a large nest of sticks and twigs lined with bark, placed high in a tree or on a cliff. Throughout the nesting period, the nest will have bits of green vegetation added to it. The female lays 2 to 4 white eggs with brown spots, which she incubates for 4 to 5 weeks. The parents both feed the nestlings. The young birds will be able to fly in around 45 days, and then the parents will teach them to hunt.

Food

 Red-tailed hawks are good hunters, feeding on small mammals such as rabbits or other rodents, birds, reptiles, and insects. They either soar, or perch on a high branch, or poll to survey the surrounding area with their sharp eyes. While soaring they may grab a bird out of the air. Hawks have binocular vision, and their incredible sight allows them to see a mouse on the ground while soaring 100 feet up.

When they spot their prey, they swoop down on it. Their dives can reach over 100 miles an hour. When they grasp their prey and clench their toes, the talons pierce the vital organs, and cause instant death.

Red-Winged Blackbird

Identification

(Agelaius phoeiniceus)

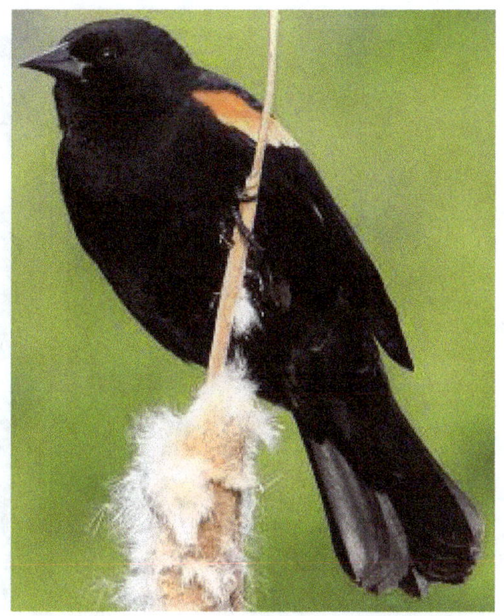

Red-winged Blackbirds are a nearly all blackbird, about 7 1/2 to 9 inches. They get their name from the distinctive red or orange-red shoulder patch also called epaulets on the male. The red shoulder patch can be seen when in flight, but when they are at rest often only the yellow margin can be seen. The birds have black, sharp, cone-shaped beaks, pointed wings, and their tails are rounded. Males can often be seen sitting on high perches with tails slightly flared.

Immature males have the red patch, but they are mottled brown.

The much smaller female Red-Wing Blackbirds have brown plumage, with dark streaking below, and often have a pink tinge on their throat. They tend to stay lower in the vegetation so they are less visible than the males.

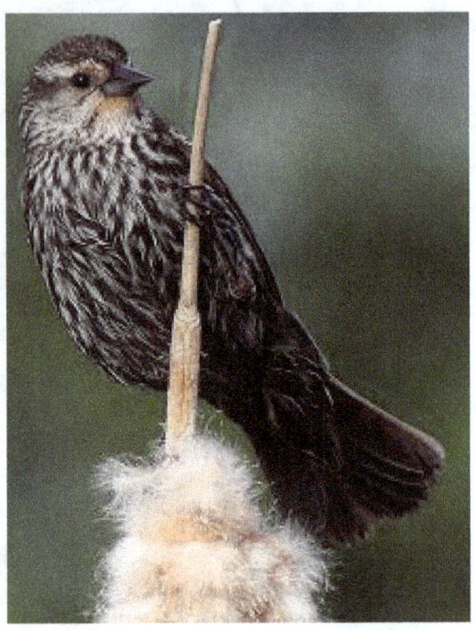

Songs and Calls

Perching on top of a cattail, with a spread tail, and displaying his red shoulder patches, the male sings oak-a-leeee. He is quick to voice his disapproval of all intruders and will often attack anything that enters his territory. He calls out check-check-check and a high trilled teer-errr to warn off other birds.

Range and Habitat

The Red-winged Blackbird can be found across the entire continental United States. In summer they extend across Canada. Any place they can find food and water, they will spend the winter. Many will migrate south to the southern United States and Mexico. In winter Red-winged blackbirds gather in large flocks to eat grains with other blackbird species and starlings. These huge flocks are incredible to see as they roll in waves across the sky. They inhabit freshwater and saltwater wetlands, and marshes, brushy swamps, meadows, fields, and prairies.

Breeding and Nesting

Breeding in colonies, males vigorously defend territories where a male may have as many as 10 females he breeds with. Groups of males do rapid chases of females, returning to their own territories afterwards. The females will also breed with other males, and may have clutches with eggs from more than one male. A pair may have 2 to 3 broods per season. The eggs and young have many predators, such as snakes, raccoons, and other birds. Group nesting helps to protect nests from the many predators. In defending their territories several birds will often mob intruders. This is especially true of males. It is common for Brown-headed cowbirds to lay their eggs in the nest of Red-winged blackbirds.

Females will build a deep cup-shaped nest of grass, leaves, and moss, lined with mud. She will attach the nest to reeds, and branches.

The female will incubate a clutch of 3 to 5 pale blue eggs for around 12 days. The eggs are blotched with dark brown or purple spots and sometimes have a pink tinge to them. Both parents will feed the young birds, which will leave the nest in about 10 days.

At the end of breeding season Red-winged Blackbirds gather in huge flocks, often with other types of blackbirds. These flocks sometimes number in the thousands.

Food

Red-winged Blackbirds feed mainly on seeds and grains, but they also eat insects, spiders, aquatic life, and small animals.

Ringed Turtle Dove

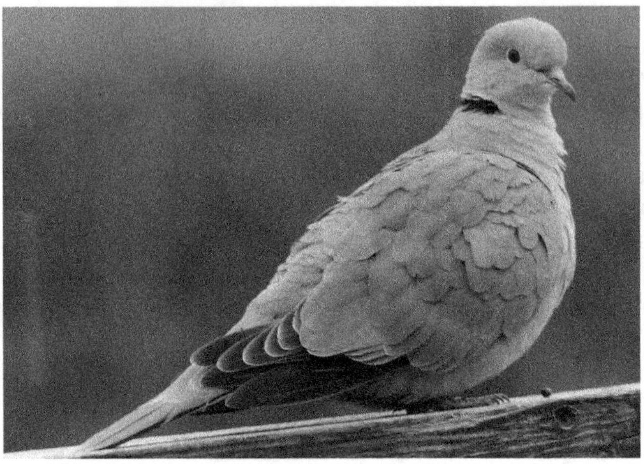

Identification

(Streptpelia risoria) Ringed Turtle Doves are about the same size
as Morning doves, about 10 to 12 inches. They are creamy tan color,
with a black ring at the back of the neck. They have a fairly long,
rounded tail with white in the corners. When they fly the dark primary
wing feathers stand out against the pale body. Like other doves their
heads bob each time they take a step. Males and females look alike,
but the males are slightly larger.

While they are usually found alone or in pairs, it is common to see
them in groups, or even flocks of hundreds, especially if they are
feeding.

Calls and Songs

Just like other doves they make a soft cooing sound. Many people
think they are hearing an owl when they hear this. They also make
laughter like cackling sound. When the birds are in flocks their wings
make quite a bit of noise when they take off.

Range and Habitat

Turtle doves like to rest in treetops, and can be found around people in
parks, and in woodlands. They may also be found in cities.
Turtle doves are one of the most popular birds kept in cages. Most
populations found in the U.S. are from previously caged birds.

I'm sure many people remember the two turtle doves in the song Twelve Days Of Christmas.

Breeding and Nesting

Turtle doves are monogamous and breed through out the year. The females usually lay two cream white eggs in a flimsy nest of twigs they build in branches of trees or shrubs. The two birds will take turns sitting on the eggs, which will hatch in around 15 days. The young birds will leave the nest around 2 weeks after hatching. The adults may breed and lay more eggs after the chicks leave the nest, but the male will continue to feed the young birds.

Food and Feeding

The doves feed mainly on seeds, but they also eat like insects. Doves drink by sucking water, unlike most birds, which will raise their heads to let the liquid run down their throats. Birdbaths will attract doves.

American Robin

Identification

(Turdus migratorius)

American Robins are a sign to many people that spring has arrived. They are one of the most familiar birds to birdwatchers. It is a treat to watch this red-breasted bird run and hop around the lawn looking for worms or other insects. You see them cock their head to one side and you know they have found a worm.

Robins have a dark gray back with dark stripes on a white throat. Their bright red to orange breast makes them stick out. The head and tail of the male are black.

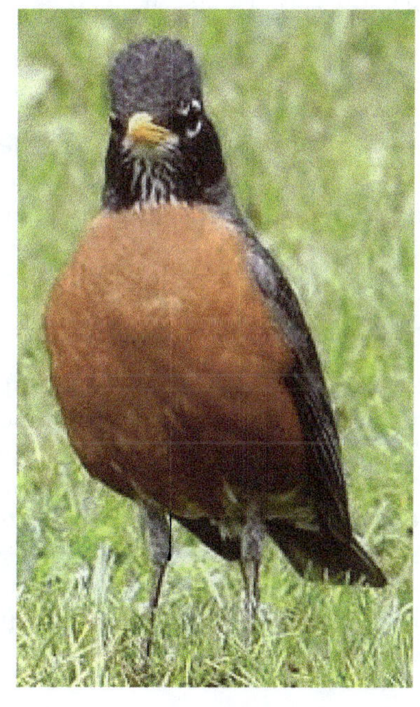

The female is a little grayer and not as brightly colored.

Young birds will look the same except for a breast speckled with black spots. The American Robin is the largest thrush in North America. Adults are 9 to 10 inches.

The early settlers, who thought that, with its reddish breast, it resembled the English robin, gave the bird the name Robin.

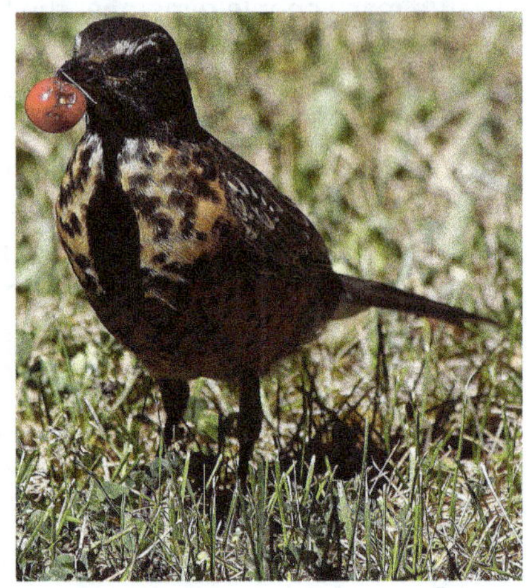

Song

Robins have a clear, cheery sound with a number of songs and calls. Many people are familiar with their cheer up, cheer up sound. They are one of the first birds to begin singing in the morning and one of the last to be heard at night. The male is the most vocal especially during courtship. The territory or whisper song is a soft hisselly-hisselly sound. The mating song of the male is accompanied by him displaying and lifting his tail higher than his head.

Habitat

American Robins can be seen in residential neighborhoods, parks, forests, and farmlands throughout much of the U.S. for most of the year. In fall and winter robins may gather into huge flocks of hundreds of birds.

Nesting and Breeding

During courtship the male feeds the female. They also do gaping, where the males and females approach each other and touch widely opened bills. Of course, there is much singing.

The birds like to nest in open woodlands, grasslands with scattered trees, and your backyard. Robins make a bulky nest of coarse grass, weeds, twigs, and mud, lined with fine grass. Breeding is in early April in the south, and mid-may in the north. Females do most of the nest building.

You can find their nests in the forked branch of a tree or shrub, on the ledge of a building or cliff, or even on the ground.

There are usually 3 to 5 light blue eggs. The female incubates the eggs for 10 to 14 days, and then both parents will feed the young, which will leave the nest in 14 to 16 days.

Food and Feeding

Robins eat mostly insects, fruit, berries, and worms. Much of their foraging is in on the ground, but they also forage in trees.

How to Attract Robins to Your Backyard

Water will attract Robins and many other birds. Robins love a birdbath and are fun to watch as they drink and bathe. They will come to a birdbath and really like running water. You will often see them under a sprinkler. **Platform feeders** are good. Robins will eat apples, grapes, other fruits, and suet. They will also come to feeders with seeds, doughnuts, bread, peanut butter mixtures, and many other foods.

Natural food sources in your yard will attract them. A damp lawn has earthworms. A pile of leaves or brush has worms and other insects that they love, such as caterpillars, grasshoppers, and beetle grubs. A good way to supply an area for them to forage in is to use fall leaves as mulch in your flowerbeds. Keep in mind that pesticides are harmful to birds.

Plant berry bushes and fruit trees. A large part of their diet is fleshy fruits and berries. A yard with natural fruit sources will be returned to over and over.

Robins will use a **nesting shelf** to build their nest in. This shelf can be attached to the side of a barn, garage, or under the eaves of a house. Since the female lines the nest with it, it is good to have it near a mud source such as a garden.

A nesting shelf can be made from three boards nailed together to form the floor, back, and roof of a house. Make it about 7 inches by 8 inches wide, and 8 inches high. Mount it in a shaded spot. A good place is on the side of your house under overhanging eaves.

Roosting, or resting in trees, is common for these birds. Groups of roosting Robins may contain twenty to a few hundred birds, especially in winter.

Roosting helps protect them from predators and they will often roost with other birds such as Starlings. Robins are highly migratory birds and can often be seen in large flocks.

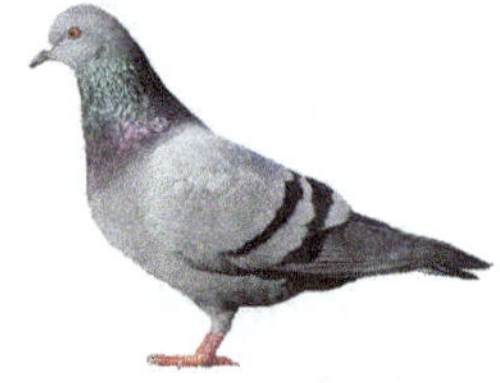

Rock Pigeon –

Domestic Pigeon

Identification

(Columba livia)

The American and British Ornithologists Unions officially named Rock Pigeons, also called Rock Doves, Blue Rock Doves, Feral Pigeons, and Domestic Pigeons, Rock Pigeons in 2004. They are about 13 inches, a little larger than Mourning Doves. They are stocky birds, with short legs, short necks, small round, bluish gray heads, slender bills, and a fleshy cere just above the bill. The eyes are usually red or orange. Typically they are gray with a white rump patch, two black bars on the wings, a large black band on the tail, and red feet. The feathers on the neck are often iridescent blue or green. There are many domestic color variations, with white, tan, black, and gray colors. Females look much like the males but have less iridescence around the neck.

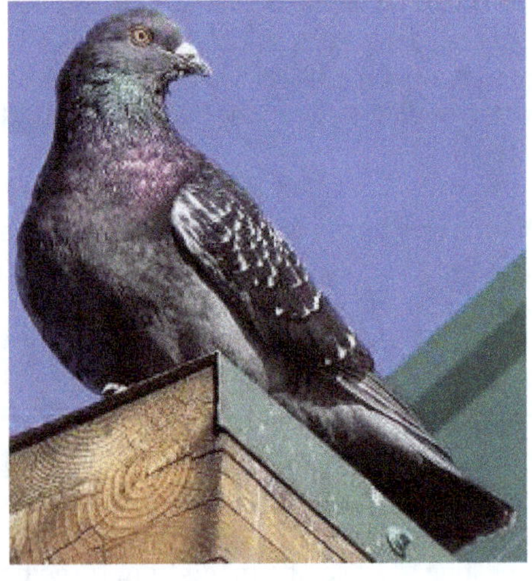

Young birds, called squabs are duller. When pigeons walk they bob their heads.

The names pigeon and dove are used interchangeably; however, ornithologists normally considered pigeons to be the larger birds. Pigeons have tapered wings with powerful wing muscles, making them very strong, agile fliers that can reach speeds of 85 miles an hour.

Carrier Pigeons

Pigeons have been domesticated for thousands of years. Although sometimes they were just pets, because of their ability to find home when released, they have been used as carrier and homing pigeons, carrying messages during wartime. During both the first and second world wars, pigeons' usefulness in carrying messages across enemy lines saved thousands of human lives. It is thought by some that their navigation abilities are a result of being able to sense the earth's magnetic fields with magnetic tissues in their heads. There are 12 recognized subspecies of Rock pigeons.

Range and Habitat

Rock Pigeons range year round, from southern Canada, across the U.S., and South America. They thrive in populated areas, and flocks of pigeons may be found in large cities, and rural areas around the world. They can be seen in crowded streets and public places, often roosting together on buildings, cliffs, and bridges.

Breeding and Nesting

In courtship the male will strut around the female with his chest puffed out and his tail spread, while bowing and cooing. Although spring and summer are their main breeding periods, pigeons may breed at any time during the year and could have 5 or more broods. They are usually monogamous. Pigeons and doves build crude nests of sticks and straw on window ledges, cliffs, under bridges, in trees, or on the ground. The male brings nesting material to the female, and she builds the nest. The female will normally lay two white eggs. Both birds will incubate the eggs for 17 to 19 days. The pair will take care of the young birds, which may be in the nest for as long as a month. Both sexes produce nutritious crop milk that they feed to the young.

Song and Call

Pigeons make a soft gurgling sound, like coo-roo-coo.

Food and Feeding

Pigeons eat seeds, grains, berries, and scraps from people. They like to feed on the ground in open areas. They are very comfortable around people and often approach them for food. Unlike many birds, pigeons can dip their bills into the water and drink without having to tilt their heads back. They can be attracted to backyards with seeds, cracked corn, popcorn, bread, and other food scraps. Because they are often in large flocks, many people discourage them by using anti-roosting pigeon spikes.

Red-Naped Sapsucker

Identification

(Sphyrapicus nuchalis)

Sapsuckers get their name from their habit of drilling rolls of holes in tree trunks and repeatedly coming back to drink the sap.

Red-naped Sapsuckers are woodpeckers, about 8 to 9 inches. The male has red patches on the forehead and throat. The back and sides are mostly black with white spots. Their wings have a prominent white bar. The belly

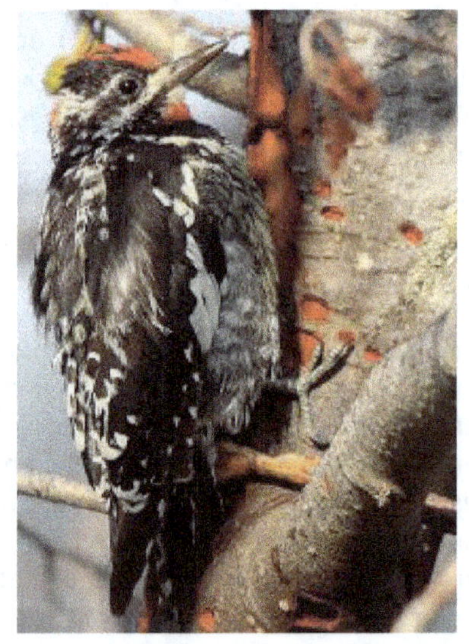

is yellowish with a black breast patch above. The head has two white stripes; one goes from above the eye to the back of the neck, and the other from the beak to the neck. Females have red, and white on throat. Younger birds are mottled brown. Yellow-bellied sapsuckers look similar but do not have the red nape. The two were previously considered to be one species but were recently split up.

They are often mistaken for the smaller Downy woodpeckers.

Sapsucker Sounds

The drumming is several rapid thumps followed by several slow thumps. The Sapsucker's call is a soft nasal cheer or mewing.

Preferred Habitat

In summer they can be found from British Columbia through much of the Western U.S. They migrate south as far as Mexico in the winter. Sapsuckers like coniferous, and deciduous woodlands, as well as orchards. They are found often in willows, aspens, and cottonwood.

Breeding and Nesting

During courtship both birds will bob and swing their heads while facing each other.

They will also perform gliding and fluttering displays. Sapsuckers nest in cavities in trees. Both birds will excavate the nest and may reuse an old cavity, but usually make a new one. They do not line the nest except with wood chips from the excavation. The female lays 4 to 6 white eggs, which both birds incubate for around 13 days. Both birds care for the young, which will leave the nest in 25 to 29 days. The parents will feed them for another 10 days. Red-naped sapsuckers interbreed with both Yellow-bellied and Red-breasted Sapsuckers.

Food

Sapsuckers drill orderly rolls of small holes from which they drink the sap. They also eat insects and fruits. Their tongue is smaller than most woodpeckers and has hair-like projections on the end that aid in sipping sap.

Sandhill Crane

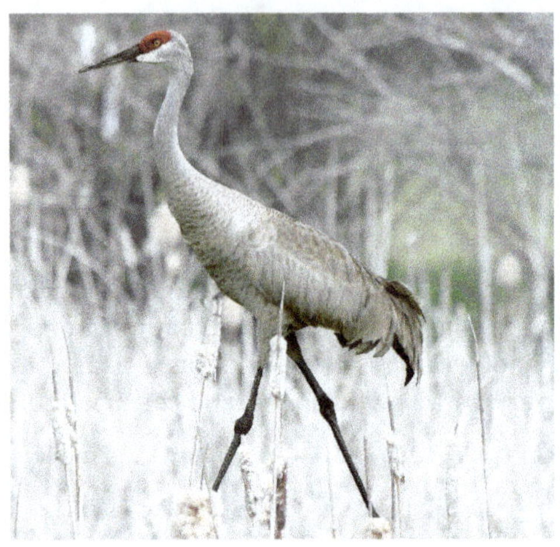

Identification

Sandhill Crane (Grus canadensis)

The Sandhill Crane is a tall gray bird, with long legs, a long neck, a bald red crown, and a thick tufted plume of long, drooping feathers over the tail. they also have a long pointed bill and white cheeks. Some birds will also have a rust color. The birds often rub mud on their feathers while preening, giving them the red or brown color. They grow to around 47 inches tall. Their wing span is 6 to 7 feet and when they fly their neck is fully extended, unlike the similar species (blue herons), which fly with their neck in an S shape. Male and female cranes look alike. The young birds are brownish and do not have the red crown. They can live for 20 years. They have been found to be structurally the same as 10 million old fossils.

Sandhill cranes are often found in large groups or pairs, and are very social birds.

Preferred Habitat

Sandhill cranes are usually found in in freshwater wetlands, marshes, river basins, wet grasslands, and prairies. There are several subpopulations, some of the cranes are migratory, and some are not. For most of those that do migrate the summer range is northern U.S. through Canada and Alaska.

They may winter in the southern U.S. and Mexico. Cranes gather in large flocks before a migration.

Breeding and Nesting

Breeding season for Sandhill cranes is from early spring to late fall. The cranes mate for life. Pairs will often do displays where they dance, bow, jump, and raise their bills together. A pair will defend its nesting territory with singing duets, displays, and sometimes stabbing with the bill or kicking aggressively. The two birds build a nest that is a hay like mound in a marsh, and the female usually lays 2 pale eggs with brown spots. Both birds incubate the eggs for around 30 days, the female is usually the only one that takes the night shift. The young birds can follow the parents and forage within 24 hours of hatching, and they can fly in about 2 months. The young birds may stay with their parents until about a month before nesting season.

Song and Call

The call of Sandhill cranes sounds like low musical rattle, and can have varied lengths, depending on why they are calling. Two other sounds they make are tuk-tuk-tuk and a goose-like honk.

Food

While the cranes like to eat grains and plants, they will also eat invertebrates, reptiles, amphibians and small mammals

Wilson's Snipe

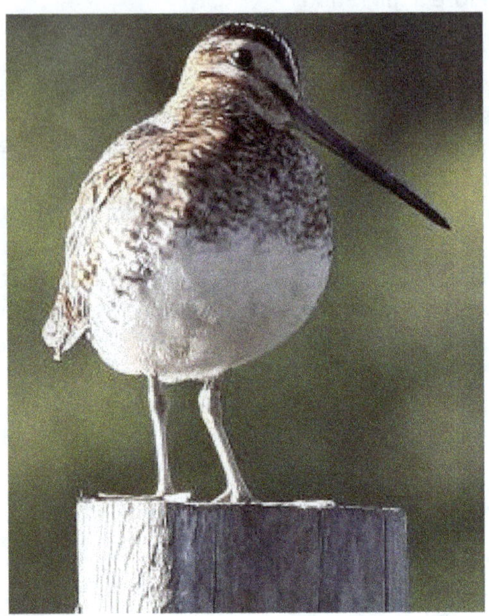

Identification

(Gallinago delicata)

Some people probably remember belonging to a group such as the boy scouts that went snipe hunting on a camping trip. Many of them came away with the belief that snipes don't actually exist. They do exist; they just can't be caught by hand.
Snipes are a stocky shorebird with pointed wings. Their greenish legs are short compared to some other shorebirds. Sometimes mistaken for Spotted sandpipers, snipes are larger, about 10 1/2 inches. It has an extremely long, slender, pointed bill useful for probing in wet mud for food. It is brown with a buff, striped back, pale breast with darker spots and bars, and the head has alternating dark and pale stripes. When it is flushed, a short orange tail can be seen as it flies off.

The sexes are similar and the juveniles resemble the adults.

They are easily concealed in ground vegetation because of their camouflaged plumage. When flushed they fly off in a series of aerial zigzags to confuse predators. Wilson's Snipe was formerly considered a subspecies of the Common snipe.

Common snipes have eight pairs of tail feathers instead of seven and a narrower white edge to the wings.

Two other similar birds are dowitchers, which have longer legs, lack the stripes on the back and down the crown, and have a white rump, and woodcocks, which are orange-buff below.

Snipe Sound

Sounds they make are a chipa chipa chipa, a flight call that is a dry, harsh rasping kesh and a hollow winnowing huhuhuhu sound.

Preferred Habitat

In summer they range from Alaska through Canada to North-Central U.S. and extend south through the rest of North America in the winter. In the Pacific Northwest, snipes are residents all year long. They like the edges of shallow ponds, marshes, bogs, stream sides, wet meadows, and damp forests.

Breeding and Nesting

Males start arriving in the breeding territory 10 to 14 days before the females. They may be seen singing from the top of fence posts. During courtship flights males perform an aerial territorial display in which they perform a series of shallow dives in a large circle, each time climbing back up to do it again. As they descend, the tail feathers make a strange winnowing sound. Females build a cup-shaped nest of fine grasses, dead leaves, and mosses lined with fine grass in a hollow ground depression in a wet meadow or marsh. The female usually lays 4 olive brown eggs marked with dark spots. She incubates them for 18-20 days. Young birds fledge in 19-20 days. Often the parents will split the young birds, each being responsible for one or two. The young birds will start to probe for their own food in around 6 days, but the parents will still provide them with food for a while.

Food

Snipes feed on wet ground for grubs, aquatic insects, worms, and plant material. Feeding in shallow water they probe into the mud with their long slender bills in a rapid sewing machine motion.

Snowy Owl

Identification

(Bubo scandiacus)

There are 19 owl species in North America and this is my favorite. This is the largest of the North American owls (21 to 23 inches) with a wingspan of 5 feet. Snow Owls are large white birds. The male is all white with bright yellow eyes, a dark beak, and heavily feathered feet. The female is white with dark spots or bars. Unlike many owls Snowy Owls fly in the daytime.

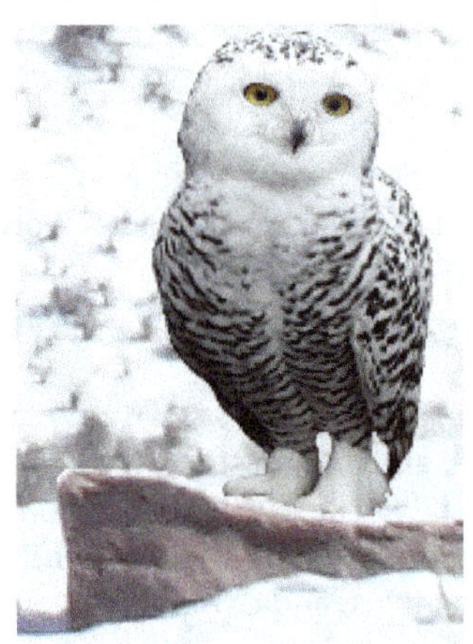

Snowy Owl Sound

While mostly silent they repeat a deep crow-ow sound as well as hooting and screeching sounds.

Preferred Habitat

In the summer they live in the artic, but will migrate to southern Canada and the northern U.S. in winter. They live mostly on the tundra, but are found in meadows, prairies, and fields.

Breeding and Nesting

In April or May males will establish and defend a territory. In courtship a male will try to impress a female with an undulating flight pattern. He may then land and offer her a lemming. They usually only nest if there is plenty of food around. Their nest is a grass lined hollow on tundra. The female will lay 4 to 8 round white eggs which will incubate for around 30 days. The male will provide food for her during incubation and brooding. Eggs will start to hatch in around 30 days. At around 3 weeks then young will leave the nest, but they still can't fly. The parents will still protect them. At 6 to 7 weeks they will start trying to fly.

Food

Snow Owls feed mostly on lemmings and other rodents. They will also eat other small animals such as rabbits, as well as birds.

Spotted Sandpiper

Identification

(Actitis macularius)

Spotted Sandpipers are a small shorebird about 7 to 8 inches. The birds constantly bob their tails with their bodies leaning forward. They are olive brown above and white with round black spots below. They have a straight beak, which is yellow or orange with a black tip in breeding plumage. There is a dusky patch on the breast near the shoulders, enclosing a white wedge between it

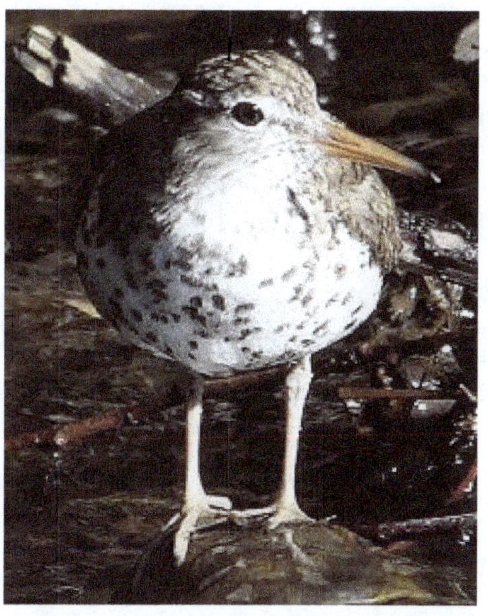

and the wing. There is a white line over the eye. In the fall and winter they lose most of the spotting. They fly with the wings held stiffly downward using shallow wing strokes. These are solitary birds not often seen in flocks. Young birds resemble the adults but have dark edges on the back feathers.

Spotted Sandpiper Sound

Spotted Sandpipers call out a clear peet or pee-weet-weet.

Preferred Habitat

This is the most widespread of all the sandpipers. The summer range is from Alaska through Canada and most of the U.S. In winter they migrate to far south U.S. and into South America. They may be found along the sides of streams and the shores of lakes and ponds.

During migration and in winter, they can be seen anywhere there is water from streambeds to seashores.

Breeding and Nesting

Unlike most birds, the female arrives at the breeding grounds before the male. She establishes and defends the territory while trying to attract a mate. The nest is made of stems and grass concealed under vegetation near rivers, streams, or lakes. The female lays 3 to 5 buff spotted eggs with blotches. When she lays eggs, they may be from several different males. After laying the eggs, she leaves them for the male to incubate while she searches for another mate. The eggs hatch in around 20 days, and the male takes care of young birds for about 4 weeks. The female may breed with up to 4 males, each raising a clutch of eggs. She may raise the last one herself.

Food

Sandpipers feed on a variety of insects and invertebrates normally feeding along the shoreline but may also grab insects from the air.

Spotted Towhee

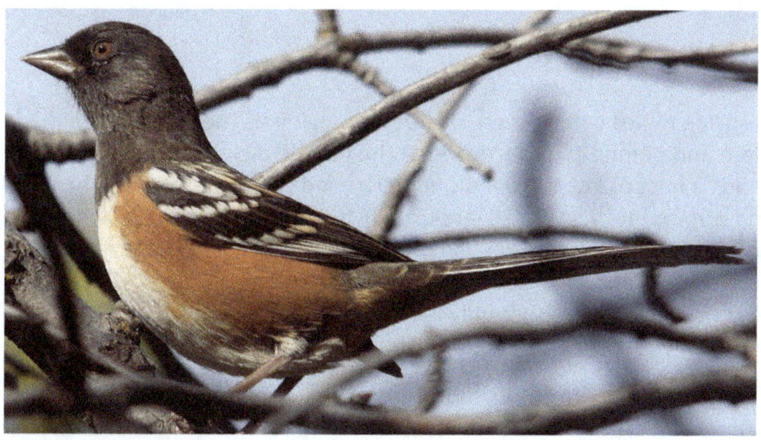

Identification

(Pipilo maculatus)

Spotted Towhees are smaller than a Robin, about 8 inches. Like many songbirds, the male has striking plumage. His head and upper parts are black. They have a thick, pointed, black bill and fire red eyes. The sides are rufous, and the breast and belly are white. White spots stand out on the black back and wings. The long tail is black with large white spots at the corners that are visible in flight. The female is similar but has brown where the male has black. The young are streaked below. Spotted Towhee and Eastern Towhee until recently were considered one species. The birds were also called Rufous-sided Towhees.

Sound

Their song is a long buzzy chweeee. In some areas the bird is called chewink because of the sound of their alarm call. Other sounds are shenk, chup-chup zedededee, and a cat-like meew call.

Preferred Habitat

Spotted Towhees can be found in much of the western half of North America. In the far west they are year-round residents and in other areas they migrate south for winter. They like open woods with thick undergrowth, forest edges, and canyons. They are often found in residential shrubbery.

They spend much time hopping around in leaves in the undergrowth
and can be hard to see but their rustling gives them away.

Breeding and Nesting

In spring males can be seen on a perch singing as they try to attract a
mate and defend their territories. The female picks the nest site and
builds a nest of grass, leaves, and bark lined with pine needles, hair,
and other materials. Nests are usually built on the ground or in low
bushes. She lays 3 to 5 whitish or slightly greenish eggs with reddish
brown spots and incubates them for 12 to 14 days. Both parents will
feed the young birds that may leave the nest in around 10 days but
will not fly for 5 to 6 days more. The parents will feed the young for
another 30 days. Their nests are sometimes parasitized by cowbirds.

Food

The Spotted Towhee's main diet consists of seeds, but they also eat
insects and fruit. Although they do search for food in trees, they
mainly forage on the ground. They scratch the ground by kicking both
feet backward at the same time to uncover food. These birds prefer to
forage in bushes with leaves on the ground, making quite a racket as
they rustle through the leaves. If you have a seed feeder near bushes,
towhees may search for seeds fallen or sprinkled on the ground.

European Starling

Identification

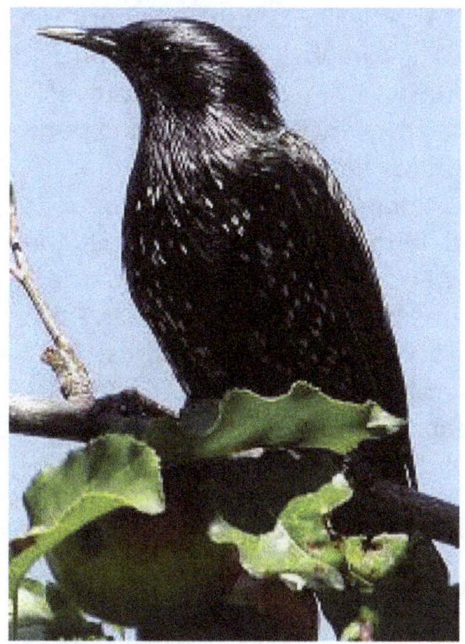

(Sturnus vulgaris)

Starlings are short-tailed blackbirds, with long pointed bills, triangular wings, and black eyes; about 7 1/2 to 8 1/2 inches. They are shaped a little like a meadowlark.   Their legs are pinkish-red. They have a purple or green iridescence and a yellow bill in breeding plumage. Later they are heavily speckled in brilliant white spots, and have a dark, bill. The male and female are similar, and young starlings are dusky gray-brown. They have a direct swift flight. Similar species are Brewers blackbird, and cowbirds.

Range and Habitat

They were introduced to America in the 1890 and are now one of our most numerous songbirds. They can be found in cities, parks, open country, and fields. They form into huge, loud flocks, sometimes covering lawns or fields as they forage for food. Flocks will often be mixed with other birds such as Red-winged Blackbirds, cowbirds, and others. Large groups will perch on power lines. The huge flocks are incredible to watch, as they form amazing flowing formations.

Breeding and Nesting

Starlings are usually monogamous. Males will establish a territory and nest site, and then attract a female. They are very gregarious, and will breed close to other pairs of starlings. During vicious fights over breeding sites, the birds will grab each other with their feet, and peck each other. Starlings prefer nesting in cavities, but will use natural cavities, holes made by birds such as woodpeckers, or birdhouses, rather than excavate their own. Both birds of a pair will help build the nest. The cavity is filled with grass, weeds, string, and other material. The female lays 4 to 7 pale blue or greenish eggs. Both birds develop a brood patch, and incubation is for around 12 days by both birds, with the female doing most of it. Hatchlings will be almost naked and will fledge in around 3 weeks. The parents will feed the young for a few days after fledging, and the young birds may stay around the parents for 10 to 12 days, but will then join other young birds in communal roosts. Starlings may have a second brood. If they do, they usually place new nesting material over the old.

Song and Call

Starlings' sounds include clear whistles, rattles and, clicks, and they often imitate other birds, and even human speech or sounds they hear around them, such as car alarms.

Food and Feeding

Starlings eat insects, worms, spiders, seeds, grains, fruit, and animals such as frogs or lizards. They forage on the ground, in fields, lawns, and parking lots. Probing the ground every few steps, they will work their way across a lawn in a zigzag pattern. They often forage with other birds such as robins, sparrows, crows, Red-winged Blackbirds or cowbirds.

Not Always a Well-Liked Bird

Many people dislike starlings, and actively try to get rid of them because they are very aggressive and may evict other songbirds from birdhouse and attack their young and eggs.

The Migratory Bird Treaty Act does not protect them, so people can legally trap or kill them or destroy their nests.

Tree Swallows

Identification

(Tachycineta bicolor)

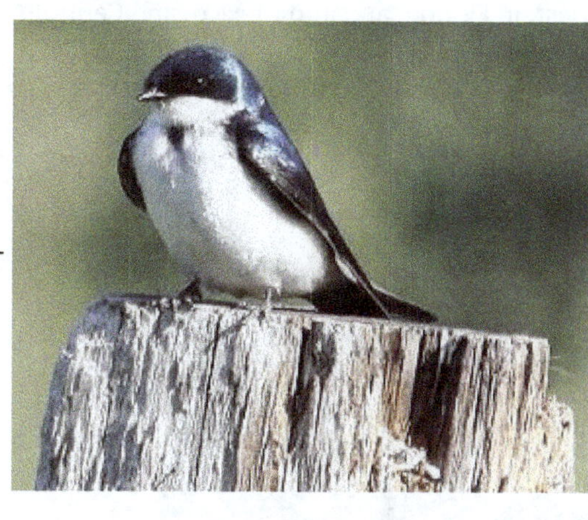

Tree Swallows are about 5 to 6 inches. They are metallic blue-black or gray black above, and bright white below. They have forked tails, and short legs for their body size. The young are dusky or brownish on top. Females may keep the dusky color into their first or second breeding season, and they may have brownish foreheads. Tree swallows are often mistaken for Violet-green swallows. Tree swallows are fun to watch as they glide in circles, ending each circle with several quick flaps of their wings as they climb higher.

Swallow family

The swallows and martins are a group of passerine birds in the family Hirundinidae, with 75 species around the world. They are all streamlined and very graceful flyers. Identifying characteristics are short legs, tiny feet, long pointed wings, and short wide bills. Swallows have a more pronounced fork in their tail while Martin's tails are squarer.

Habitat

Tree Swallows like open country near water, such as lakes, streams, or rivers, and open areas near woods. They can be found through much of Canada, Alaska, and the U.S. in summer. They winter along the Gulf Coast, in Florida, and into Mexico, and Central America.

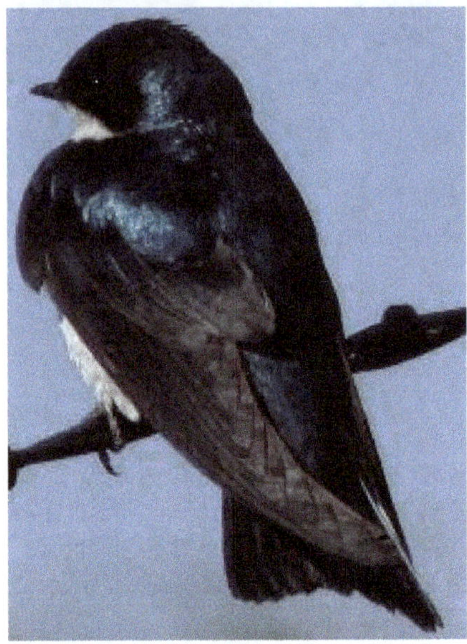

Breeding and Nesting

During courtship the male shows the female possible nesting sites. They build a cup-sized nest lined with feathers in a tree hole, building, or nest box. Often they will use nest boxes put up for bluebirds.

The female will lay 4 to 6 white eggs. She incubates these for around 15 days. Both parents feed the nestlings, and the fledglings are able to leave the nest in about 3 weeks. The young birds will be strong flyers when they leave the nest. They will be fed by the parents for a short time, but it is not long before they are skilled at catching insects.

After the breeding season swallows migrate to their wintering homes in southern U. S. or Central America.

Sound

The Tree Swallow song is a liquid gurgling twitter repeated with
variations. Their call note sounds like trit or chi-veet.

Foods

Like all swallows, the streamlined bodies of Tree Swallows give them
the flying ability to be excellent at hunting insects on the wing. While
flying insects are their main diet, they will also eat berries in the
winter.

Violet-Green Swallow

Identification

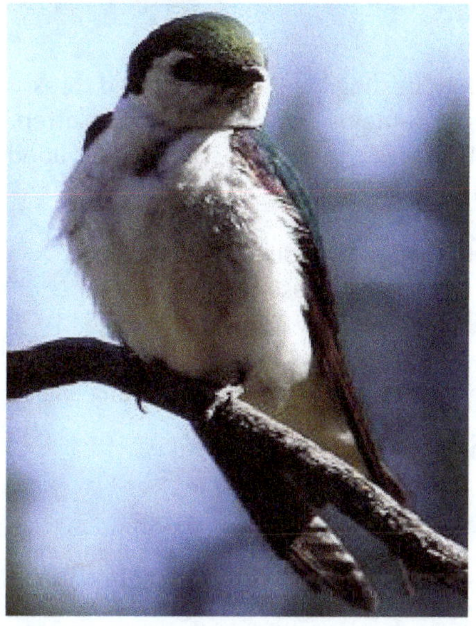

(Tachycineta thalassina)

Violet-Green Swallows are about 5 1/4 inches. They are often
mistaken for Tree swallows. One way to tell the difference is Tree
swallows have no white above the eye. When the birds are perched,
the wings of Violet-green swallows extend beyond the tail, and they
don't on Tree swallows. Adults have an iridescent violet-green helmet
and back. The rump is purple with white below. The white patches
almost meet over the base of the tail.

Below the green helmet the face is white, and the white almost circles the eyes.

Swallow Family

As with all swallows, they are streamlined and very graceful flyers. Identifying characteristics are short legs, tiny feet, long pointed wings and short wide bills.

Habitat

Violet-Green Swallows may live in small colonies, or just as single pairs. They can be found in a variety of habitats from forests, wetlands, prairies, and cities. The birds are very social and are often seen in flocks with other swallows.

Breeding and Nesting

They breed from April through July, nesting in holes in cliffs and trees in open forests, woods, canyons, mountains, and in towns. They often use birdhouses. The nest is built of grass, straw, and string, and is lined with feathers, and is built by both birds.

Females incubate 4 to 6 pure white eggs for around 14 days. Both parents will feed the nestlings. The birds will usually only have one brood but have been known to have a second. The young fledge in 23 to 25 days, but the parents will continue to feed them for a while. If swallows start nesting in your birdhouse, they and their young will most likely return to nest again.

Sound

The sound they make is a rapid chit-chit and high cheep cheep. They also make a series of notes like wheet wheet given in flight.

Food
Swallows eat mostly insects and are constantly swooping through the air for their prey.

Warbler

Yellow Warbler

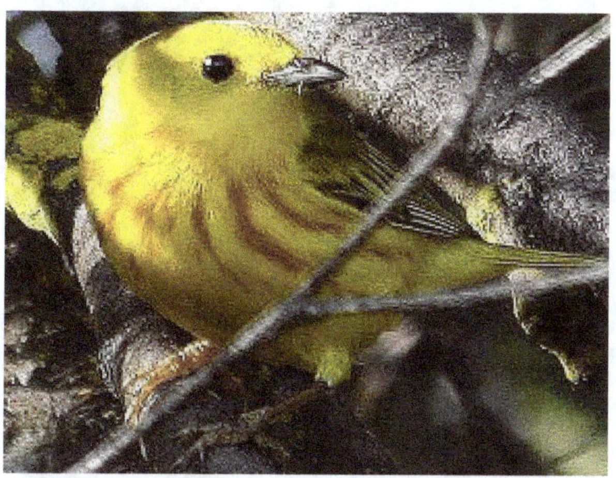

Identification *(Dendroica petechia)*

Warblers are small, very active birds, about 4 ½ to 5 ¼ inches, with thin, pointed bills in the Passerine family. There are a quite a few different warblers. The most widespread and brightly colored is the Yellow warbler. The Yellow Warbler is the most yellow of all the warblers. The male shown here has red streaks on his breast. The females and young are not as bright, and if they have streaks, they are not as pronounced as the male. Other common warblers are the Yellow-throated Warbler, Wilson's, Prairie, and Orange-crowned Warbler. One of the easiest ways to tell most warblers apart is with the head pattern.

Common Yellowthroat
(Geothlypis trichas) Males stand out
with a bright yellow throat and black
mask. Both sexes are brownish below
with yellow tail.

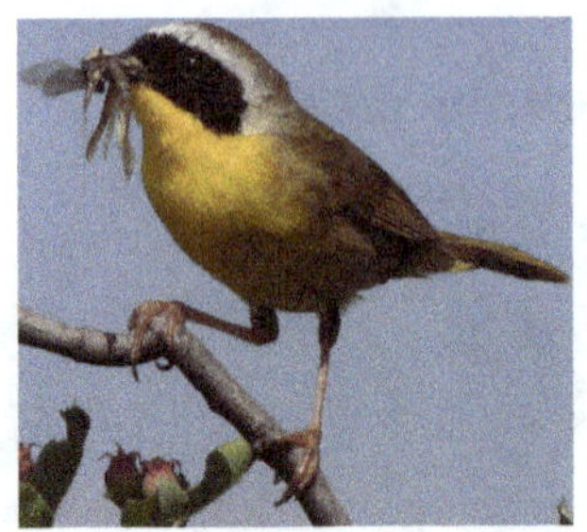

Wilson's Warbler (Wilson's pusilla) is yellow
with an easily recognizable black cap.

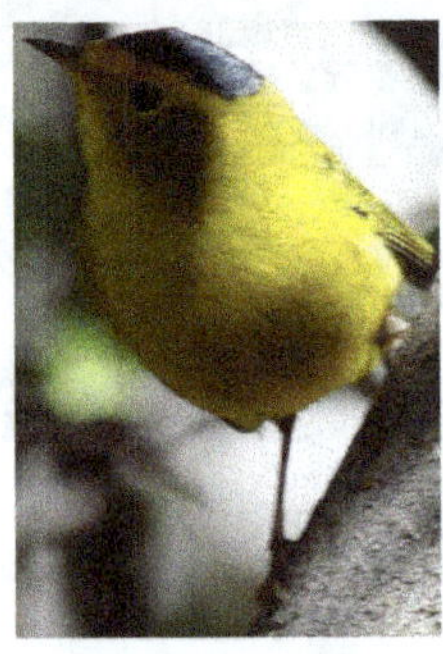

Orange-crowned Warbler
(verminova celata) are olive-green above, and
yellow below, with a small orange crown that
often can't be seen.

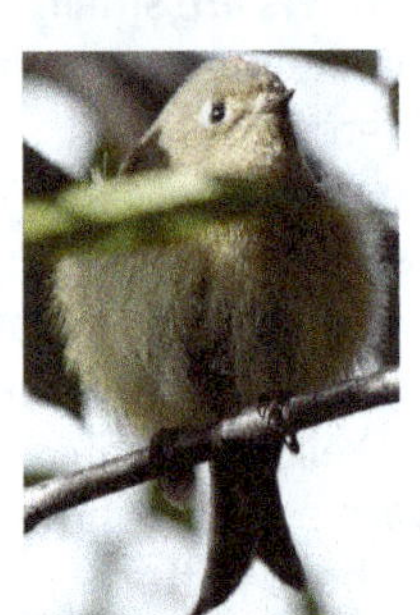

Prairie Warbler (dendrocia dicolor) have a yellow
head with a dark half circle under the
eyes, and dark spot on the neck. They are
yellow with dark streaks on the side. The
females look like the males but are much
duller.

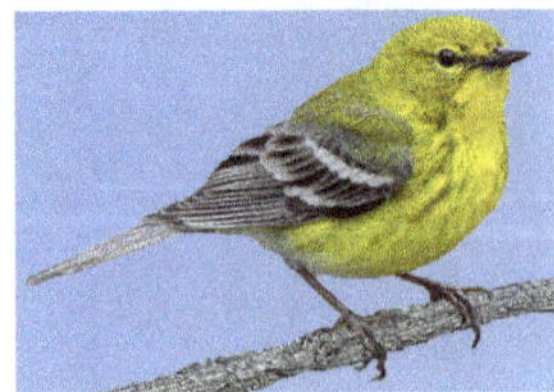

Breeding and Nesting

Female Yellow Warblers usually arrive at the breeding grounds a few days after the males, and they will bond into pairs. She will build a cup-sized nest of grass, stem fibers, and plant down. The nest is lined with plant down or other soft materials, and may be held together with webbing from caterpillar nests. It is usually placed in low shrubbery. Warblers are one of many birds that are parasitized by Brown-headed Cowbirds. Cowbirds lay their eggs in the nest of other birds, so the host bird raises their young. Warblers often build one or more new nests on top of a nest with cowbird eggs in it. Their eggs can be gray, pink, or greenish white. They are speckled with grayish or purple spots, which often form a band around the larger end.

Food and Feeding

Insects and spiders are Warbler's main diet; however, they will visit suet feeders.

Warbling Vireo

Identification

(Vireo gilvus)

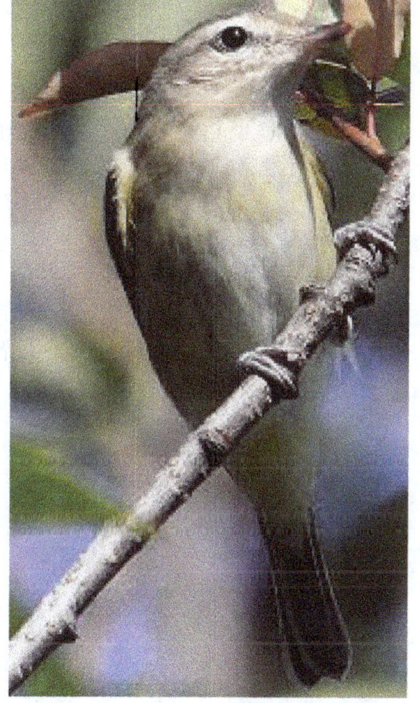

Warbling Vireo is a small North American songbird, about 5 1/2 inches, somewhat like a wood warbler. Unlike some vireos, this one does not have wing bands. They have a dull greenish back, olive-gray on the head, with a light eyebrow stripe that arches above a dark eye, and they are whitish below. Western birds have yellow below and on the sides. They have a stout bill, and thick blue gray legs. Male and female birds look the same. They are often difficult to spot, being easier to locate by their song.

Range and Habitat

Warbling Vireos range across most of the U.S. and much of Canada in summer, migrating south to Mexico and Central America for the winter. They like deciduous shade trees and mixed woods, cottonwoods, willow, aspens, riparian woodlands, and pastures. They prefer forest edges and trees near river and stream banks. They are most often found in high treetops.

Breeding and Nesting

Vireos are monogamous. Breeding is late May through July. Both members of a pair will build a basket like nest that hangs from a forked tree branch or shrub. The nest is made of grass, leaves, bark strips, plant fibers, lichen, hair, and spider webs. They incubate 4 smooth, white eggs for 12 to 14 days. The male helps in incubations and often sings from the nest. Both parents will care for the young birds for around 2 weeks in the nest, and another 2 weeks after they fledge.

Song and Call

The vireos' song is a weak, cheerful warble. Their call note is a wheezy twee.

Food

Vireos eat insects, spiders, snails, berries, and fruit. They forage mostly in treetops by hopping around branches and also hovering in the air to grab insects.

Waxwings

Identification

There are three types of waxwings, two of them in America.

Cedar Waxwings

(Bombycilla cedrorum)

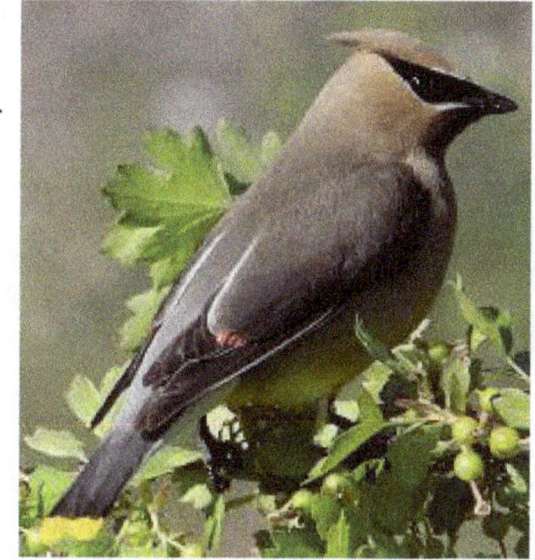

Cedar Waxwings are sleek golden brown birds a little larger than a sparrow, about 6 1/2 to 8 inches in length. Their fluffy soft feathers almost look like fur. The fawn-colored plumage blends into an ashy gray.

Waxwings get their name from the red teardrops at the tip of the secondary wing feathers. The drop, which looks like red wax, can be seen on most adults. Sometimes it will also be on tail feathers.

The breast will sometimes be a yellowish color. Both sexes look alike. They have a head crest, much like cardinals or Blue Jays. There is a yellow band at the tip of their tail, and under tail coverts are white.

There is a black patch or mask that starts above the eyes and crosses over above the beak. Waxwings, like many birds, have specialized beaks. Their short beak is slightly hooked, to help the bird easily pick berries and catch small insects.

Young birds are more of a gray color with light streaks on the under parts. Instead of a the black mask that the adults have, young birds have white on their cheeks and behind their eyes.

Bohemian Waxwings

(Bombycilla Garrula)

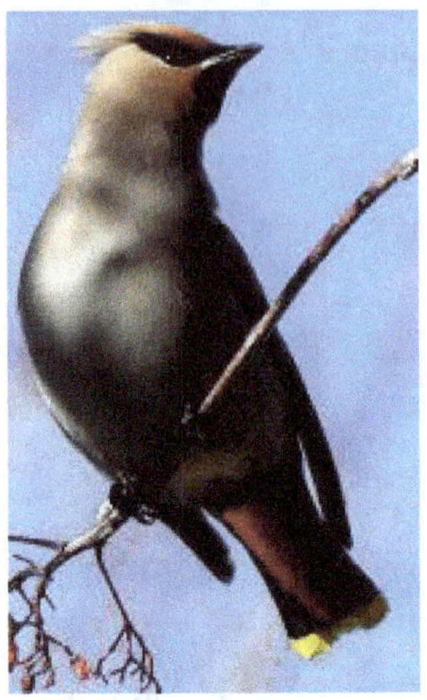

Bohemian Waxwings are similar to the Cedar waxwing but a bit larger. They have a rusty crest and face, but are more of a gray color, with no yellow on the belly. Bohemians have white and yellow markings in the wing, and tail feathers have yellow tips. The under tail coverts are a deep, rusty color.

Song and Calls

Most of the time waxwings are not heard. Their song is a quiet, high-pitched hissing whistle. This is often given when they are in flight or are just taking off. It sounds something like seee.

When perched, they can be heard giving a light cricket like call and high bzeeee trill.

Range and Habitat

In the summer waxwings can be seen across Canada and the Central U.S. They are in the Pacific Northwest, as well as central and northeast U.S. all year long and will stay in woodlands, orchards, and open areas where there are trees, and shrubs with berries. They like to spend the winter in the southern half of the U.S.

Breeding and Nesting

In late spring males can be seen hopping around doing their courting dance. During breeding season they feed in flocks. Males also pass berries to females. If a female is interested she dances with the male. The two birds will hop from side to side and pass a berry back and forth. This goes on to the end of summer.

The female chooses the nest site. The nest is a bulky structure of grass, leaves, fibers, bark, twigs, and moss. They will use bits of string or cloth set out by people.

The female will lay three to six pale bluish gray eggs with dark markings.   She incubates the eggs for 10 to 12 days. During this time the male stands guard and brings her food. Both parents feed the chicks, which fledge in about two weeks. Adults store food for the young in a crop or pouch located in the throat.

Food and Feeding

Waxwings love fruit, their favorite being berries. If you have trees and shrubs with berries on them you may see large flocks of these extremely social birds. Waxwings will fly in and stay as long as the fruit lasts, then they will be gone. Often the birds eat fermented berries and become intoxicated.

They will also eat insects, which provide a good protein source, especially during breeding season.

Waxwings will eat raisins or sliced fruit such as apples or oranges.

Western Kingbird

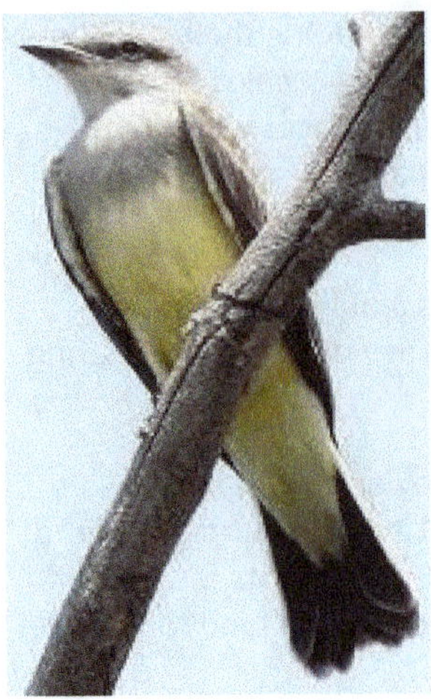

Identification

(Tyrannus verticalis)

The very aggressive Western Kingbirds are about 8 to 9 inches. They are light grayish green above. They have a black tail with white edges and dark wings. The throat and upper breast is light gray, below that and under the wings is light yellow. Just like the Eastern Kingbird, they have a bit of red in the crown that is not often seen. The two sexes look alike.

Young birds look like adults but are paler; they do not have the red crown, and the wings have a buff edged.

Kingbirds that look similar are the Tropical, Cassin's, and Couch's. Western Kingbirds have a white edge on each side of the tail.

Eastern Kingbirds (Tyrannus tyrannus) look much the same, but are gray-black above, and white below, with a white band at the tip of the tail.

Sound of the Western Kingbird

The Western Kingbird's song sounds like kip-kip-kip, followed by a high-pitched chitterling. Often there will be just a single kip.

Preferred Habitat

Western Kingbirds have a wider range than Eastern kingbirds because the Eastern Kingbirds prefer to be near water. They like open country, and can be seen perching on trees in open areas, fence posts, or utility poles. They are often found around ranch buildings where there are places to perch.

Breeding and Nesting

The male does a courtship display of twists, and turns in the air to attract the female. In this display he will fly as high as 60 feet up, and then do flips and twits as he falls toward the ground. Western Kingbirds like to nest in pine trees, on a utility pole, building ledges, or even in deserted nests of other birds. A cup-sized nest of weeds, grass, and plant fibers is built by the female. She lines this with plant down, and feathers. Kingbirds will attack any larger birds that dare to get near the nest.

The female incubates 3 to 4 creamy-white spotted eggs for about 2 weeks. The young are fed by both parents and will leave the nest in 14 to 16 days. The parents will feed them for additional 2 to 3 weeks.

Migration

Western Kingbirds will migrate in small flocks to southern Mexico and Central America in late summer.

Food and Feeding

Insects are their main food, but they also eat small fruits, and berries. Kingbirds can be seen perching on fences or posts, from which they will swoop out to grab Insects. They often hover over fields, and drop down to grab their prey.

Western Tanager

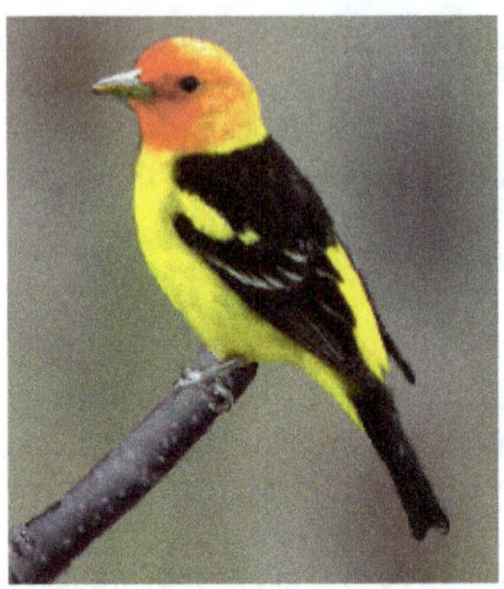

Identification

(Piranga ludoviciana)

Western Tanagers are medium-sized songbirds, about 6 1/4 to 7 1/2 inches. The males stand out with their striking colors. They are yellow with black wings and tail, and a red head. The wings have two white or yellow wing bars. They have short, thick, pointed bills, and the legs and feet are gray. The red pigment of the male is a result of his diet of insects, and he will lose most the coloration in autumn.

The females and juveniles are dull greenish above, and olive-gray back, yellow below, with a whitish belly, and white or yellow wing bars. Females are sometimes mistaken for female orioles, which have thinner bills, and longer tails. The tanager's flight is swift, and direct with rapid beating wings.

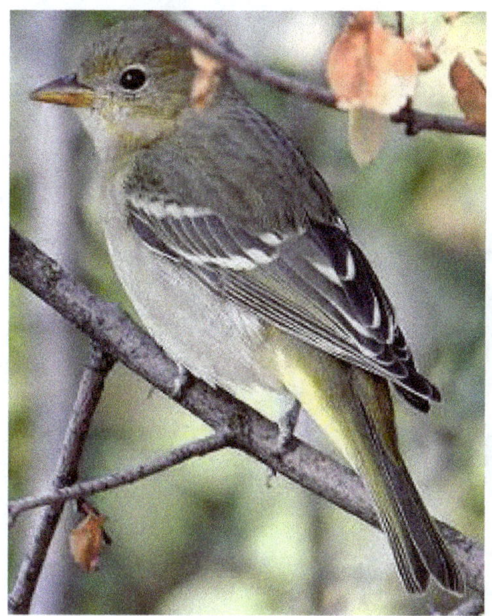

Sound

The Western Tanager's song consists of short phrases, somewhat like the American Robin. They also have a call that sounds like pre-tee-tic and chip.

Preferred Habitat

They can be found in the western half of the U.S. Their preferred habitat is open conifer or mixed forests. They migrate south to southern California, Mexico, and into Central America for winter. They migrate at night, and travel at high altitudes.

Breeding and Nesting

During courtship the male chases the female through the trees. Western tanagers are monogamous. The female builds a cup-shaped nest of twigs, grass, and bark lined with hair, and rootlets on a tree branch. The female incubates 3 to 5 blue spotted eggs for about 13 days. Both parents feed and care for the young, which fledge in around 11 days. The young birds will stay near the parents for about two more weeks.

Food

Their diets consist of insects, fruits, and berries. They forage in trees, and shrubs, also catching insects in the air. They are often hard to see since they like to forage high in the trees.

White Pelican

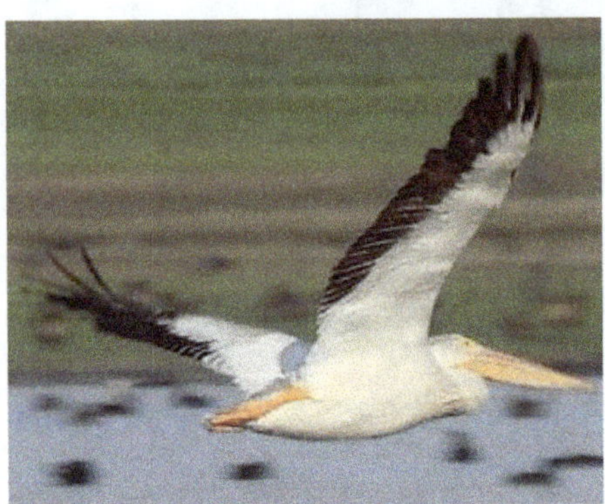

Identification

(Pelecanus erythrorhynchos)

White Pelicans are large water birds, 54 to 70 inches, with a wingspan of 8 to 9 1/2 feet. They are white with black primaries, visible when they fly or flap their wings. They have orange legs and feet. They also have large flat orange-yellow bills with large throat pouches. During breeding the adults have a horn on the top of their bill. The sexes look similar. Juvenile birds have a light gray color on their heads, necks, and wings. They are very buoyant swimmers and scoop fish into their throat pouch as they swim.

They congregate in flocks that fly in lines and broken V formations, often circling on thermal currents high in the air.

Sound

The voice of the adult pelicans is a low groan, but they usually make little noise. Younger birds make whining sounds.

Preferred Habitat

White Pelicans form into very large colonies, and they can be found near water sources such as lakes, marshes, and beaches. Most populations are migratory.

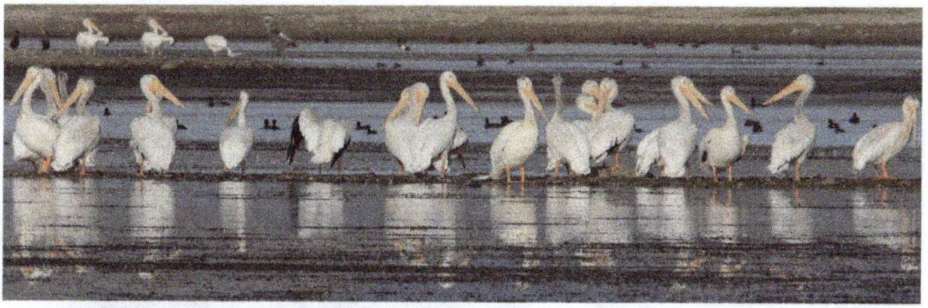

Breeding and Nesting

During courtship the birds take short flights, strut and bow displaying their large orange bills. Once they pair off the two birds will select a nest site, usually on open ground. They prefer to nest on isolated islands, or sandbars to avoid predators. The nest built by both birds is a shallow depression surrounded by dirt or vegetation. The female lays 2 to 3 large whitish eggs, and both birds incubate them for a month. After hatching both parents feed the young birds regurgitated food for about 30 days. They will fledge in about 10 weeks. The parents care for them during this time. The young birds will form into groups called crèches or pods.

Food

White Pelicans eat fish, frogs, salamanders, and aquatic invertebrates. They fish while swimming, scooping up fish in their large throat pouch. The birds often cooperate while fishing by circling the fish or driving them towards shore. They will forage at night during breeding season.

White-breasted Nuthatch

White-breasted Nuthatches are very agile and you will often see them hopping down a tree trunk headfirst.

Identification

(Sitta Carolinensis) or the Upside-Down Bird

White-breasted Nuthatches are compact little birds, about 6 inches long, with a short neck, stubby tails, and short wings. This is the most widespread of the 4 species of nuthatches in North America. They have a black cap on a white face with a beady black eye. The back is blue-gray. The chest and under parts are white with a bit of chestnut. Their head is large for their size, and they have a strong bill like a woodpecker, good for probing in crevices. Their bill is longer in proportion to their head than other nuthatches. The sexes look alike, except the male may be a bit more colorful, and the female's cap may be gray instead of black. Their strong feet enable them to climb up and down tree trunks. There are nine subspecies, and the looks and songs vary from one to another.

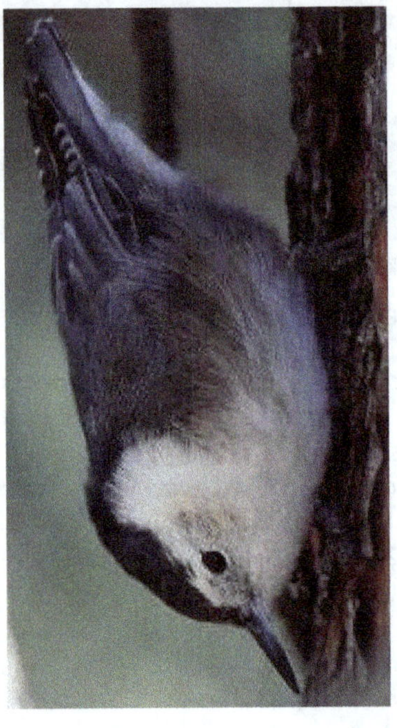

The name Nuthatch came from the way it wedges nuts into the crevices of bark and hacks them open with its strong bill.

Three other similar but smaller nuthatches are the Red-breasted, Brown-headed, and Pigmy Nuthatches.

Nuthatch Songs and Calls

They sing a vibrant series of nasal notes like whi whi whi, who who who, eh eh eh, yank yank yank, or too too.

Range and Habitat

They can be found year-round from southern Canada through the U.S. to southern Mexico. White-breasted Nuthatches like deciduous and coniferous forests, woodlands, river groves, shade trees, and backyards with trees and feeders. Especially liked are old trees with large trunks. Unlike other North American nuthatches, which prefer pine trees, White-breasted Nuthatches prefer deciduous trees. In winter they will travel with mixed flocks of birds such as chickadees and titmice, making it easier to find food, and providing more protection from predators. Recent studies show that nuthatches understand the alarm calls of chickadees.

Breeding and Nesting

Breeding season varies by region. White breasted Nuthatches are monogamous. During courtship, the male sings from a perch. When the female approaches he starts bowing and waving as he sings. They will feed each other as the courtship moves forward. A pair stays together all year. Although a pair may stay close together during winter, and even visit your feeders together, they will roost in separate holes at night, unless the weather is cold, in which case several may roost together.

The nest will be in a natural tree cavity or even an old woodpecker hole. They may use your birdhouse. The cavity floor is pieces of bark and lumps of earth. The female builds the nest alone, and it will be lined with shreds of bark, grass, fur, hair, and feathers. They often rub a beetle around cavity hole. It is thought that this leaves a chemical residue that helps deter predators. White breasted Nuthatches raise one brood per year. The male feeds the female while she incubates 5 to 9, smooth slightly glossy eggs for around 2 weeks. The eggs are white, cream or pinkish, and spotted with light red, reddish-brown, or purplish spots. Both parents will feed the young birds. They will fledge in 18 to 26 days, and will be fed after leaving the nest for another 2 weeks. The young birds will then leave the territory and either establish their own or become what are called floaters.

Food and Feeding

Natural foods of the nuthatches are insects such as beetles and caterpillars. They like acorns, nuts, and seeds from pinecones. They will forage on tree trunks, much like woodpeckers, but they do not use their tail for support.

Their strong legs and feet allow them to climb up and down trees and they will often be seen head down. Nuthatches will store food in bark crevices and small holes in trees for winter use, and for the female to eat while she is incubating eggs. You can attract them to your yard with suet, and feeders with sunflower seeds and nuts. You are more likely to see them if you have shade trees. They can be quite aggressive at feeders. With wings spread they will swing from side to side to keep other birds away.

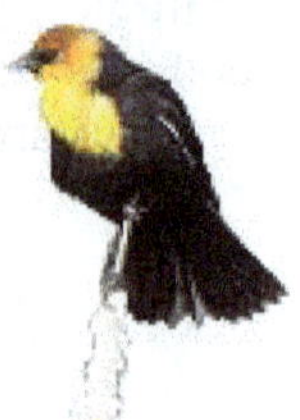

Yellow-headed Blackbird

Identification

(Xanthocephalus)

Usually perched on a Cattail, Yellow-headed Blackbirds are marsh birds, about the size of a Robin (9 to 9 3/4 inches). The most striking feature of the adult male is its yellow or orange-yellow head and breast, which stands out against a mostly black body.

They have a pointed black bill, and a white wing patch is visible at the right angle or while the bird is in flight. Young males are brownish with red shoulder patches.

The female is brownish with a dull yellow throat and breast with white streaks.

Songs and Calls

The song consists of low hoarse rasping notes almost like a rusty hinge. They also call a very distinctive low (kruuck) sound. Their unique, loud song helps in locating them in a marsh.

Range and Habitat

Yellow-headed Blackbirds range across much of the west-central portions of Canada and the United States, inhabiting freshwater marshes and wetlands in summer breeding season. They winter from California and Texas through Mexico.

They like large wetlands with deep water. They are often present in areas with Red-winged blackbirds, preferring the center of the marsh.

The birds will live in open fields during the non-breeding season. They form large flocks often mixed with other blackbirds. In the winter these flocks may consist of only males or females. Blackbird flocks will fly in what looks like large flowing waves, where the birds in the back fly over the rest of the flock.

Breeding and Nesting

Males arrive at the breeding area first and will sit on top of cattails or other reeds singing with a spread tail and half-open wings.

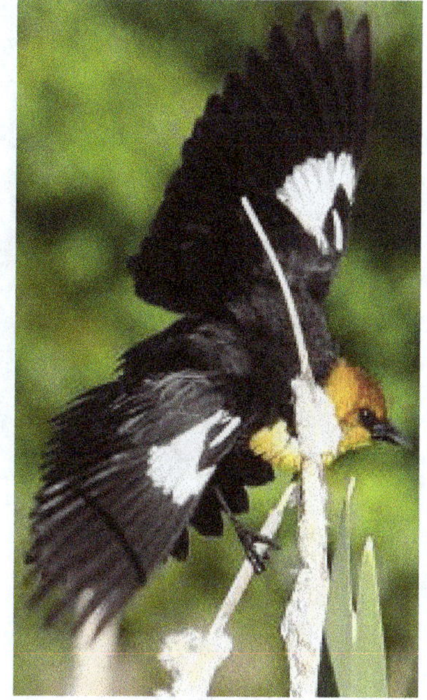

They breed in colonies with males usually having 3 to 4 mates at one time, however they can have 6 or more. These pairs will only last for 1 breeding season. The nest is a woven cup of grass, stems, and leaves which the female secures to cattails, reeds or other aquatic vegetation, about 1/2 feet above the water. She incubates 3 to 5 greenish-white eggs with dark blotches for 12 to 14 days. The male may help, but the female does most of the feeding. The young will leave the nest in around 12 days, staying near water until they can fly. She will usually only have one brood for the season but may have two.

Food

Foraging in fields and marshes, Yellow-headed Blackbirds eat seeds and insects.

Greater Yellowlegs

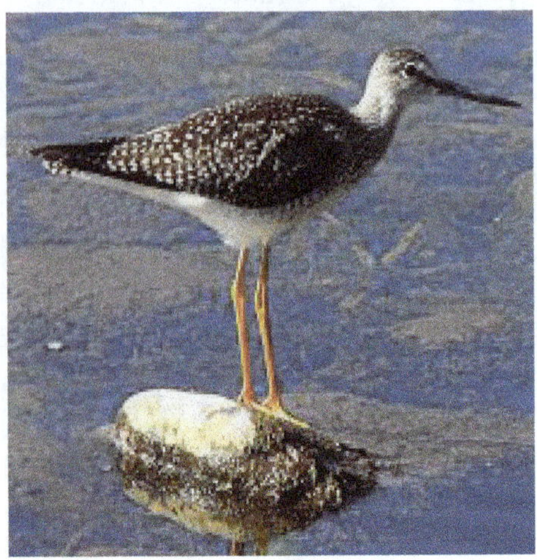

Identification

(Tringa melanoleuca)

Greater Yellowlegs are a slim gray sandpiper, 12 1/2 to 15 inches with black, white and gray-checkered back. As the name implies, it has long yellowlegs. They have a white eye ring and the under parts are whitish. In breeding plumage they are heavily barred below. The bill is long and slightly upturned. The white tail, barred at the end can be readily seen in flight. Young birds look similar to the adults but are not has heavily marked. Like other birds in this genus they bob their body up and down.

The Lesser Yellowlegs looks similar but are smaller and have a slim straight bill.

The Sound of the Greater Yellowlegs

Males do a loud, ringing, whistled song. Their call is a clear, squeaky whew-whew-whew.

Preferred Habitat

Greater Yellowlegs breed in muskeg bogs in Canada and Alaska. In summer they can be seen in streams, ponds, and marshes throughout the U.S. while they migrate south to the Atlantic and Pacific coasts of the United States and to South America.

Breeding and Nesting

In courtship the male performs display flights, gliding, rising, and falling while he does his loud whistled song. They nest in depressions on the ground lined with twigs, grass, leaves, and lichen. Females will lay 4 buff, blotched eggs which they incubate for around 23 days. Soon after hatching the young are able to leave the nest.

Food

In breeding season, insects and insect larvae are their primary food. During migration and winter they feed on fish and other aquatic insects and animals, swinging their beaks back and forth in the water to stir up their prey.

Creating this Book
I photographed most of the birds for this book right around my home town of Missoula Montana. I spent many hours watching birds. I also spent hours at libraries to verify details. I used valuable resources on the Internet. One is the Open Content Alliance. The OCA is an effort by nonprofit and governmental organizations from around the world to make thousands of books and other materials searchable and accessible online. All bird details in the book are common scientific knowledge.

Bibliography

Alderfer, Jonathan, ed. *National Geographic Complete Birds Of North America:* National Geographic, 2005.

Alsop, J. Fred. *Birds of North America*: Smithsonian handbooks, 2001.

Audubon, J. James. *Birds of America,* 1967

Baicich, J. Paul and Harrison J. Colin. *Nests Eggs and Nestlings of North American Birds,* 2005.

Bailey, M. Florence. *Birds of Village and Field: A Bird Book for Beginners*. 1898

Bailey, M. Florence. *Handbook of Birds of the Western United States*. 1902

Blanchan, Neltie. *Bird Neighbors*. 1922

Chapman, Frank. *Bird-life, a guide to the study of our common birds*. 1901

Cleveland B. Arthur. *Life Histories of North American Birds*: 21 volumes, 1919 to 1968.

Dunn, L Jon. *The Birds Of North America*. National Geographic field guide, 2006.

Ehrlich, R. Paul, Dobkin, David and Wheye, Darryl. *The Birder's Handbook*: A field guide to the natural history of North American birds, 1988.

Griggs, L. Jack. *All the Birds of North America,* 1997.

Harrison, Kit and George. *Favorite Backyard Birds,* 1983.

Jellis, Rosemary. *Bird Sounds and Their Meanings,* 1984.

Kaufman, Kenn. *Lives of North American Birds,* 1996.

Kaufman, Kenn. *Birds of North America*. 2000.

Lotz, Aileen. Birding Around the World, 1987.

Palmer, S. Ralph, ed. *Handbook of North American Birds vol. 5, Diurnal Raptors*: Yale University Press, 1988.

Pearson, T. Gilbert, ed. *Birds of America,* 1936.

Peterson, T. Roger. *Birds of North America. A Field Guide to Western Birds*: The American   Ornithologists' Union, 1961.

Savage, Candace. *Bird Brains*. 1997.

Sibley, A. David. *The SIBLEY Guide to Birds,* 2000.

Terres, K. John. *The Audubon Society Encyclopedia Of North American Birds,* 1980.

Trafton, H. Gilbert. *Bird Friends*. 1916.

Useful Websites
https://www.audubon.org

Patuxent Wildlife Research Center https://www.mbr-pwrc.usgs.gov

Open Content Alliance https://archive.org/details/opencontentalliance